D0841605

Purrs of Praise!

"*Makin' Biscuits* provides an entertaining look at feline behavior, but don't be deceived by the lighthearted tone of this book. Deborah Barnes provides solid, well-researched information for cat parents who are trying to understand their feline charges better."
~Ingrid King, award-winning author and publisher of *The Conscious Cat*

"Deborah Barnes treats readers to an inside look into the world of cats and cat people in *Makin' Biscuits*. Those of us who are cat parents are quite emotional about our love for our fur-kids, but sometimes, well, we just scratch our heads and wonder why the heck our cat is doing what they're doing. The delight in this marvelous book is in the stories by those who contributed. It's both entertaining and educational—an honest and real look into the world of cat parenting. I loved every page of it, and cat people should share it with anyone who has ever said cats are boring!"
~Yvonne DiVita, co-founder of the BlogPaws Pet Community and publisher of *Scratchings and Sniffings*

"In today's world where the popularity of cats has soared, there are still shelters overflowing with cats in need of a home. Many wound up there for behavioral problems that could have been solved by understanding the instinctual mindset of a cat. In *Makin' Biscuits*, Deborah Barnes tackles this subject in an enjoyable, easy to read manner as she shares a compilation of funny, sweet, and poignant stories from ailurophiles around the globe. FOUR PAWS UP!"
~Caren Gittleman, publisher of *Cat Chat with Caren and Cody*

"In *Makin' Biscuits*, Deborah Barnes uses humor and a conversational style to deliver a serious message about responsible pet ownership. With anecdotes from cat lovers, as well as her own experiences, Barnes gives us a candid look at life with cats, sharing funny, eccentric and often touching tales of cats and their people, plus tips and references to help keep them happy. My favorite—the story about an owner who "time-shared" Tux the cat with loving neighbors for eight years. Read on to find yours!"
~Ramona D. Marek, MS Ed., author of *Cats for the GENIUS*

"Just when I thought my cats couldn't get any sillier, more resourceful, creative or cunning, I'm realizing the possibilities are endless and they're in good company. Deborah Barnes' collection of real life stories of those funny habits our cats have is endearing, enlightening and often hilarious. Not only have I giggled at the funny quirks my own cats share with cats across the globe, I've now learned many of the whys behind their curious behavior. It's like a secret glimpse into what makes their clever minds tick and what brings me so much joy each and every day."
~**Debbie Glovatsky**, award-winning blogger and photographer, *Glogirly.com*

"I expected a collection of cute-and-funny kitty tails, but *Makin' Biscuits* is so much more. Each chapter introduces a particular "feline foible" followed by real life examples that prompt smiles, gasps, sometimes welling eyes, but always delight. The author could stop there—but bookends these *Mews From Others* sections with pithy *Purr Points to Ponder*, complete with explanations, speculations and cautions. This is a treasure of a book cat lovers will lap up like cream!"
~**Amy Shojai**, CABC, author of 30 pet care books and a founder of the Cat Writers' Association

"What a delight to read! Deb Barnes has gathered a terrific collection of touching cat stories that are sure to make you smile. She marries these stories with important cat behavior lessons, resulting in a unique and enjoyable book that sheds light on so many misconceptions about cats."
~**Kate Benjamin**, founder of *Hauspanther.com* and co-author of *Catification* and *Catify to Satisfy*

"*Makin' Biscuits* is a fun read that reminds us through anecdotes from both the author and other cat parents of the odd, unexpected and entertaining things cats do that keep our hearts and homes full of love and laughter."
~**Tamar Arslanian**, author of *Shop Cats of New York* and publisher of *IHaveCat.com*

"*Makin' Biscuits* helps humans feel not-so-alone in the quirky day-to-day life of living with cats. It's a funny, sweet, and informative page-turner that's sure to entertain anyone who's owned by a cat or three...or five."
~**Angie Bailey**, author, *Texts from Mittens* and *Whiskerslist: The Kitty Classifieds*

"No matter how quirky, odd, or crazy you think your cat is, Deborah Barnes' *Makin' Biscuits* lets you know you're not alone. Ms. Barnes and the others, who share their stories about the eccentricities of their kitty companions will make you laugh, cry and identify. An absolute must for any cat lover!"
~Stephanie Piro, nationally syndicated cartoonist and the Saturday Chick of King Features' *Six Chix*

"Not only does Deborah Barnes know cats but she also understands cat lovers—and the extremes we'll go to make sure our felines are happy. Tips and tricks are deftly interwoven with personal stories and advice in this volume that will be a fun addition to every cat lover's bookshelf."
~Paris Permenter, author of 33 books on pets and travel and blogger at *CatTipper.com*

"Author Deborah Barnes is the consummate cat lover, wearing her love of cats on her sleeves. Her third book, *Makin' Biscuits* is no exception. A true delight, it's finally the book that allows her to fulfil a dream of hers: to keep cats out of shelters and increase adoptions. With her trademark wit and conversational tone, she deftly shares experiences from an array of cat lovers, seamlessly intertwining them with nuggets of wisdom and hands-on solutions and tips to help keep cats in tune with their natural instincts—all of which equates to a happier cat and a stronger feline-human bond."
~Christine Michaels, award-winning blogger, *Riverfront Cats*, and founder and president of Pawsitively Humane, Inc.

"Is your cat dropping toys at your feet or staring into space for no apparent reason? *Makin' Biscuits—a* fascinating read for any cat lover pokes fun at these age-old questions!"
~Dusty Rainbolt, ACCBC, award-winning author of 12 books including *Kittens for Dummies*, *Cat Wrangling Made Easy* and *Cat Scene Investigator: Solve Your Cat's Litter Box Mystery*

THE INSTINCTUAL MINDSET OF CATS REVEALED!

MAKIN' BISCUITS

Weird Cat Habits and the Even Weirder
Habits of the Humans Who Love Them

Deborah Barnes

With a Foreword by Gwen Cooper

ZZP PUBLISHING, LLC

Makin' Biscuits

Copyright © 2016 by Deborah Barnes

All rights reserved. Except as permitted under the U.S. Copyright Act of 1976, no part of this publication may be reproduced, distributed, or transmitted in any form or by any means graphic, electronic, or mechanical, including photocopying, recording, taping, or by any information stored in a database or retrieval system, without the prior written permission of publisher; except in the case of brief quotations embedded in critical reviews, press releases, and articles.

ZZP PUBLISHING, LLC
PO Box 770625
Coral Springs, FL 33077
www.zzppublishing.com

Printed in the USA
Charleston, SC

Acknowledgements:
Book cover/back layout and graphic design: Deborah Barnes
Book interior layout and design: Deborah Barnes
Book cover/back cartoon illustrations: Stephanie Piro
Photos: Dan Power
Editing: Karen Robinson

First Edition: November 2016

Library of Congress Control Number: 2016913207

ISBN 978-0-9834408-3-3

To my sweet Mia—the cat who started it all when she decided napping on my toweled head after I got out of the shower was our normal—and to my equally sweet Jazmine whose passion for biscuit making inspired the rest to follow.

Foreword

For a few years now, I've been trying to resist the urge to become one of those people who talks endlessly about her cats' quirks, oddities, and frequently charming (to me, at any rate) behavior. My efforts are somewhat complicated by the fact that I write about my cats for a living, that I'm frequently invited to speak at events where direct questions are asked about my cats by audience members, and by my natural writer's impulse to tell a story and tell it to completion—even if my sense of when "completion" has been attained may have long exceeded my listeners' interest and patience.

Recently, at a fundraiser for a no-kill cat shelter in Louisiana, I found myself expounding at length upon my three-legged cat, Clayton's, habit of leaping into my lap while I'm writing, flipping over onto his back, and demanding that I cradle him like a baby in the crook of my arm.

"Like a *baby*," I insisted several times. "Cats are supposed to hate that, but Clayton gets so upset if I *don't* do it. Isn't that so *odd*? Of course," I added, by way of providing all relevant information, "Clayton is incredibly needy. He needs a *lot* of attention. He has no idea that there are cats out there whose humans *aren't* self-employed writers who get to stay home with their cats all day. I always think that if Clayton ever got to talk to other cats whose humans have office jobs and are out of the house every day for nine or ten hours at a time, he'd be so…"

Well, you get the idea. I like to think that I reined myself in before the actual moment when my audience's eyes glazed over and they started sneaking glances at their watches. But I can't really be sure. This is an area in which I've come to doubt my own judgment.

My one comfort is in knowing that I'm not alone in this. "Cat people" love to share stories about our cats, about the various ways in which they're unique and "weird" and entirely unlike any other cat we've ever lived with or even heard of. This isn't because cat owners are "crazy" or "obsessed" in the ways that popular culture loves to accuse us of being. It's because we're human, and humans—as pack animals who can talk to each other—are hard-wired with a desire to share news and information of the unusual with each other. It's baked into our very DNA.

Of course, definitions of what's legitimately interesting will vary from person to person. Personally, I'll never understand why people are so gung-ho to hear about the latest Brad and Angelina goings-on, or discuss who won on *The Bachelor*. Give me a good cat story any day! But one woman's pleasure is another woman's poison, and to each her own, and all that sort of thing.

If it's true that we're wired to exchange descriptions of the unusual with our fellow humans, then cats certainly provide ample fodder. Dogs are pack animals (like humans), the conventional reasoning goes, and thus more like us in their ways. Cats, however, are solitary hunters (unlike humans), and will forever seem a bit mysterious to us. Your dog's instinct is to please you and conform to your expectations. Your cat, on the other hand, cares very little for your opinions *or* your expectations, and will therefore pursue any path or behavior that strikes him as fun or desirable without concerning himself very much with what you think is "weird."

And, so, every person who's lived with a cat long enough will have at least a couple of stories about the things his or her particular cat does that are unlike anything she's ever heard of any other cat doing—the cat who has a passionate love of carrot cake, even though carrots (or cake, for that matter) aren't a food that cats are supposed to be interested in; the cat who's learned how to open the drawer where you keep all your rubber bands, so she can sneak them out one at a time and add them to the hidden rubber-band stash she's collecting in a spot under the couch for no discernible reason; the cat who loves rolling around in the wet bathtub just after you've taken a shower, even though conventional cat wisdom dictates that cats hate getting wet even worse than a gossip columnist hates a stable celebrity marriage.

When it comes to cats, tales of the unusual abound. Being in the position I occupy—having written a popular memoir about my own cats—I've heard from (quite literally) tens of thousands of cat owners over the past few years. They write to me about their joys and concerns. They share stories of oddities and uniqueness. Many of these stories are funny, all of them are laced with obvious affection, and a handful attain, "Okay—even *I* think that's weird!" status.

And yet, for all the differences among these tales, there are a handful of themes that I hear repeated so continuously that the only conclusion to be drawn is that they represent experiences common to every person who lives with a cat. People write telling me about the divorce, depression, major illness, job loss, or overseas military service they wouldn't have made it through if not for the warmth and inexplicable understanding of the cat in their life. They write of that moment when even a previously aloof cat will come over to deliver an affectionate head-bonk or biscuit-making session, a moment when the supposed distances between human and cat as two very different species are closed entirely, and all that's left is the certainty of loving and being loved in return.

The stories in this book will entertain you, will startle you at times with their oddness or make you laugh at others. But the one common thread you'll find is a shared love that defies all set expectations, even as it resists easy explanation.

Not everybody likes hearing stories about cats. To each his own, as they say. But those of us lucky enough to be owned by cats know exactly where we stand. And we wouldn't have it any other way.

Gwen Cooper is the New York Times bestselling author of the memoir *Homer's Odyssey: A Fearless Feline Tale, or How I Learned About Love and Life with a Blind Wonder Cat*; the novels *Love Saves the Day* and *Diary of a South Beach Party Girl*; and the crowd-sourced collection of cat selfies, *Kittenish*, 100% of the proceeds from which were donated to support animal rescue in Nepal following the 2015 earthquake. She is a frequent speaker at shelter fundraisers and donates 10% of her royalties from *Homer's Odyssey* to organizations that serve abused, abandoned, and disabled animals. She also manages Homer's ongoing social-media community, which reaches nearly two million cat enthusiasts and rescuers around the world each day. Gwen lives in Manhattan with her husband, Laurence. She also lives with her two perfect cats— Clayton the Tripod and his litter-mate, Fanny—who aren't impressed with any of it.

Table of Contents

Our Family Tree

Dan & Deb

Engaged couple living in the lovely tropics of South Florida and human servants to resident cats—Zee, Zoey, Mia, Peanut, Rolz, Kizmet, and Jazmine. Dan is the photographer of the family, taking all the stunning pictures featured in the book. Deb is the book's author, including creative layout and cover design.

Zee & Zoey

Feline power couple featured in Deb's first book, *The Chronicles of Zee & Zoey – A Journey of the Extraordinarily Ordinary*. Zee is a lovable male Maine Coon who was given to Dan as a housewarming gift from Deb when he moved in with her in 2004. Zoey is Deb's soul-mate kitty—a petite and pretty Bengal with a strong personality to boot. She joined the household in 2008 and when Zee first laid eyes on her, he was instantly smitten. They fell deeply in love, and as a consequence, several months later a litter of four kittens was born.

Mia, Peanut, Rolz, and Zeuss Catt

Zee and Zoey's beautiful kittens. They have Zee's dark grey/black coloring, with the leopard spotted markings of Zoey, as well as her sleek and slender build. Mia, Peanut, and Rolz stayed on as permanent house cats of Dan and Deb, and Zeuss Catt went on to live with a family friend in Boston. Despite that Mia, Peanut, and Rolz have all been raised in the same environment since birth, they have very distinct personalities. Mia is shy, Peanut is a lover, and Rolz is aloof.

Kizmet & Jazmine

Two cats that unexpectedly came into Dan and Deb's life as rescue kittens. Kizmet was discovered by Deb at a Pet Supermarket adoption event—he's a Maine Coon mix with a sweet and lovable personality; and Jazmine was found by Dan and Deb when they were traveling together for a pet-related conference. She's a gorgeous ginger cat with a white bib and mittens, most probably of the Siberian breed.

Jazz & Harley

Angel cats of Dan and Deb. Jazz was a wise and kind Ragdoll who was a Mother's Day gift for Deb. He crossed the Rainbow Bridge in 2013 and consequently shared his story in his meow memoir, *Purr Prints of the Heart – A Cat's Tale of Life, Death, and Beyond*, a book written to help people with the grieving process after losing a pet. Harley was a rescue cat—a torbie mix—who died in 2014, very unexpectedly. She was a gentle cat, preferring to spend most of her days napping on the living room couch with Deb at her side.

The Gang

Introduction

I've had cats all my 50 plus years of life, so honestly there's very little any of them do any longer that surprises me. Cats opening doors. Cats closing doors. Cats stealing my underwear. Cats bringing me gifts in the dead of night. Cats sleeping on my head and cats giving me hugs. Even cats visiting me in the afterlife—you name it; I've probably seen some variation of it. But naturally, cats being cats, they'll prove otherwise, if for no other reason than because they can.

One day, I was showering like I had thousands of other mornings. Typically, one cat or another is on the wicker hamper we (we, being me and my fiancé, Dan) keep on the opposite side of the shower, waiting for me to finish. They like to provide me with kitty companionship while I'm in the bathroom, and on this particular morning, Mia was my designated furry friend. What you need to know about Mia is despite her living in the same house her whole life (she was born in my bedroom closet, or even possibly, on my lap) and being surrounded nearly 24/7/365 by Dan and me—two people who adore her and dote on her every whim and desire, she's an extremely shy and reserved cat. You know the kind I mean—the kind you pick up to pet and who contort their bodies into a pretzel shape, looking at you with wide-eyed horror you would even dream of petting them, let alone pick them up.

Mia would let me randomly pet her, but there were **RULES**. First off, I could only pet her on the hamper in the bathroom—or occasionally the bed in my bedroom—but only if I didn't get all emotional about it. If I treaded slowly and acted nonchalant enough, like it wasn't a big deal she was letting me pay attention to her, I could get a victory pet in here and there.

You can only imagine my surprise then, after I got out of the shower and bent over to wrap a towel around my dripping wet hair, to suddenly feel something land on my head. I blindly reached up and realized it was Mia! She was right smack on top of my head, purring up a storm and passionately making biscuits into the towel!

There's a cat on my head!

I remained stooped over—she let me continue to pet her and soon settled into the soft towel for a contented nap. Being the loving cat parent I am, I remained in the stooped position (with my back in excruciating pain, mind you), clothed only in said towel for as long as I possibly could. I was running dangerously close to being late for work and knew the "my cat was sleeping on my head" excuse would only go so far.

It was at that very moment it dawned on me. This wasn't your typical weird. Besides being a pet parent to one assorted cat or another over the course of my life, I'm also an award-winning cat blogger (*Zee & Zoey's Cat Chronicles*) and author of two well-received books about cats: *The Chronicles of Zee & Zoey – A Journey of the Extraordinarily Ordinary* and *Purr Prints of the Heart – A Cat's Tale of Life, Death, and Beyond.* By this point in my life, I knew cat behavior so well I was practically a cat myself, having been told that on many an occasion.

I decided to test it out with my readers—I shared Mia's story on my blog and quickly found from the comments I received that her weird was only the tip of the weird litter box. Weirder story after weirder story came in. *Cats have weird habits*—that became abundantly clear. But it also became clear the humans who love them are just as weird. Not that there's anything wrong with that, says the person who was in her bathroom, nearly naked and shivering, stooped over in pain because she didn't want to spoil the special bonding moment she was sharing with her introverted cat.

An idea formed in my toweled, cat-covered head—this stuff would make an entertaining book—and that's how *Makin' Biscuits – Weird Cat Habits and the Even Weirder Habits of the Humans Who Love Them* initially started. I put out an open call on my blog and social media sites for cat lovers to share some of the silly, strange, sweet, amazing, heroic, or off-the-beaten-path things their cats have done or some of the weird or crazy things they've personally done for the love of a cat.

I heard from cat lovers around the globe of every lifestyle, sex, age, and occupation—bloggers, authors, celebrities, musicians, behaviorists, friends, family members, and more all opened up to share one cat story after another. But once I started writing, I realized it was so much more than a book of weird cat habits.

Patterns emerged, and I began to question the behaviors. *Why were cats doing all these weird things?* After doing some research, it became evident cats do the things they do because that's how they're instinctually wired, not just because it's a random weird habit.

Once I made the connection, I knew I wanted the book to explore the feline mindset alongside the strange habits by explaining why these behaviors occur in the first place, as well as to offer well-researched, practical advice to help cat guardians provide their feline friends with the proper resources and environment to ensure they can live an optimally happy and healthy life.

I wanted to make a difference in a larger sense, too. Despite the U.S. being a cat-loving nation—according to the 2015-2016 American Pet Products Association (APPA) survey[1], it's estimated that the total number of cats owned in the U.S. alone is somewhere around 85.8 million—cat overpopulation remains an epidemic problem.

The American Society for the Prevention of Cruelty to Animals (ASPCA) indicates each year approximately 3.4 million cats enter shelters nationwide—add to that all the homeless cats living on the streets, and it's a collective total of nearly 70 million cats without a home because the staggering numbers of available cats far exceed willing adopters. And even more tragically, each year approximately 1.4 million cats are senselessly euthanized for a myriad of reasons.[2] Cats might have crazy habits, but those statistics are what's really crazy.

As a cat advocate, I want *Makin' Biscuits* to be part of the solution. I want every cat to have a good home, and I want the world to know what wonderful companions they make. So, not only will the book bust outdated misconceptions, such as that they're too aloof to make good pets, it will enlighten the reader with easy-to-understand information to help enhance the feline-human relationship and correct certain common behavioral problems that often land a cat in a shelter in the first place—such as litter box issues or scratching furniture.

So, if you can, grab a cat for your lap and enjoy the read! *Makin' Biscuits* is a full-range of cat chat—many of the anecdotes are your average, simple, everyday kinds of things that generally any cat lover can relate to, such as the universal love most cats seem to have for an empty box. And some of the stories are so bizarre or amazing you'll marvel how they ever came to be in the first place! Some will make you smile, some will tug at your heart, and I promise you'll laugh on more than one occasion. You'll most certainly say— "Oh yeah, my cat has done that," or you'll read it and say, "Ha, I have that beat—my cat does X, Y, or Z." And you might just learn a feline fact or two along the way!

Meows, purrs, and head bonks to you all!

[1]http://www.americanpetproducts.org/press_industrytrends.asp

[2]http://www.aspca.org/animal-homelessness/shelter-intake-and-surrender/pet-statistics

You Can Pet Me, Just Don't Touch Me

I like to call these my "teenage" cats. Not that they're of teen age—just that general Jekyll and Hyde teenage personality that can switch on a dime when affection is involved. You know what I mean—the kind of affection that causes a cat to recoil in horror if you dare try to pet them or pick them up.

You can pet me, just not in the house. Or outside. Or anywhere I am. And if you must, please do it without touching me or without anyone seeing you do it. Yes, you can give me treats, but that doesn't mean I've succumbed to your desire of you wanting to hug me. If you're like me, you go for it anyway—how could you possibly not? Your cat is just so darn cute, so irresistibly fluffy, and sooooo huggable.

As predicted, their darling little bodies squirm in wild banshee abandon as they attempt to disengage from your loving embrace as quickly as possible. These, of course, are the same cats that will snuggle contentedly into your lap while you're on the computer and settle in for a deep nap, rendering it impossible for you to get up to refresh that now-cold cup of coffee.

They're also the same cats that follow you around from room to room, happily chirping and meowing a conversation with you, and the same cats that will possessively swat at you from the kitchen counter as you walk past, just because they want you to acknowledge their presence.

With my gang of seven, I have a full range of what my cats will tolerate. Some, like Peanut, are the polar opposite of a teenage cat.

You—yes, I literally mean *you* reading this book—could pick her up and cradle her in your arms like a baby all day long. From family members to virtual strangers, she's a Robert Palmer cat—addicted to love.

Rolz is my "TMBS" cat. Meaning he'll patiently hang out at all hours on the kitchen counter next to the pantry where we keep the cat food because "there might be something," i.e., an opportunity for a treat, and he needs to ensure he'll never, ever miss that chance. I can possibly give him a relatively quick pat once I dispense a treat, because, yes, his eternal patience always does yield a yummy reward from me, but if I attempt to hold him or give him extended pats, his body shivers in complete abhorrence—he's a "you can look, but don't touch" type of cat.

Then there's my Bengal, Zoey, who's the epitome of a teenage cat. She's a tiny thing—a leopard shrunk to miniature size—but she packs a powerful punch, complete with a loud yowl of protest letting me (or anyone else who foolishly dare try to pick her up) know that she finds PDAs unbearable and completely unacceptable. *Hmmpf. Pick me up?* As if, her eyes glare in steely indignation.

I've learned not to take it personally with her. We have our special time—when I relax at the end of the day to watch TV on the couch—when she comes and lies on my outstretched legs for the duration. If I inadvertently forget to stretch out my legs, she'll perch on the armrest of the couch next to me and stare deep into my eyes, her nose practically touching mine, to remind me I've forgotten something—i.e., Her Majesty's needs. I'm allowed to pet her smooth-as-silk fur as much as I want, and she's a devoted mama's girl for the rest of the night. My legs will be thoroughly numb and in pain within minutes, but that's okay. A short three hours later, I'll be getting up off the couch to go to bed. I've also long since trained my bladder to work around her schedule; after all, being graced with her presence is far more important than catering to something as mundane as a necessary bodily function.

Pick me up? Think again...

~MEWS FROM OTHERS~

My cat, Russell, is an absolute lover if I stick to his rules. If I try to pick him up to hold him, he'll wiggle out of my arms, but if I'm sitting down, and only if I'm sitting down, he'll venture onto my lap and grace me with some personal time. He has to pick the spot on my lap where he'll sit, and when he's had enough, he leaves for his kitty yoga session—a rather unusual routine which entails him rapidly making biscuits into an old blanket lying next to me, while at the same time stretching his back legs and, then, lifting them up, one at a time, midair for a few seconds before lowering them again! This leg up and down pattern, combined with the biscuit making, will continue until he finally settles down for a nap.

Jobi Harris, cat blogger, *Ask-Fisher.com*

My tortoiseshell, Vixen, was feral the first year of her life and didn't like to be held. Any time I would try to hold her, she'd struggle and wiggle out of my grip. If I continued, she'd give me "the look," and if I persisted, she'd bite me. Not just a little nip, either—she would grab my arm with her claws to pull it toward her while biting and holding it on the other side. Blood was usually drawn, and I would surrender in pain. As Vixen aged, she spent most of her days sleeping in a bed I placed underneath my desk for her. After consulting Pet Psychic, Laura Stinchfield, I discovered Vixen had a touch of vertigo and didn't like being up off the floor. She was happiest when lying in her bed at my feet, so I didn't pick her up any more than necessary. She got to where she'd come over to me and stand, looking up at me, while I was sitting in my chair. Her intent was perfectly clear—she was asking me to pick her up for hugs! I didn't understand her reasons, but as she was nearly 24 years old, it was probably because she sensed our time together was growing shorter and she wanted to feel closer to me.

Lynn Maria Thompson, founder of *OldMaidCatLady.com*

My cat, Seren, never likes to be held, pushing her front paws against my chest in a "NOOOOO! Let me DOWN!" posture any time I make an attempt. Her only exception is she will lap sit on cold/cloudy days— but she still hates being picked up, and the affection has to be her choice.

Amy Shojai, CABC, author of 30 pet care books and a founder of the Cat Writers' Association

I adopted my loveable orange and white cat, Rusty, when he was 8 weeks old. About a year into our relationship, he started getting upset anytime I'd pick him up. He'd cry and put his head under my arm to hide his eyes, but then, minutes later, without a care in the world, he'd jump onto my lap, wanting to sit with me for hours!

Linda Stapleton, retired, Miamisburg, OH

My rescue cats, Bessie and Lulu (mother/daughter) had a strict "do not pet me or pick me up" policy when I took them in. Lulu was the first to allow me to touch her, somewhere in our first year, but I had to be careful how I approached her and where I placed my hands. Any slight movement that suggested I wanted to pick her up sent her into a panic and she ran. Her mama Bessie was a different story. She was fiercely against my gestures to pet her, even though I would catch her watching me snuggle with my other cats from afar. One day Bessie was sitting on my bed and I casually approached her, putting my hand on her back, closer to her tail. She didn't move. I managed two more strokes before she pushed away. This small feat took over three years for me to accomplish, and after that, she began to allow full-on pets, but only on my bed. Bessie and Lulu both sleep with me now, and I can pet them, but to this day I have yet to hold either of them in my arms. I even had to have our vet come by with his cat-catching net to snag them before my apartment was sprayed for moths because we all had to leave while it was done.

Laura Zaccardi, blogger, *Squeedunk, Whiskers and Warehouse*, and co-founder of PAD PAWS Animal Rescue, Jersey City, NJ

My cat, Chevy, is a squirmy, "don't pick me up" little dude unless he "needs" attention which typically happens when I'm just out of the shower. He'll weave around my wet legs, the signal I can pick him up, and then I'll be rewarded with equally wet head bonks and kisses!

Sassenach MacConney

My ex-husband learned the hard way that my cat, Kitty, was not a fan of being held, especially by him. She would act all come-hither, lying on her back to expose her fluffy belly to him, which he couldn't resist, and then she'd attack him! It got to the point when she purposely flopped down in front of him, he'd say, "Yeah, I'm not falling for that again!" Kitty would occasionally allow moments of affection and jump onto my lap, but that would last about 30 seconds before she'd jump back off. Or she'd wait until I was asleep and then snuggle next to me, which I wouldn't realize until I woke up and saw her next to me. I once took a cat personality quiz that labeled Kitty a "secret service cat." It was a joke, but I liked thinking of her that way. She didn't interact much with me, but always had to be in the same room as me, much like a secret service agent guards a particular person, but isn't allowed to fraternize with them!

Katherine Kern, writer/blogger at *Momma Kat and Her Bear Cat*

Carson is a gorgeous lynx point Siamese. He was supposedly feral, but it turned out he was just upset about the library-style book deposit he was unceremoniously dumped down. Used by some shelters for people to drop cats off after hours, the cats are shoved into a large door that dumps them to the feral cat area where they stay the night. Understandably traumatized, many of them end up incorrectly evaluated as feral. The woman who intercepted Carson couldn't calm him but saw something special in him and asked me, whom she knew had a farm, to take him. I did, and by day 30, he was eating out of my hands, purring like a motorboat and rolling around in my lap. He's an indoor cat now and can't seem to get enough human or cat contact (I have seven cats), but despite that, I can't pick him up. He knows when it's "that time of the month," i.e., flea medication and nail trimming. The only way I can administer the medication or clip his nails is when we're in the bathroom with the door closed—that's okay, but nowhere else. He no longer shakes uncontrollably when I have to pick him up, and any time I have to take him to the vet, all seven cats go, which makes him happy.

Adrienne Usher, researcher, Kearneysville, WV

My long-haired Persian, Brulee, is the Queen of Squirmy. On her very first vet visit, the tech couldn't take her temperature because she was squirming so much. If I try to pick her up, she immediately wiggles out of my arms to get down. And when I try to brush/comb her belly, she can twist so quickly, it's a major challenge to groom her. Even if I just reach over to pet her, she moves away—probably because she thinks I'm going to clean her eyes, even when I'm not, so she runs away just to be safe. Despite all that, first thing in the morning when I wake up, Brulee is usually on the bed before her fur-sister, Truffle, and she'll give me the cutest little squeak for a meow, and will climb into my lap and begin purring. As long as I sit on the bed, she'll stay on my lap and snuggle into me, but if I try to get her to sit on my lap any other place in the house, she refuses.

Paula Gregg, blogger, *Sweet Purrfections*

One time my upstairs neighbor knocked on my door—he had taken in a beautiful Tonkinese cat, Tiffany, which he wasn't able to keep. She had a history of several owners, probably having been abused along the line, and didn't trust people at all. I agreed to take her and sure enough, she didn't trust me and would try to bite and scratch if I tried to touch her. I was disappointed not to have a cuddly cat, but vouched I wouldn't be another in the long list of those who had abandoned her. A year later, I had to move and friends watched Tiffany until I found a place that allowed cats. True to form, she hid, coming out for her food only when they were out of sight, which is why their jaws dropped one day when she came into the living room, jumped up on the side table next to them, and started rubbing herself on the phone. A minute later, the phone rang. I usually called them at work, so this was the first time I called them at home. Tiffany knew—somehow—and was there, waiting. When I finally brought her home, I let her out of her carrier, and respectfully, didn't try to touch her. I lay down for a quick nap—moments later, she came up on my chest and put her paws around my neck and clung to me for hours until I eventually had to get up. Over the years, she became so trusting that I could cradle her in my arms like a baby.

My mom also had a cat with trust issues. Cali was a rescue—she wasn't overly friendly and had a low, acid meow, letting you know to leave her alone, though she never scratched or bit. She loved classical music and often when my dad played his record albums, she would place herself between the speakers and lie on her back, writhing with unbridled delight to the rhythm of the music. When the music stopped, she would promptly run off with an air of "that never happened."

Jacqueline McKannay, owner of ThirstyCat Fountains

~PURR POINTS TO PONDER~

Why do cats have such varying degrees of how much affection they'll allow? One minute all is seemingly well and you can pet them, the next the claws come out, ready for war. What just happened? Well, just like people, cats have different personalities and levels of tolerance for physical attention, often dictated by the current circumstances surrounding them. Just because your cat might not seem friendly, or lashes out, doesn't mean he doesn't appreciate your company. You just need to recognize the unique signs of feline love he's giving you and respect the boundaries he's setting at that particular moment.

Following you from room to room like a loyal puppy dog, sleeping next to your computer while you're doing whatever, napping on your favorite chair, and meowing a greeting of hello when you come into a room are some of the many ways your cat is giving you a nod of approval.

Follow your cat's lead and build your relationship with positive reinforcement. Aggressively chasing him to pick him up or looking him straight in the eyes can be intimidating. He doesn't intend to be mean, but if he feels threatened, he'll react. Talk in gentle tones and focus on petting him in small doses and in areas he'll tolerate. For example, most cats aren't fans of tummy rubs, so don't provoke him, no matter how adorable and fluffy his tummy is.

A cat that doesn't tolerate petting might enjoy some gentle grooming with a brush—not only will it reduce the chances of him developing hairballs, it feels good to him and can strengthen your bond. Cats are also drawn to soft blankets and pillows. Try placing one next to you when you sit on the couch; maybe he doesn't want to snuggle on your lap, but he might not mind snuggling next to you.

Interactive play can also be fun for both of you—a wand toy with feathers typically entices most any cat. Or try a healthy and yummy snack—there are very few cats that won't turn on the charm for a tasty morsel, allowing you to be his best friend for at least a few minutes. If you establish a daily routine with these types of efforts, it shouldn't take long before he associates you with good things.

Be mindful your cat comes with history, especially if you found him as a stray or adopted him from a shelter. You don't always know what kind of life he had and much of his behavior will be triggered by situations from his past. Be patient and listen to how he communicates to you—a wave of the tail, a twitch of the ear, a meow and more—all of these are ways he's "talking" to you.

Current circumstances will also dictate what he'll tolerate—if he just had an altercation with another pet or has been startled by something outside or is wary of visiting company or anything else out of his perceived norm, it's not the time to be experimenting with hugs.

If he's growling, hissing or spitting, with flat, backward ears, dilated pupils, and a twitching or waving tail, he's telling you to leave him alone. He's annoyed, frightened, or angry and might become aggressive—this is also not the time to be picking him up. The same goes if he becomes a "Halloween" cat—ears back and flat against his head, whiskers back, back arched, fur standing on end and tail erect or low.

But if he's arching his back up to meet your hand when you pet him, with his fur flat and tail high, proud, and erect, that's a signal he's enjoying your touch! This is often accompanied by chirps and trills, which probably means he wants something from you—such as food or attention. This is how a mother cat communicates to her kittens to follow her, so this could be a good time to take advantage of his pleasant mood with some lovey-dovey attention!

If he's lying on his back, purring, he's very relaxed and would probably welcome some affection. Purring is generally a sign of contentment, but it can be deceiving, as sometimes a cat may purr when he's anxious or sick, using his purr to internally comfort himself. Just pay attention to the signs he's subtly (and sometimes not so subtly) giving you, and it will help you determine what is, and isn't working as you build your loving relationship.

Cats in Toyland

There probably isn't one single toy I haven't bought for my cats. I'm addicted to making them happy, so as a result, we have baskets (yes, baskets, plural) filled with every cat toy imaginable because I can't walk past the pet aisle in any store without getting them something. This includes getting them stuff we already have dozens of, such as fake mice, because goodness knows it takes them less than a minute playing with one before it goes to that magical toy graveyard under the couch, only to be resurrected from the dead if and when I ever decide to pull the couch out to vacuum.

Poor Jazmine doesn't have enough toys.

I also get to review really cool cat products on my blog. I'm talking the *good* stuff—the kind of stuff that requires an engineering team who have graduated with PhDs for the product to make it to store shelves. My cats get to be the study group; their typical verdict—the box the stuff came in is better than the product.

Dear so and so. Thank you so much for sending me that really expensive item for my cats to test out and review so lots of people will buy it. I'm sure it's a really super product—as soon as my cats get out of the box it came in, I'll let you know.

But truthfully, if I were a cat, I think sometimes I would prefer the box over the toy too. We've had some epic fails in our house—for example, a plastic mouse that's supposed to simulate the real thing. It's powered by a mini battery and moves around the floor in circles. The problem—it's as loud as a cat in heat, so they'll only come near it when it's turned off and, thus, completely dead. And, for a cat, what's the fun of prey if it's already dead?

I think the most unusual "toy" I've ever seen any of my cats (and by that, I mean Jazmine) play with is a string bean. I love to buy fresh string beans, and in order to cook them, I cut each end with a paring knife. I'm really quick at it, and Jazmine likes to sit on the counter and watch me while I do it. Her head goes back and forth, just as quickly as my cutting hand does, as she watches the rhythmic procedure: cut the stem from one end of the bean, let it drop to the sink, cut the stem from the other end, and repeat.

If I slow down for even a second, she swiftly grabs a cut stem from the sink with her stealthy little paws and runs off with her treasure—I know this because I'll find remnants of little bean stems all over the house. And when I'm all done and I'm wiping down the counter, she does the same thing with the sponge I'm using—she watches my wiping motion, and I get the impression she thinks I'm flinging a threatening mouse back and forth!

~MEWS FROM OTHERS~

Cathy Keisha (CK) has always been a different kind of cat. Kind of playful, but kind of feral too, and she's never really liked traditional cat toys. She'd easily get bored batting any of the plush mice that I would throw to her, so I needed to think outside the box to keep her properly entertained. At the $1 & Up store, two toys caught my eye— a gun that shot round plastic discs, and a launcher with foam rockets. I bought them both—the disc toy quickly broke, but the foam rockets held up and CK loves playing with them. When playtime begins, she'll get into one end of her cat tunnel and I crouch nearby with the rocket launcher. Then I say, "On the count of three, I'm going to fire the rocket. One! Two! Threeee!" and every time I do it, she runs at the count of three and makes a mad dash through the tunnel to chase the rocket.

Pattie Kleinke, blogger, *Stunning Keisha*

I remember a time my cat, Rose, was staring intently at something on the kitchen floor. Since she has an obsession with twist-ties, that's what I thought she was looking at, probably getting ready to pounce on it for a game of twist-tie toss. Upon inspection, it turns out it was a tiny lizard, stretched out in a twist-tie shape that had gotten in the house. While she probably was planning on pouncing on it, and would have preferred it to a twist-tie, I saved the lizard before any harm was done!

Jason Manocchio, attorney, Plantation, FL

I took in Mouse (aka Maggie Mouse) at 2 days old. She was born in a metal scrap yard—the owners thought the mom had abandoned Mouse and her sibling sisters, and I stepped in. After round-the-clock feedings for several weeks, I bonded strongly with my kitten charges, all of them consequently becoming "foster fails." One of my favorite stories is Mouse's obsession with balls of rolled-up foil she uses to play a weird bathtub game I call "Keep Away Tub Soccer." It goes like this: Mouse brings the ball to the tub, hits it fast, toward the drain, and then she races to the end of the tub after it to keep it from going in the drain. All the while, she's meow-singing in her little high-pitched voice. Shortly after, she'll appear and drop the ball in front of me to throw again, and the game starts anew. I can always tell when she's done because she either drops the ball out of my reach or doesn't bring it back at all.

Catherine Fleming, Spring, TX

To each her own when it comes to toys. My cat, Tigtig, has a very unusual favorite toy—a cheap, plastic flyswatter! She likes to be lightly spanked with it and will become completely unhinged during the process. She rolls her head, bumping it on anything close by, and will plop over and grab hold of any object that will make her slide around on the floor!

Melissa Formby, Lampasas, TX

For some cats, it's a particular toy in the house that piques their interest, for my cat, Barney, it's the house that's the toy! Barney has an evening habit of playing King-of-the-Mountain that involves possession of nearly every nook and cranny he can lay his paws on. He starts out by running though the catio and diving through the cat door into the sunroom. A quick right turn to tear through the living room and down the front hall where he makes a U-turn (pushing the throw rug up against the front door), and dashes up the stairs and down the hallway to my office where he begins a very loud series of meows. Sometimes he does this routine several times in an evening, and I often wake up in the morning to the front hallway rugs akimbo. He stopped his routine for a few months after his "mom" (my dog) passed away, but is once again back on schedule, treating me to a nightly show.

Marci Kladnik, president of the Cat Writers' Association, award-winning writer, photographer, and feral cat/TNR expert

~PURR POINTS TO PONDER~

Toys and playing are extremely important to the health and well-being of your cat. Not only does playing help to keep her physically and mentally fit, but using interactive toys to play with her will hone the bond you have with one another, relieve any stresses she might have by allowing her to exert energy, and permit her to act like the skilled hunter she was born to be.

I schedule playtime every night with my cats using an interactive pole/string toy with a feather dangling on the end, and I make sure each of them gets time to engage with the toy. I've nicknamed the toy "Bird," and there have been numerous "Birds" in our life because they have a limited lifespan with my active clan before they have to be retired to the garbage can.

Jazmine loves the activity so much she'll go on her own to get Bird—I learned that one night when I heard a huge ruckus (you know what I mean—the indiscernible sound of crashing and banging of goodness knows what) and saw her come proudly prancing into the living room with Bird in her mouth—stick, feathers, string, and all. The closet was in shambles—boxes and blankets knocked to the floor—and as a consequence, Bird now lives behind a locked door.

Strings can be dangerous to cats, so it's best not to keep them out with an unsupervised cat. And by hiding Bird, it also makes the playtime more exciting—if Bird were constantly out in plain view, the thrill of the hunt would be lessened. All I have to do is say "Bird" and Jazmine will run ahead of me to the closet, waiting for me to open the door. And if I ever think about not bringing Bird out because I'm just too tired at the end of the day to play, I've got another think coming. Jazmine will give me the saddest look ever, so naturally she wins.

Kizmet prefers the simplicity of a glittery pompom ball that he will bring to me to throw (over and over and over). Like Bird, there have been many pompoms, as they can virtually disappear into thin air. Thankfully I was able to buy them in bulk—I got a package of 100 from *Amazon.com*. I probably could just pull the couch away from the wall to restock, but that seems far too logical. Mia is my high-tech kitty—she loves to play interactive "fishing" games on my iPad, and Zee's my old-fashioned cat—he likes to carry around 10-year-old plush toys that he's had since he was a kitten, as if they're prey he caught.

Kizmet and his pompoms.

Regardless of the activity, maintain a regular schedule with your cat—you'd be surprised what a half hour a day of playtime can do for a cat's emotional and physical health. And it's also a good way to keep your cat mentally fit—especially as they age and become more sedentary. Some toys can be too difficult for a senior cat to engage with so you want to find something that can help keep their mind active.

I had great luck with a particular item called the Turbo Star Chaser Toy from Bergan Pet Products with my senior cat, Jazz, when he was still with us. It's a circular-shaped toy with a scratch pad in the center that's surrounded by a tubular track with a motion-activated LED ball that lights up when your cat touches it. He was instantly attracted to the toy, stretching his body full out to scratch the scratching pad and swatting at the ball to make it go around the track. Zee, our current resident senior cat at age eleven, has now claimed the toy as his own.

My turbo toy.

If you can't afford to buy toys, there are lots of great do it yourself projects to make fun stuff for your kitties—just do a quick Internet search or go to a bookstore or library for ideas. And quite honestly, in my house, some of the best toys are 100% free: a human toe, a wadded up ball of paper, wiggly fingers under a blanket, and a random bug that wanders into the house, to name just a few.

Is This Seat Taken?

What's up with cats and chairs? If your place is anything like mine, chances are good you could open your own pet store with the number of cat beds, cat pillows, cat mats, cat condos, cat shelves, and cat trees you have all over the house to make certain kitty has a warm, safe, and comfy place to nap.

So where's kitty now? Napping on your chair. One morning I went for a brief walk, and when I came home, Zoey was sound asleep on my office chair like she'd been there for hours. I'm a loving and fair-minded person—no big deal. Rather than wake her (I believe it's cat rule number 42.6a, humans aren't allowed to do that anyway), I got a spare chair from the guest bedroom for me to sit on. What did it matter it was old and rickety and super uncomfortable?

At some point I got up for a quick second to refresh my coffee. I'm literally talking about walking to the kitchen and back. I don't live in a mansion—it's a short walk—and surprisingly, there were no pit stops or distractions along the way—like a cat to pet or say hello to. I came back to find Mia napping on the spare chair like she'd been there all along. Zoey on my chair, and Mia on the spare. At this point, I was fresh out of spare chairs, so I did what any logical cat parent would do. I precariously perched myself on the edge of the chair Zoey was on and sipped my coffee (cat rule number 42.6b—if you must sit in the same chair as your cat, make sure you put their comfort ahead of yours).

Zoey in my chair,
Mia in the spare.

There's more to it, of course. I can't tell you the number of times I've been typing away on my computer in my office only to be suddenly ambushed by Kizmet. He'll bound out of nowhere and jump up and behind me, wedging in between my back, and the back of the chair, like he's morphed himself into a plush toy. Not only is there a comfortable couch in my office with lots of pillows to snuggle into, but also a shag rug to nap on and a specially designed cat perch mounted to the wall on the other side of my computer. But no, he prefers to tuck himself behind me. I will admit, though, he does make a fine pillow and I do enjoying feeling his fur and the warmth of his body against my back.

Countless times I've gone to sit down, quite innocently, only to find I'm about to squash a cat I didn't know was sitting on my chair. I would name names, but in these instances, the cat usually skedaddles so quickly I can't identify them! And anytime we have company over for dinner, it's a given one cat or another will suddenly decide our dining room chairs are *the* place to be, despite not having sat on the chairs at all for the months prior to the company visiting. It's an adorable battle of wits as the guest tries to politely get said cat to move. Which they won't. Typically, it ends with the cat sitting on the person's lap, forcing them to figure out how to eat while sitting with a cat on their lap.

As long as you're comfortable Peanut, that's all that matters...

~MEWS FROM OTHERS~

I work from home, and my cat, Valentina, initially demanded my computer chair be her own personal office space. To solve the dilemma, I found a second chair for her that I adorned with a blanket and soft tulle netting. She instantly took to it—now every time I sit down to work, she cries until I pull up her special-helper chair, and then she promptly curls up and settles in for a sound sleep. I also use tulle as a cheap and cheerful attempt to decorate the tops of my warehouse apartment to soften the industrial feel of the space.

The first time I took the tulle down to launder it, Valentina's cat-mate, Coco, fell in love with the fabric, so I bought some just for Coco's personal enjoyment. I came home one evening and caught Valentina walking down the hall with Coco's tulle in her mouth, dragging it between her legs and behind her. She just stopped and looked at me as if to say, "What? We think this piece belongs over here," and it was not uncommon for me to find the tulle had been magically reassigned a new spot during any time I was away from the apartment.

Laura Zaccardi, blogger, *Squeedunk, Whiskers and Warehouse*, and co-founder of PAD PAWS Animal Rescue, Jersey City, NJ

My 25-pound cat, Pepee, doesn't mind sharing the couch as long as he can sit next to me while I watch the nightly news. As soon as I sit down, he rushes over to be with me, especially enjoying the weather reports. When he's not sharing the couch with me, he's watching shows on his own—I tape Animal Planet's My Cat From Hell *and* Cats 101 *for him to watch.*

Elizabeth

Some cats are quite bold about stealing chairs; others are rather sneaky about it, with ulterior motives. My husband, Paul, has a cat named Chance who likes to climb up behind Paul's chair every night, being very slow and secretive about it. He then somehow magically ends up in Paul's lap and will stare at him, with squinty eyes, until Paul puts his hand on Chance and presses him onto his belly, upon which Chance promptly curls up and falls right to sleep.

Lynette Noykos, Freeland, MI

Being a good cat-parent, I made sure to buy my orange tabby cat, Abby, a brand new cat tree at the same time I purchased new furniture for my living room. I didn't want her to feel left out—but where does she sleep? On the new recliner, of course! Abby's cat tree sits in the corner of the living room, completely unused! My husband Mark and I are relegated to the couch—and not only does Abby rule the recliner, we have made it even more comfortable for her by putting a plush cat bed atop the recliner cushion!

Toni Nicholson, owner, RCTees

My Bengal, Milo, is very possessive with my husband John's computer chair—I found this out when he was out of town for a few days and I invited some musically inclined ladies to come by to play music. I warned them not to pet her, as she doesn't take well to strangers. I suggested they ignore her, letting her come to them on her own terms. As they were playing, one of the ladies giggled that Milo touched her back with her paw, no claws, just touched. They continued playing, and Milo sat on the floor watching one lady for a really long time. Thinking it was an invitation from Milo for some approved interaction, she reached down to pet her. Milo took a swipe at her hand—she didn't use her claws—and after the swipe went to her cat tree and slept until all but one guest left—a guest that was sitting in John's chair! Milo woke up, stretched, eyed the situation, jumped onto John's desk and hissed at the lady sitting in his chair. I told Milo to be nice and picked her up and put her on the floor. She jumped back up and hissed some more, walking toward the lady in stalking mode. The lady said, "I don't think she wants me sitting in John's chair," so she moved to another one. Milo then jumped up onto John's chair and stayed there, glaring at the lady until she left. On the second day John was away, Milo completely took over his chair. She would occasionally come to me to be held, but because I couldn't type and hold her, I'd put her down and she'd go back to John's chair. Other than her wariness of company, she's actually a very sweet and loving cat.

Sue Ward, Fredericton, New Brunswick, Canada

~PURR POINTS TO PONDER~

Much as you love your kitty, sometimes having her sleep in your chair isn't always convenient, and believe it or not, you actually can move her! I know you don't want to break her heart or maybe you think she'll hold a grudge, but there can be a happy medium. She just wants to be near you, so try providing alternatives that work for both of you. There's a wonderful array of cat shelves, cat trees, window seat treatments, and more specifically designed for your cat's needs to fit in nearly any room of your house or apartment. A trip to your local pet store will provide you with lots of great ideas to pick from. Or try shopping online—along with a mind-boggling selection, many of these sites offer free shipping. One of my favorite sites is *Hauspanther.com*—they're always featuring the latest and greatest in cat paraphernalia for design-conscious cat people, complete with reviews, tips, and suggestions.

My Jazmine insists she be only inches away from me when I'm on the computer. Rather than let her walk all over my keyboard, I put a shelf over my computer. I keep it padded with a bath towel so she's comfortable, and this way I can also easily remove the towel to throw it in the wash. It's a great solution—she's happy and I'm able to get a lot more work done (notwithstanding that I'm easily distracted and feel compelled to talk to her or pet her every other minute).

Supervising a human sure can be exhausting work for a cat...

As a matter of fact, she actually "reports for duty" every morning! As soon as I get my coffee and turn on the computer, it's her signal it's time to begin her busy day of supervising me. She jumps up to her spot, does a quick couple of circles to find the most comfortable area, and plunks herself there for as long as I stay. She's quite the loyal and courteous employee—granted, 99.9% of her work efforts consist of napping, but I do give her an "A" for her devotion to the task!

For those who aren't too keen on cat hair on couches and chairs (if you have a cat, it's inevitable), throw blankets are a wonderful solution. Cats love to nap on them and they come in a wide array of beautiful colors and designs—just drape them over your furniture and wash when need be.

If you have a cat that's extremely possessive of a certain chair, like Milo, who doesn't want to share with others, that will require some patience and trial and error to break the habit. One suggestion is to "share" the scent associated with the chair with the person the cat doesn't want to share with. In the case of Milo, that would translate to taking something John's scent is on, like an unwashed piece of clothing, and transferring some of that scent onto the guest by rubbing the clothing on their hands and arms. This will allow the strange person to be less threatening to the cat by smelling safe and familiar. Another tactic is to have the person sit in the chair, armed with treats and a fishing pole type of toy to play with the cat, so the cat associates that person with positive outcomes.

Love Hurts

Love hurts. Literally. One time Dan and I were innocently sitting on the couch watching TV, and Zee unexpectedly lunged up from behind us. We were caught completely off guard and couldn't duck in time, which resulted in Zee using Dan's head as a springboard to propel himself across the room in pursuit of whatever life-threatening predator had fabricated itself in our living room. Because Zee did not retract his claws, they dug so deep into Dan's head that his scalp started bleeding.

I was also blessed with a temporary love scar by Zoey early one morning when she was cuddling next to me in bed. She heard a noise that I didn't, so naturally I had no forewarning to protect myself. She jumped up and ran across my cheeks with her razor sharp claws, fully outstretched, causing me to bleed instantly. I had an interesting track-mark pattern that lasted for several weeks, and ironically, I was traveling to a cat-related writing conference a few hours after the incident happened. It made for a great conversation opener if nothing else.

Zoey also has an interesting habit when I sit on the couch at night to watch TV. Even though we live in Florida and the temperatures rarely dip below 70 degrees, I'm always chilly and will have an afghan wrapped around me. The only body parts not covered are my head and toes. I will be innocently sitting, completely immersed in whatever mindless show I'm watching, only to find my toes brutally under attack! It will be Zoey biting them. I jump, and then she quickly tunnels herself under the afghan to crouch on my lap while bleating a victorious meow. This lasts until she's satisfied all the toe monsters have been rendered dead, at which point she comes out from under the afghan to sleep on my legs the rest of the night, like nothing out of the ordinary ever happened.

And then there are the times when Zee and Peanut make biscuits on my belly, which is frequently. They do it with such passion that I can literally feel my insides moving around. My stomach will start to rumble and gurgle, and it's a rather weird and painful sensation. I typically have a full bladder at the time, so that doesn't help matters. Maybe if I had a nice, flat, toned stomach it wouldn't hurt as much, but the chances of that happening rank next to me winning the lottery.

Waking up in the morning is also a precarious endeavor. Between trying not to trip over seven cats impatiently waiting for breakfast (can I please at least go to the bathroom first?), trying not to trip over the landmine of toys Zee has left on the floor (I can't tell you the number of times I've stepped on a squeaky toy, with the loud noise echoing jarringly in the early morning hours), and trying to dodge any potential hairballs or any other surprises left by them on the floor, it's a miracle I make it to the kitchen unscathed and without a broken ankle.

~MEWS FROM OTHERS~

Sometimes love hurts, and sometimes it just plain smells as I know only too well! I was traveling to Jacksonville, Florida, with four of my show cats, including my Blue Point Mitted Lynx Ragdoll, Lover (aka Drama King), along with the two cats of my traveling partner. One of the cats farted, causing us to find a rest stop as quickly as possible to evacuate the SUV for a few moments of fresh air! Come to find out, my partner's husband thought it would be funny to feed her cats sardines about an hour before we left. Needless to say, two very angry human blondes plotted his demise the remainder of our way to

Florida! Lover is also a plotter, only his target was my Bichon Frise, Cheri. I was cleaning Lover's eyes—he didn't take too kindly to it, proclaiming so in a low meow that progressed to an ear-piercing loud whoop. When I was done cleaning and allowed him to get down, he walked over to Cheri who was innocently sitting on the floor and took out his frustration by slapping her.

Elizabeth Roberts-Berg, retired clinical psychologist, Ph.D., TX

My cats, the Captain and Gilly, have a special language between them—not really meows—but unlike any other sound I've heard a cat make. The Captain will "call" his brother to play with him, but Gilly takes a more direct approach—he will usually just start annoying his sleeping brother when he wants to play, up to and including biting him right on the butt to get up!

Lynn Maria Thompson, founder of *OldMaidCatLady.com*

Finn is a gorgeous black cat who came to me as a rescue "drop out." He was three weeks into his rescue, but since he lacked the social skills to know it wasn't proper to bite people, he was headed back to the field as a TNR (Trap/Neuter/Return) cat. But to me, he was just a kitten and deserved a chance. While teaching him some manners, I also decided to teach him something fun, something cats just aren't known to typically do—sit on command! Now socialized, he acts more like a dog and has proven cats can be friendly, involved, and responsive if you take the time and patience to work with them.

Cindy Rein, co-founder of Catopia Cat Rescue

My cat, Minko, is obsessed with shoes and sandals—in his case, he uses them as a scratching post. The trouble is, I'm wearing my shoes at the time when he feels the urge to scratch! I don't really mind, but when I'm wearing sandals, it can be rather painful!

Ingrid Rickmar, Battle Creek, Michigan

~PURR POINTS TO PONDER~

What do those "zoomies"—when a cat seems to randomly decide to run around like a two-year-old toddler high on sugar, and then stops as if nothing has happened—mean? Basically, since cats are crepuscular (meaning they are instinctively more active around dawn or dusk), it occurs as a result of their natural need to expel energy. It also stems from the fact cats need to keep their hunting skills sharp. Considering they nap most of the day, the random running and jumping helps keep their bodies in top physical form. To help your cat release that pent-up energy, it's essential to provide her with plenty of opportunities to exercise throughout the day.

Accidental scratching is a different issue, and it's important to understand your cat is not purposely trying to hurt you with her claws. Getting mad or punishing her will not help matters. The first thing you need to do is take action. For a surface scratch, disinfect your hands by washing them with soap and warm water (avoid overly hot water as it may prolong bleeding), rinse thoroughly, and apply an antibiotic ointment such as Neosporin. Let the wound air dry to heal and apply ointment several times a day.

For a deeper scratch that has punctured the skin and is bleeding heavily, stop the bleeding before you start cleaning the wound. Apply firm pressure with a clean towel to the bleeding area until the bleeding subsides. Wash your hands as above and gently clean the wounded area with soap and rinse. Dry the wound with a clean towel, apply antibiotic ointment, and cover it using a bandage or clean gauze dressings.

Deeper wounds might require medical treatment and the use of oral antibiotics to prevent infection. Typically, a wound from a fully vaccinated indoor house pet shouldn't pose a problem, but if you're scratched by a stray cat, or an unknown cat, complications could occur. Symptoms of fever; swelling of the head or neck; red, itchy, or scaly patches of skin; severe headaches; or dizziness are reasons to contact your physician as this could be the sign of a severe infection or other ailment.

To prevent further injuries, clip her nails every 2–3 weeks. You can use regular nail clippers or clippers made specifically for cats, such as the Zen Clipper brand, and with some practice, you should be able to get your cat to accept nail trimming.

If possible, start young. It's easier to get kittens used to trimming than an adult. And because paws are one of the most sensitive parts of a cat's body, take it slow. Your cat will probably squirm and try to pull away from you, so practice warming her up to the task in a positive manner. When she's most relaxed, touch one of her paws and push on her paw pad to gently extend a claw. Talk to her in gentle, soothing tones, praising her. When she's had enough, stop.

When you feel comfortable she's accepting of the feeling, try clipping. If you aren't able to trim all ten nails at once, that's okay. Few cats remain patient for more than a couple of minutes, so clip what you can, praise her (maybe give her a treat) for being good, and then be on the lookout for the next clipping opportunity. Since cats are frequently in nap mode, chances are good you'll be able to clip a nail or two on an unsuspecting cat with no undue stress.

Clip the sharp, clear end of the nail. Don't get too close to the pink part of the nail called the quick, where blood vessels and nerve endings lie as the quick is very sensitive and cutting into it will likely cause bleeding and pain. If this happens, apply slight pressure to the tip of the claw (don't squeeze the entire paw as it will increase the blood flow), dip the claw in a bit of styptic powder or cornstarch, or rub the nail across a dry bar of soap. Stop clipping and keep an eye on her to be sure the bleeding stops. Make sure your trimmers are sharp, as dull trimmers will crush and splinter the nail, making the job more difficult and stressful on your cat.

Keeping your cat's claws trimmed not only protects you, but will also protect furniture and household items from being damaged. And unlike a drastic alternative such as declawing that can adversely affect your cat's health, well-being, personality, and behavior, it's safe and humane. Declawing is a procedure that involves the amputation of each of the ten front toes of the cat's paws (something that would be equivalent to us losing the entire tip of every finger at the first knuckle) and it can cause serious, lifelong changes to a cat.

Removing the claws changes the way a cat's foot meets the ground, so walking for them would be comparable to the painful "pebble-in-the-shoe" sensation we feel when they stand or try to walk. This condition can lead to abnormal posture and movement and may even produce arthritis in the legs, which, in turn, may cripple the cat further and cause more suffering. Since cats tend to hide symptoms of pain, much of the pain is masked by behavioral tendencies that could unfortunately lead to litter box problems, which often lands them in a shelter as a result.

Ahh...Nothing like a good scratch to make kitty feel happy and healthy!

Along with keeping your cat's claws trimmed, provide her with several well-placed scratching posts. There are also products, such as vinyl Soft Paws, which safely adhere to the tips of your cats nails to prevent them from harming furniture or humans when they scratch.

Are You Going to Eat That?

Cats are obligate carnivores, and my Jazmine thoroughly lives by that inherent mindset. But she also believes in a` la carte entrees to complement the meat—a salad, side dishes, and dessert, *thank you very much*. She's a lasagna-loving Garfield wannabe cloaked into one gorgeous and sneaky ball of ginger-colored kitty fluff. Not only will she steal your heart, she'll steal the food off your plate—chickpeas, spinach leaves, green beans, grated cheese, pineapple cubes, Cheez-It® and more—she's a girl that wants it all. Basically, she's saying, "If you can have it, then I can, too."

Being the disciplinarian of the house, I carefully monitor what I feed my gang, and I try to rein her in. Dan, well, he's another story. Jazmine is the apple of his eye, and all it takes is one dainty, white-mitted paw pat to his cheek, a flirtatious blink of her golden topaz eyes, while tilting her head in the most compelling of possible ways, along with a sweet meow chirp, and he's putty in her paws. Or should I say her mouth.

Friday night is when we do our grocery shopping. It's also the night we treat ourselves to something from the deli. I'm a vegetarian, so I get whatever power-packed salad is available, and Dan gets his guilty pleasure—chicken tenders and southern potato salad. I don't cook any meat, so unless he wants to take over my role, this is his one opportunity to indulge. Much as he loves the diversion, I think he loves sharing his chicken with Jazmine even more.

Is this adorable enough yet?

Jazmine knows Friday night means treats for her. The rustle of plastic bags and the thud on the counter when we come back from shopping is a sure sign it's her night. After the groceries are put away, she runs to the couch to assume her position (yes, we eat in front of the TV) and is already waiting for us (Dan) in anticipation of some fowl goodness before we sit down.

Dan sits next to her—thoroughly trained in the Pavlov school of classical conditioning, he puts a piece of chicken in his mouth so Jazmine can take it from him. If he puts the chicken on the floor, she looks at him like he's crazy. It *has* to be from his mouth. That's their little ritual. None of the other cats do it, and in all my 50 plus years of loving cats and going to some pretty wacky extremes for them, I've never done it either.

I do have an interesting food story, however. My cat, Kit, was 15 years old and seemed to be minutes away from death's door. She had stopped eating, and for some strange reason, I decided to see if she would eat a small piece of a Kraft cheese slice. It wasn't something I'd done before, so I had no idea if she'd like it, but I was out of options and just wanted something in her stomach before I lay down with her, to what I was sure would be her last night with me.

I woke up the next morning, terrified to what I would find. And there she was—up—seemingly fit as a fiddle! She regained her appetite and lived an additional 3 years with me. I don't recommend cheese slices as a cure-all to what ails a cat, but I can say without a doubt, in this instance, Kraft saved her life.

~MEWS FROM OTHERS~

My cat, Lola, is a lush. Not wine or mixed drinks, just beer. The minute I open a bottle, she comes speeding in to perch on my shoulder. She's not given any beer to drink, but for whatever reason, she's fascinated with watching me imbibe! No other food or drink causes this reaction, just beer.
Samantha Rembo, designer, San Diego, CA

When I was a child, my cat, Oskar, was absolutely crazy about tomato soup. No meat, cream, or anything like that. Just your average cold, vegetarian tomato soup with little spaghetti chunks in it. I guess he developed a taste for tomato when he was treated to canned mackerel in tomato sauce!
Thomas Clausen, custom pet portrait artist, *www.tclausen.net*

Most cats "magically" appear at the whirr of a can opener or the rustle of a treat bag or with the heady aroma of cooking fish. And while our beloved angel cat, Moosey, did enjoy those things, the snack that always brought him running into the kitchen was lettuce. We discovered it by chance when Tracey accidentally dropped a piece on the floor, and Moosey quickly moved in for an up-close inspection. "Kitties don't like lettuce, Moosey," Tracey said. Moosey's response? He gobbled up the lettuce, licked his chops, looked up at her with his big blue eyes, and meowed for more. In a state of disbelief, she fed him another piece by hand, and he nearly bit her finger off! From then on, when we had salad, we all *had salad.*

Tracey and Kevin Hattori of the award-winning blog, *Animal Shelter Volunteer Life,* **and volunteers at PAWS of Norwalk, CT**

Kitty loved the smell of onions and came running anytime I chopped one up. She never ate one, but Bear, one of my other cats—that's another story! I had taken a bite of Bodacious Onion Dip (a dip with a fiery kick) and quickly ran for water. I was gone for only a minute and Bear had already downed a few bites of the dip. Thank goodness it didn't make him sick and I now know better—the only reason I left the dip out unattended was because I was sure he wouldn't touch it.

Katherine Kern, writer/blogger at *Momma Kat and Her Bear Cat*

My husband, Brandon, and I have taco night a couple of times a month for dinner. It used to be uncomplicated until our cat, Chewbacca, discovered he liked tacos, too! Chewbacca's a food-hound and Brandon would always let Chewbacca eat off his dinner plate. The first time Chewbacca tasted a piece of taco, he quickly munched it down and promptly decided he wanted more! Now I have to make extra tacos so Brandon can prepare a couple just for Chewbacca! Rather than let Chewbacca eat them from his plate, which can get a bit messy, Brandon puts them on the floor on a piece of wax paper and Chewbacca will growl at our other cats if they dare try to steal his tacos from him!

Toni and Brandon Armstrong, Thomaston, GA

My angel cat, Lucy, was very particular when it came to beverages. She liked milk, but there were rules. It could not be straight from the jug—it could only be room temperature milk from a bowl with cereal in it. But she would only drink it after the cereal was completely gone!

Allison Hunter-Frederick, part-time teacher and blogger

~PURR POINTS TO PONDER~

While it's nearly impossible to resist your cat's insistent and adorable plea for human food, feeding her your food really must be done in moderation and with caution. First, certain human foods just aren't safe for kitty, and second, your cat should be eating foods specifically developed for her dietary needs so she can live a healthy lifestyle befitting her specifically feline requirements.

When it comes to cooked meat, a bite or two of your meal is okay, but don't go overboard, and no cooked bones because they have the potential to splinter if ingested. Make sure the meat is fully cooked to prevent salmonella bacteria. Some tuna now and again is okay too, but a steady diet of tuna prepared for humans can lead to malnutrition because it won't have all the nutrients a cat needs. And too much tuna can cause mercury poisoning.

Garlic, onions, and shallots in all forms—powered, raw, cooked, or dehydrated—can break down a cat's red blood cells, leading to anemia, and raw doughs with yeast and eggs could cause gastrointestinal upset or possible food poisoning from bacteria such as salmonella or E. coli.

As for that bowl of milk for kitty—while some cats can handle it, most cats are lactose-intolerant, so their digestive system cannot process dairy foods, which results in digestive upset and diarrhea. Grapes and raisins are also dangerous—a cat can easily choke on them, and they can also cause kidney failure. Chocolate and caffeine are also highly toxic—even lethal—and should be avoided at all costs.

The best advice, if you do give your cat human food, is to do it in moderation, avoiding any foods that are known to be dangerous to them. The ideal diet for your cat is a raw food diet or a high-quality canned food diet where protein is listed as the first ingredient on the label, with the meat/poultry fit for human consumption, and grain-free.

Dry kibble diets, while convenient, can be bad for your cat. Cats need moisture to support their bodily functions and a dry food only diet can leave them in a state of low-level dehydration which can lead to urinary tract, kidney, and bladder problems. If your cat is a dry kibble only eater, transitioning her to a raw/canned food diet can be tricky—I know from my own personal experience because I had been feeding it to my gang (mixed with canned) for years, not realizing the complications of dry food until recently.

My Mia was completely addicted, and time, patience, and tricks were necessary to get her to eat anything else. But it's no wonder—dry food is actually made with that intention in mind by pet food manufacturers. They coat the kibble with extremely enticing animal digest sprays and additives, such as pyrophosphates—making a poor quality diet preferable to the target animal, i.e., your cat.

The other problem is that cats can be highly resistant to change. If your cat has been eating a crunchy texture for years, introducing a canned or raw food product can be challenging. It's best to promote a healthy diet when your cat is young so she's accustomed to it, but if that's not possible, the key to a successful transition is to be patient and to not give up in frustration. Cats can be very stubborn, so you need to be even more stubborn!

What's Mine Is Mine and What's Yours Is Mine

This is so rudimentary to the feline-human relationship I almost considered not mentioning it, but for those of you reading this who might be new to the whole "you've-got-a-cat-in-your-life-thing," let me set the record straight so you can move on. Regardless of the mountains of cat paraphernalia you will buy for your darling feline (and trust me, *you will* buy mountains of it)— expensive cat beds, cute cat feeding bowls, designer cat condos, new-fangled litter boxes and state-of-the-art litter, fancy grooming tools, cat-specific toys, cat food that costs more than human food, kitty treats, and more—it's really quite simple: *those things belong to your cat, and everything else in your house also belongs to your cat.*

Your bed. The kitchen counter. The kitchen sink. Book shelves. Dresser drawers. The top of the refrigerator. Any and all chairs, couches, ottomans, and recliners. Your shoes. Your clean laundry. Your dirty laundry. The food you eat. The straw in your drink. Your toes. Your legs. Your purse. Your suitcase. Your computer keyboard. The top of your printer. Empty boxes. Full boxes. Your lap. The top of your head. The bottom of your feet. The list is endless, so for simplicity's sake, it's just easier to boil it down to everything and anything.

Even the oddest things you think your cat would have no interest in, they do. Rolz was endlessly fascinated with the stainless steel drain plug in our master bathroom shower stall. I heard a weird clinking noise one day and, after investigating, saw it was him diligently trying to lift the plug with his front paws. It wasn't easy, so it kept hitting the shower tiles as he partially lifted it, only for it to fall back down, thus the clinking noise. Perennially patient, he finally freed it, and it made a loud, echoing clinkkkkkkkkkkkkkkkkkkk noise as it sprung lose from the hole and hit the tile floor. I put it back, but since he now knew what he was doing, he immediately pulled it back out like I was some sort of dingbat for thinking it was meant to be there. This went on for quite some time until I finally gave up and we no longer have a shower plug. It's been sitting on the floor of our shower for approximately three years now.

~MEWS FROM OTHERS~

My cat, Barry McNaughtypants, lives up to his name and takes the "mine is mine" concept to whole new levels—he opens doors in our house and lets himself outside! He doesn't get out intentionally—I try my best to keep the doors locked, but sometimes he's quicker than I am. Once outside, he sits and follows anyone who walks by. Then, if someone should pass them, he turns and follows that person instead. He has ended up as far away as a mile before someone called me to let me know he was found. I once got a call that he was having breakfast with one of the neighbor's kids and was welcome to stay for lunch; they were having one of his favorite foods—Spaghetti-O's. Another neighbor called to say he followed her husband in from taking out the garbage and was asleep on the couch with their dog—they had never met him before. Barry rarely comes home on his own and would be a world traveler if he didn't have a collar on with his name on it!

Heidi M. Shields, Portage, WI

My life changed the day I found a black and white tuxedo cat, Tux, sitting unattended in the hallway of my apartment building. Dubbed "Mayor of the Hall," he would be seen on one side of the hallway one day and somewhere else the next, often patiently sitting next to the door of whatever apartment he hoped might be friendly enough to let him in. Over time, he came to me for some cautious pets, but it never occurred to me to let him in as I didn't even know his owner. But Tux settled it—he was out to lay claim to not only the apartment I shared with my daughter, Jennifer, and my wife, Leslie, but our hearts. The fateful day occurred when Leslie came home with grocery bags in tow. Tux hid behind one of the bags, and as Leslie came in, so did he—leading us on a mad chase around our apartment before we could finally get him out. The next time I saw him, his owner was in the hall, and introductions were made. I had initially believed his name was "Tox," as that's what I thought I heard his owner calling him. I remembered thinking what an awful name for a cat —was it short for toxic? But no, it was Tux. I then asked if Tux could visit, she said yes, and the rest was history.

I was given a cardboard box for him to sleep in, some of his favorite toys, and food dishes. Tux loved the arrangement and would spend the entire day with us, only to go home when it was litter box time or the end of the day, and he never volunteered— he was always escorted home by his owner. He would sometimes even go so far as to get into his cardboard box, curl up in a ball, hide, and put his paw over his face, as if to say "you can't take me home if I can't see you!" His daily routine was simple—he'd go by his front door and meow until his owner brought him over to our place. If she was busy at her desk, he'd push the papers off her desk until she brought him over. When he needed to go home for a litter break, he'd "ask" for a treat first (no self-respecting cat could possibly expect to take that long trip down the hall on an empty stomach). He would then open the closet door next to the entrance door and stare at it—his signal to be let out. This continued for eight years until the moment we feared came—his owner had to move and we would never see Tux again. Some two months after moving, his owner called to say Tux had suffered a saddle thrombosis and couldn't be saved. Our grief was profound, but we were grateful for every moment we were able to share with our custodial, tuxedoed friend.

John Brindisi, cat care giver from New York

Some cats lay claim to physical items, others, like my cat, Ruby, lay claim to music! She loves music so much; that whenever I'm playing Pandora on my phone, she has to be right next to it or almost on top of it. And when I play Pandora on my TV, she'll lie on top of the TV. I used to wake up to music every morning with the alarm on my phone but had to stop because Ruby would jump on the phone and shut it off before I'd even wake up! Thankfully, I've never been late for work as a result of her musical obsession. If anything, I'm grateful for it— Ruby's not a very affectionate cat, but if I'm lying in bed or lounging on the couch looking at my phone and music comes on, she immediately jumps up to lie on my chest to get as close to the phone as possible.

Mari Brandy, registered nurse, Jacksonville, FL

My cat, JB, gets into my stuff all the time, but he usually leaves telltale evidence behind like a random whisker, a clump of hair, or a hacked up hairball. How was I to make the connection between him and my iPad one morning, when suddenly, for no discernable reason, I could no longer insert the charger into the charging port of my iPad? Nothing worked and I became anxious, envisioning having to be without my iPad for an indefinite timeframe while it got repaired. Resigned to knowing I had no other choice, I drove down to my local electronics repair shop and ran inside. After a quick explanation of the problem to the technician, I reluctantly handed the iPad over. The repair man took a glance in the port and said, "There's something in there." He then grabbed a pair of tweezers and extracted a tiny object. "What is it?" I asked. He placed the item in the palm of my hand. I looked in disbelief, and then looked closer. No. It couldn't be. But it was—he had pulled out a tiny piece of claw that clearly came from one place—the paw of JB! I looked at the repair man with embarrassment, dressed in my cat T-shirt and kitty earrings, and after it was confirmed I wasn't going to be charged any fees, I grabbed my iPad and went home. JB greeted me at the front door with a sweet, innocent meow and a very mischievous look. To this day, I don't know what JB was doing with my iPad, let alone how he got one of his claws stuck in it!

JB Bean, author of *Mister's Garden*

I'm a University of Florida graduate so it's no surprise I have an Arthur Court silver tray adorned with gators in my possession. What was surprising, however, was when my cat, the Captain, was a kitten. He loved lying in it as if it were some sort of cat bed instead of a tray to serve food! As he grew, I had to put the tray away because he was hanging over the sides too much and I figured he wasn't doing his skeletal system any favors!

Lynn Maria Thompson, founder of *OldMaidCatLady.com*

I began my career as a talent agent quite by accident in the 1960's after befriending Janis Joplin and Jimi Hendrix, whom I met at an apartment building I had just moved to from Queens, New York, to Los Angeles. Armed only with a degree in sociology, I unwittingly became one of the most influential wheeler-dealers in show business, managing such diverse stars as Alice Cooper, Anne Murray, Blondie, Pink Floyd, Teddy Pendergrass, Luther Vandross, Raquel Welch, Frankie Valli and Groucho Marx. But underneath my extravagant lifestyle of sex, drugs, money, and fame was a man with a soft spot for cats. One of them was Mr. Sensitive, a wild cat I found living under some bushes on my property that I adopted. Mr. Sensitive has a story that could only happen in Hollywood—I shared custody of him with my neighbor—actor Cary Grant! I've since given up the Hollywood lifestyle and moved to Hawaii to concentrate on culinary arts and my beloved cats. Mr. Sensitive has since passed on—he lived a full ten years with me—but since then, I've found another wild cat to adopt who lived 13 years (Mocha), along with my newest adoption, Squirt, whom I got from a shelter.

Shep Gordon, talent manager, film agent, producer, and author

~PURR POINTS TO PONDER~

It's all well and good our cats feel comfortable enough to "own" everything in the house, but for the practicality of keeping your possessions and your sanity intact, and for the safety of your cat, certain things need to be considered. For example, if you have a mantel, shelf, or bookcase with breakable decorative items, you might want to hold them in place with museum putty, pack them away altogether, or replace them with unbreakable knick-knacks so your cat doesn't jump up and accidently knock them over.

Or maybe you don't want your cat jumping up somewhere such as the kitchen counter and claiming it as his bachelor pad. Cats are intuitively drawn to counters as a social outlet—both for your company and as a source of food. Keeping him off might be a test of wills, but with some patience and training, the habit can be broken. Try a motion-activated air blaster to startle him or put double-sided tape on the counter to deter his jumping. It's also important to provide a positive outlet to redirect what you consider negative behavior from him. Put a designated stool (or chair, or cat condo) near the counter so every time you tell him "no" and remove him from the counter, you can put him on the stool and reward him with a "good boy" and a treat so he associates the stool with something good.

I actually allow my cats on the counter—I enjoy having them around me, and as a matter of fact, Jazmine "helps" me cook dinner every night. Our counter is double tiered—she sits on the top shelf, intently following my every move as I do whatever chopping, stirring, and mincing that needs to be done like she's an apprentice studying to become a seasoned chef. She likes to flop over onto her back, exposing her belly while cocking her head upside down to give me the most heart-melting look imaginable. And yes, if appropriate, she does get a human treat. You try resisting that cute face of hers.

Uh huh. So you cut the artichoke up into tiny pieces. Then what?

If "non-cat" company happens to come by (what? how dare they not be a cat person), I just pretend to act shocked when any of the cats are on the counter (around dinner time, all seven of them can be hovering), and I'll feign an "Oh my goodness, I've never seen them do *that* before."

I've also learned some invaluable lessons about leaving breakable stuff out. It started with Zee when he was younger. He had an extremely militant clock in his furry little head, and for him, he was adamant Dan and I go to bed on schedule at 11:00 p.m. One night we had family over and were socializing in the backyard. The window was open and Zee could hear us laughing. We could see him pacing on the counter—clearly agitated, he was telling us it was past our bedtime.

Unfortunately, I didn't realize the seriousness of his pacing. Ker-rashhhhhhhhhh came the sound of a glass bottle filled with grenadine that plunged to the floor, exploding in an impressive display of bright pink liquid all over the floor and cabinets. If I didn't know better, I'd swear he knocked it over to let us know of his displeasure. And back when Mia, Peanut, and Rolz were kittens and realized they could jump up onto the counter, the first victim of that achievement was a glass coffee carafe I had left out to air dry. It went crashing to the floor, smashing into thousands of dangerous shards of glass. We no longer keep anything breakable on the counter.

Houdini Cats

I remember one 4th of July—normally we stay at home, but this particular year Dan and I decided to take a trip to the beach to watch the spectacle. We live in South Florida and had never seen a display over the ocean before and thought it was about time we gave it a try. We were getting ready to leave and I did my standard cat check—one, two, three, four, five, six, seven...eight...eight? Where was cat number eight? Cat number eight who happened to be Rolz in this case.

We did the typical—we looked in every closet and then looked in the same closet again. And again. We opened every closed door. Shook bags of kitty treats. Opened cans of cat food. Called his name—a zillion times. Even though we hadn't been outside all day and had seen Rolz in the house earlier (not to mention, he's not allowed outside), we looked outside for him. We looked under furniture, on top of shelves, and then we just got plain ridiculous. We looked in the refrigerator, in closed drawers, and in the garage—somewhere else we hadn't been all day.

Rolz, our big, hulking cat had vanished into thin air. He was purposely hiding—probably due to the combination of the panic Dan and I were emitting and the fact he was just bothered by the random people in the neighborhood letting off noisy firecrackers. Common sense dictated he was in the house, and logically, we knew he was around, so we decided to go see the fireworks.

I think we lasted about a block before we made the decision to turn the car around and go back and look for him. My heart was beating a mile a minute—I was a nervous wreck as to what we might find, and when we opened the door, Rolz was sitting on top of the cat condo in the dining room, washing his front paws in the most matter-of-fact, bored way imaginable. I swear he looked at me and was laughing, as if to say, "Ha! You fool, I knew you were looking for me the whole time and I was just making a game of you finding me!"

Yawn.
Humans
can be so
predictable.

I had another cat, Harley, who had been living with me for years and was rather shy and timid by nature. My mom happened to be cat-sitting while Dan and I were out of town. I got a text from her asking who my newest cat was. I didn't have a new cat. It was Harley who had scurried past her like a scared bolt of lightning.

~MEWS FROM OTHERS~

One day I was looking for my beautiful, long-haired kitty, Big Eric, or Almost Feral Eric as I called him. Even though he was born on my property, he was shy around most people except for me and my husband, John. I heard a pitiful mewing and there he was, hidden in the rafters of our shed, acting helpless about getting down. I tried everything, including tossing slices of ham up to him, which he ate, but he refused to come down. His cat-brother, Conor, raced up the side of the wall and then down, showing him the way. Finally, despite my hate of heights, I had to climb up a stepladder and grab him. I had a quick vision of the two of us stuck up there—but I finally got him down. He then looked at me as if nothing had happened and demanded more ham!

Stephanie Piro, nationally syndicated cartoonist and the Saturday Chick of King Features' *Six Chix*

My cat, Calvin, is perfectly fine making himself visible until the alarm is sounded, i.e., three dogs barking madly that there might possibly be a new human (aka "Unapproved Person") entering the house, and then he runs for the nearest hiding place he can find to disappear. Generally, those spots are your basic under the bed, under the sofa kinds of places, and occasionally they require more effort, such as threading himself between some photo albums or into such a tiny space, I swear he must fold himself up like an origami cat. Sometimes he completely miscalculates and doesn't have time to get to a designated safe spot, such as the time he ended up on the top shelf in my kitchen where I keep my flour, sugar, and coffee canisters! When the "all-clear" signal is given—either the dogs go back to sleep, or

the new person is quietly settled in one place—Calvin will tentatively creep up and perform an unseen sneaky sniff to determine if the person is friend or foe.
Susan C. Willett, writer and humorist, *LifeWithDogsAndCats.com*

I once spent hours looking for my cat Lucy. I checked all my closets, bureaus, and under my bed. I recalled opening the bottom bureau drawer earlier in the day, so I checked that one twice just to be sure—no Lucy. Several hours later, I checked the bureau again, this time checking the middle drawer that I hadn't previously looked at. There was Lucy, sound asleep! It turns out she had crawled through the side and into the middle drawer, but since I hadn't opened that drawer, I didn't see her!
Ellen Pilch, blogger at *15andmeowing.com*, Ware, MA

The cats in my family are masters of disguise. Shortly after I moved into my new house, Dude went missing. I only had a one-bedroom ranch, with very little in the way of furniture for him to jump on or crawl under, so his whereabouts were a mystery. It was dead of winter—no windows opened, doors all shut—and I was searching places he could not possibly have gone. Running out of ideas, I called my mom who lived nearby to help and as I was dialing, I turned around and there was Dude sitting in the middle of the floor with what looked like a grin on his face.

My parent's cat, Daisy, also vanished one time. They had been searching for over an hour and were just about to call me for help when they spotted her. She was sound asleep on the curtain rod in their dining room! She probably used the dining room table as a launch pad, but how she stayed on the curtain rod is anyone's guess—even though Daisy's a tiny cat, the curtain rod is only two inches wide, if that. But it's their other cat, Boomer, which takes the cake for being the ultimate magician. He has a knack for climbing things—ladders, deck railings, curtains and more—typical cat stuff—but what he accomplished in their basement laundry room was astonishing. The basement has exposed cross beams, with maybe a three-inch "ledge" on each side of the beams. My mom was doing laundry—she heard the noise of a cat making a fuss and looked up. It was Boomer—he was standing on the crossbeam ledge. How he got up there remains a mystery, as there were no jumping points near the cross beam, either under it, beside it, or anywhere else.

Da Tabbies O Trout Towne

I found myself in a panic one day thinking my cat, Waffles, had somehow gotten out of the house. After searching high and low, I finally found him holed up inside a box spring mattress after I had shined a flashlight under the bed and the light caught his eyes. I couldn't get him to come out and had to wait for him to finally reappear. There were workmen on the roof earlier in the day that apparently really freaked him out. He wouldn't even come out for food! Meanwhile, my older cat, Katie, didn't care at all about the noise and was next to me while I was trying to talk Waffles out, looking like "What the heck, Waffles?"

Debbie Glovatsky, award-winning blogger and photographer, *Glogirly.com*

My family was pet-sitting a black cat for a friend at our home. I was about ten at the time, and cat lover I was, I wanted the kitty to stay in my room. I had no idea, however, that the cat could turn invisible! Within the first hour, the cat vanished, and after searching everywhere, it was assumed she must have gotten out. The night before the friend would be returning for her beloved kitty, I opened my closet and looked toward the back. The farthest corner was pitch black and always gave me the creeps. I wondered and slowly reached my hand back but felt nothing. I was shaking with fear of crawly things lurking in the dark, so I gathered all the strength I had and reached farther. My hand touched a warm ball of soft fur! I still couldn't see the cat, but I felt around until I could get a good hold on her and pulled her out. The invisible cat was right in my room all *along! The cat immediately tried to hide again, but I barred her from the closet.*

L. E. Mastilock, author and artist

~PURR POINTS TO PONDER~

Cats are reactive to even the slightest change—strange company visiting, being in a house they don't recognize, or hearing unusual noises outside—which can cause them to vanish into thin air, looking for a safe spot to hide. So a day and night like the 4th of July—something out of their typical norm—can be especially unsettling and dangerous to them. Even in the best of circumstances, it's safer for a cat to be indoors, but on a holiday like this, it's especially important.

If your cat is an indoor/outdoor cat, try to keep him indoors a few days before and after the 4th, as people tend to let off fireworks for days at a time to prolong the holiday. Fireworks can be dangerous to an unsuspecting cat, and some ill-intentioned people even purposely try to harm an outdoor cat with fireworks.

If you're having an outside cookout, be careful as you go in and out the door, as your cat might be lurking nearby and try to escape. Double check that doors are securely latched and that window screens don't have any tears. And even if you always keep your cat indoors, make sure her identification is current and that you have a picture of her. It's easy for kitty to slip out the door while in a panicky state and end up lost, injured, or worse.

You should also set up a sanctuary room for your cat that includes safe hiding places, food, litter, etc. Some cat parents have success using pheromone therapy to de-stress their cat (using a product like Feliway spray), and playing music or having a television on to diffuse noises also helps. If these suggestions don't work and your cat is unable to remain calm, don't leave him alone if you plan on watching fireworks. Notwithstanding my Jazmine who actually enjoys watching the fireworks from the comfort of our guest bedroom window, not all cats are that brave. Hire a pet sitter if need be, or ask a neighbor to stay while you go out.

Remember as well that picnic foods and alcohol are not appropriate for kitty and can cause problems ranging from mild stomach upset to extreme toxicity. Glowsticks that kids use outdoors at night can cause irritation if chewed and don't give your cat any calming medication unless you've been instructed to do so by your veterinarian. You don't know what side effects may occur or how your cat may react to a particular medication the first time it's administered.

Laws of Attraction

Much as it boggles my mind, *there are actually people who don't like cats.* Some of them say it without understanding why—meaning they may have never even had a cat yet still feel compelled to say they don't like cats or they're a "dog person" (it is okay to like both cats and dogs in case they weren't aware). And some might have a specific reason, such as maybe they're allergic.

My mother-in-law Dotty is someone who doesn't like cats. She will avoid a room if there's a cat in it, and petting one is out of the question. Naturally, any time she comes to visit, my cats are drawn to her like she's sprinkled in catnip, she's that irresistible. Just ask Zoey.

Zoey's the kind of cat that gives cats the reputation of being standoffish. Her glare alone causes people to tiptoe around her and I'm one of the few people she trusts to bond with (as long as I don't dare pick her up for a quickie hug). She even growls at her kittens, which are all now full-grown adults (and much bigger than her, mind you), if they try to cuddle on the couch with me if she's already napping on my legs. Her growl is worse than her bite, and they just ignore her, but it's a testament to her rather persnickety ways.

You can only imagine our surprise then, when one night Dotty was nodding off on the couch and Zoey jumped out of nowhere to settle herself for a nap on her lap! Granted, she might have initially associated Dotty with me, as our routine every single night for years now has been her sleeping on my outstretched legs while I sit on the couch, and Dotty was sitting in "my spot." But even after Dotty screamed and nearly jumped out of her skin, Zoey didn't flinch, and she and Dotty spent the rest of the night together until Dotty got up and went to bed.

We also have a CPA who comes to the house every year to help with our income taxes. He's visibly uncomfortable around our cats, and Peanut fell Pepe le Pew madly in love with him the first moment he sat at the dining room table and took out his computer to begin business. She loudly purrs a love song to him and makes biscuits in his lap as he punches numbers into his calculator, despite his not reciprocating her attention at all. What accountant doesn't want a cat butt in his face and a cat tail in his coffee? I have to pick her up from his lap at least a dozen times (um, super awkward) and eventually I have to bring her into my bedroom and shut the door so he can get some work done (I *am* being charged by the hour).

One time many years ago I adopted a cat for my ex-husband, Bill, as a birthday gift. We were in the mall—it happened to be a Friday, and it also happened to be Bill's birthday. I saw this forlorn, very sickly looking grey striped tabby sitting in the display window of a pet shop (this was back when pet stores were common), and my heart broke—I had to rescue him! I said to Bill, "Surprise—you're getting a cat for your birthday!" and promptly went in to adopt him. I aptly named him Friday, and it turns out he wasn't sick at all, he just didn't like living in a store front window. Friday adored me and I was the love of his life. He never liked Bill, and until the day he died, he would avoid him as much as possible. There was even a time Friday somehow managed to finagle himself into Bill's cowboy boots, upon which he left him a nice gift—a puddle of pee.

There are also those times when your cat picks you. I went to a cat rescue years ago with my youngest son, Joe. We wanted to pick out a kitten together and were having a hard time deciding which bundle of fur to bring home from the dozens of adorable available kittens. We finally found a rambunctious torbie that won us over and were getting ready to leave with her. I then felt a tiny thud on my shoulders. It was a shy kitten that initially didn't come out to socialize with us, that somehow managed to jump up onto me!

She was also a torbie—and with that one bold move, she stole our hearts and we brought her home. We named her Harley for her orange and black markings like the Harley Davidson motorcycle, and ironically, she never jumped after that—not on counters, not on cat condos, shelves, or anything else. It was like she knew that was her one jump of a lifetime.

~MEWS FROM OTHERS~

When my personable Siberian cat, Ivan, was one year old, he had his first sleep over at his pet sitter's home, which included a teenage daughter, three cats, and a frisky ferret named Bear. Ivan's a true social butterfly who adores people, cats, and well-behaved dogs, but a ferret was a new experience for him. Before I left, I politely explained to him that Bear was a family member, not a delicious snack to munch on. Within 24 hours I received email photos confirming my worst fears—Ivan had eaten Bear! No, actually what happened was that Bear was latched onto Ivan's cheek, and they were engaged in a rambunctious wrestling match. Ivan and Bear became fast friends, playing at full tilt. Since I believe in the importance of environmental enrichment for my cats, I travel 25 miles round trip for Ivan and Bear to have play dates in between sleep overs!
  Ramona D. Marek, MS Ed., author of *Cats for the GENIUS*

My token canine, Abby, an odd-looking Chinese Crested mix, loved cats. In the five years my husband and I had her, Abby helped raise many a litter of orphaned kittens, but she had a particular fondness for a kitten named Emily. Emily's rescuers found her at three weeks old under a mobile home with her head trapped inside a block of fiberglass insulation, and as result, Emily suffered from permanent eye and lung damage. Abby became her protector, and they quickly formed an unbreakable bond. When Emily was about four months old, Abby began pushing her around the living room floor with her nose, as if she were dust-mopping the tile. Horrified, I freed the kitten and scolded Abby. Emily immediately jumped down and the mopping resumed. Obviously Emily enjoyed it as much as Abby. Since most people didn't want a kitten with chronic health issues and because Emily was Abby's favorite dog toy, we adopted her. After three years of the daily floor exercises, Abby began suffering from seizures. Treatment failed to control the episodes, and one evening she passed during a violent attack. As is our ritual, we laid Abby to rest on the floor in repose to help provide our other pets with as much understanding and closure as possible by letting them see (and smell) that Abby's soul had left her body. We buried Abby under the pecan tree in our backyard, and Emily observed the interment from a few feet away. As I read a prayer for Abby, Emily approached the grave and sat down on the mound as if to say goodbye to her beloved canine friend.

Dusty Rainbolt, ACCBC, award-winning author of 12 books including *Kittens for Dummies* and *Cat Scene Investigator: Solve Your Cat's Litter Box Mystery*

My Siamese cat, Rosie, was part of a TNR project. She was slated to be returned to her feral colony, but luckily, someone saw potential in her and didn't release her back. When my husband and I adopted her, Rosie was a scared and skittish three-month old kitten who was afraid of her own shadow. One small fish, a Panda Corey Catfish, named Bandit—a fish that has lived well beyond his expected years—changed that. When Rosie joined our family, Bandit wasn't looking so good. Before long, Rosie found that the spot next to Bandit's tank was one of her favorite places to be, and since then, he's looking much better and they're the best of pals! He comes out to see her and swims right to her, up and down the glass, when she's sitting next to him. I'm convinced they help each other, and if you ask Rosie, "Where's Bandit?" she immediately runs over to the table and sits next to the tank—and Bandit's right there to greet her!

Lynna Reese Walter, South Florida

When I was 10, my family adopted a Siamese kitten. We named her Pyewacket and she was an exceptional cat, often displaying dog-like behaviors (fetching superballs, following me to the bus stop) while managing to be the center of attention most of the time in our household. She was a beautiful and charismatic creature, who either didn't know she was a cat or didn't understand that not everyone would adore her, because I recall a few people coming to our home, declaring their general dislike for cats. One such person was a bridge partner of my father's, sitting in our living room waiting for my dad so they could leave for a tournament. He stated, "I really don't like cats," just as Pye walked into the room. Pye looked at him, then at me, and proceeded to jump onto his lap while purring and looking into his eyes. She was quite a little charmer, and because he was so amazed that she approached him, he patted her and said, "Well, she's not so bad."

Laura Zaccardi, blogger, *Squeedunk, Whiskers and Warehouse*, and co-founder of PAD PAWS Animal Rescue, Jersey City, NJ

When I lost my beloved soul-cat, Jasper, I was devastated. One evening, feeling extremely low, I Googled tuxedo kittens like my Jasper, and when I found some, it gave me a happy feeling inside. I decided I was ready for a kitten and one stood out—I knew he was the one. I emailed the owner who informed me she was holding him for someone else, but he had a brother. I told her Jasper's story and politely declined. But to my surprise, the woman wrote me back—she had shared Jasper's story and the people decided to take the brother instead. I was elated—it was meant to be! I named him Jax and tried bonding with him, but he wouldn't have it. And it's not because he's not affectionate; he just had someone else in mind—my husband,

Johnny. My husband, mind you, who doesn't necessarily like cats. He's a dog person who was always amazed by my close relationship with Jasper. Jax isn't very vocal, but he runs up to Johnny and meows and rubs against his legs until Johnny picks him up, and when Johnny goes to put him down, Jax bites him in protest. When Johnny naps on the recliner in the living room, Jax will run up to him, full of purrs, rub his face, circle a couple of times, and then cuddle with him until they both are napping. If I try to get him to lie down with me, he won't have it. I've resorted to buying his affection with food—now when I come home, Jax will rub my legs and "let" me give him treats—but I'll take whatever I can get!

Terri Tye, medical billing specialist, Corbin, KY

My dad is not a cat guy. He grew up on a farm, and cats were not allowed in the house. He doesn't mind my house cats but doesn't want them on his lap or anything of the sort. One evening he was over watching a basketball game on TV. Of course, there were snacks out since you can't watch basketball without snacks. The rule I have with my cats is this—sniffing is ok, stealing or eating snacks is not. The head cat at the time was a large, long-haired orange male tabby named Butterscotch. Once the snacks were laid out, he came over to investigate. My dad tried to get him to leave and finally, in frustration, threw a piece of popcorn at Butterscotch. Butterscotch sniffed it, ate it, and like it or not, decided my dad was his new best friend!

Jeanne Kudich, cat blogger, *Random-Felines.com*

A large and caring dog found an orange colored cat lying in some bushes, picked her up by the scruff of the neck, and brought her home to his humans for help. They, in turn, brought her to a rescue that took her in, naming her Ginger for her fur color. Unbeknownst to the humans or the benevolent dog, a few small puncture holes had been put into her neck when she was picked up. As a result, when my family and I went to an adoption event and saw her, falling in love with her on the spot, the rescue group was reluctant to release her because we already had a 109-pound Rottweiler (Zeus) and a cat

(Clementine). I plead our case—Zeus and Clementine were best friends and I was in the pet industry—I would never put Ginger in harm's way. The rescue relented and my family and I were right— Ginger was just fine—she never missed a meal, a chance to go out in the yard, or an opportunity to hang with Zeus. When Zeus passed, all of us were heartbroken, including Ginger. A year later, we brought home Lacey, an Australian Shepherd and once again, Ginger was not afraid. She and Lacey were best friends until Ginger passed away in December 2015.

David Levy, owner of Zen Clippers

When I was eleven, I picked out the runt of the litter and named her Sachi. Sachi had her fair share of health problems and was a cranky cat who didn't like anyone, human or animal, except for me. I loved her unconditionally and secretly relished the fact she didn't like anyone else. After college, she came with me to my first apartment and finally lived in a peaceful environment without being bothered by any of my family's other animals. That was until Chilly sauntered into our lives. I had not planned on bringing another cat into my life. In fact, my now husband was dead set against it, but I couldn't help feeling sorry for her. She was skin and bones—it was the start of an already bitter cold winter—and I worried she wouldn't make it. After weeks of feeding her on the sidewalk outside my apartment, I spotted her one morning squeezing herself out of a broken basement window into the building courtyard. Chilly spotted me and from then on, she would climb up to the window and meow at me to let her in for some food and warmth. My husband was not pleased at all, and one evening he caught me with Chilly in the apartment. Chilly took one look at him and was smitten. She ran right over to him and started weaving herself between his feet, purring the entire time. I couldn't believe my eyes, but that was exactly what she needed to do to secure a place within our family!

Akemi Blanchard, industrial designer and founder of Akemi Tanaka, Inc.

~PURR POINTS TO PONDER~

It seems counterintuitive to logic, but we've all been there. You go to someone's house with a cat and you long for the cat to come see you, but he doesn't. You're a cat lover, and being withheld affection by a creature you adore is excruciating and embarrassing. Who does the cat go to? The person who's completely ignoring them. The reason why is actually simple—cats find direct eye contact intimidating so they gravitate to the one person who has the courtesy not to stare or make a fuss.

You *can* win him over; it just takes some patience so he can get to know you. Slowly show him your hand to let him give you a thorough sniffing. Or sit next to him but ignore him until he becomes accustomed to your presence. Don't jump in by trying to pick him up or by loudly talking to him. In no time at all, he'll be your friend or let you touch him or, at the very least, let you sit next to him. Bribing him with a treat or two wouldn't hurt either.

For those people who say they don't like cats because of allergies, the good news is that in many instances with some preventative measures, you *can* co-exist peacefully with a cat in your house rather than deciding to cut them out of your life altogether or opting not to adopt in the first place. I know this for a fact because I was allergic to cats at one time in my life, but have long since been able to overcome the symptoms.

Many times, a shot or medication will do the trick, but there are other steps, such as cleaning the air with strategically placed ionizers and HEPA (High Efficiency Particulate Air) purifying systems throughout the house to reduce allergens.

It's also best to keep the cat out of any bedroom of the person who is allergic, and don't let them sleep on the bed. Provide other comfortable sleeping areas for your cat to nap and if you do allow him to sleep on the bed (for some cat lovers, it's impossible to say no), wash all bedding in 140-degree hot water at least twice monthly. This will eliminate both dust mites and cat allergens, and products are available, such as DeMite, which can be used with laundry detergent to kill harmful particles.

Put throw blankets on couches and furniture where your cat might nap so you can wash the linens frequently and change air conditioning filters on a regular basis, as they also catch a large amount of cat hair. You can also use an anti-allergen spray to deactivate allergens. Allersearch ADS, for example, made from non-toxic substances, can safely be sprayed throughout the house to take the sting out of household dust by rendering allergens harmless.

Carpet is a magnet for allergens, so vacuum frequently with a high-grade HEPA vacuum. Use the hand tools to get into hard to reach spaces—cat allergen particles are very small and invasive, so you have to do a thorough job. This includes furniture, throw rugs, drapery, walls, under furniture, and more.

Hardwood and tile floors, especially in corners where cat hair tends to drift should be swept frequently. If you find your allergies are being triggered while vacuuming or sweeping, wear a protective mask to cover your nose. Damp mopping these surfaces (including walls) also helps minimalize dander. Dust frequently and use liberal amounts of spray furniture polish, as this dramatically limits allergen particles from becoming airborne.

Wash your hands after petting your cat, using a strong anti-bacterial soap, and avoid rubbing your eyes. You should also avoid excessive hugging and snuggling with your cat. And since the dust from cleaning litter boxes can trigger allergy attacks, either find someone who is not allergic to do the cleaning, or use a protective nose mask to reduce the chances of allergens entering your body.

What's in a Name?

All my cats—Zee, Zoey, Mia, Peanut, Rolz, Kizmet, and Jazmine—know their names. They also know the endless silly nicknames Dan and I feel compelled to give them. For instance, I like to call Rolz, Roley-McPoley and Mia, Missy-Moo. I don't know why, I just do. Not to mention the names they're given based on circumstances that warrant otherwise. For example, if Zoey has jumped up to the counter for the umpteenth time while I'm trying to prepare them dinner, she'll get an exasperated, "For the love of God, Zoey Barnes, *pul-lease* get down," from me. Not that she ever jumps down, but the need for a last name just seems necessary. And for good measure, sometimes I call her Zoey Marie Barnes when I'm even more frustrated. Why Marie? No idea—it just came to me one day and stuck.

There are also the times that I inadvertently become all discombobulated and call one cat by the long name

"ZeeMiaPeanutRolzKizmet—aggh—whoever you are" because my brain just can't connect the dots fast enough! And when Mia, Peanut, and Rolz were kittens, I'm certain they thought their names were "No-no Mia," "No-no Peanut," and "No-no Rolz" because I was always telling them "No-no" for whatever mischief they were constantly getting into!

It always amazes me when people act surprised that a cat knows his or her name. Of course they do. If you're anything like me, you must say their name a million times a day. Every time you walk by them, you hug them, pet them, or give them a loving word or two. And you certainly carry a conversation with them, speaking to them in lovey-dovey, high pitched tones to further let them know how endearing they are to you.

In my house, a cat's name primarily equates to good things happening. "Hi, Jazmine, here's a treat for you, sweet princess." Or "Muah, give Mama a kiss, Jazmine." Or "Go get it, Jazmine" when you throw a fake mouse for her to catch, followed by a "good girl" of praise when she brings it back.

There are exceptions, of course. Generally, when you are trying to prove a point, such as when company comes over and you call your cats to come say hello. Then, either they hide, seeming as if you don't even have cats, or they stare blindly at you, as if to purposely make you look a fool. Naturally, the moment your company leaves, they will come when you call them.

Very rarely will a cat come when you call their name while you're holding a cat carrier. Somehow a cat understands what a carrier is and acts accordingly. Surprisingly enough, if you take an empty box and cuts air vents and windows into it with a door for your cat to play games, all is good. But even whisper the word "carrier"—that box-shaped item with air vents, windows, and a door—your cat will flee the vicinity immediately. This phenomenon applies to all cats in the household, regardless of whom you're actually trying to get into the carrier.

~MEWS FROM OTHERS~

When Max came into my home as a foster, he was known as Smokey, but he would never answer to that name—so I let him choose his own. I shortlisted a few names I liked and called them out to him one by one. When I yelled "Max," he came running and leapt into my lap. I said, "Good choice Max—your name means 'the greatest,' and it stuck ever since.

Tracy of *Pawesome Cats*, a cat-centric lifestyle blog in Australia

My cat, Jaq, is the king of selective hearing, especially when the word "no" is involved. I'll yell "No kitties on the counter!" He interprets that as me saying "lie down so I can rub your belly." This interpretation problem, among other choice things, has earned him the nickname Booger. His selective hearing is also why he responds to Booger and not Jaq.

Jenny Carlson, blogger, *As the World Purrs*

I have a previously feral cat named Dilettante, after the famous premium chocolatier in Seattle, Washington. His nickname is Dilly, and whenever I call him to come into the house or from another room, he often worries he's in trouble, so he's very apprehensive about coming to me. He's since been trained—if I call to him, "Dilly, Dilly, Dilly," then he knows all is safe and he'll come running without fear. If it's just one "Dilly," he'll check things out first before determining if he should come or not.

Vicki Farretta, a member of the TNR Community in Seattle, WA

In 2009, I won a contest hosted by Petfinder.com for "Best Group Name for Felines." My story went like this: One day a cat followed me home. The cat was hungry, so I gave her something to eat and drink, and no surprise, she soon started coming by at night for me to feed her. She was black and white, so I named her Domino. I saw her on and off, and about three weeks in, my family and I heard noises in the crawlspace in our attic. We didn't think too much of it until about a week later when it sounded like a herd of buffalo was running back and forth above us. Then we heard the meowing. Domino brought the kittens down a couple of weeks later, and one of the kittens looked exactly like her, so I named her Ditto. Because Domino was feral, she was not able to be handled and, as a result, had a couple more litters of kittens before she was finally able to be captured and spayed. One litter was born behind the washing machine in our carport and one of the kittens looked exactly like Domino and Ditto, so I named him Etcetera. In the litter to follow, she had two kittens who looked exactly like the other three—I called them Andsoon and Andsoforth.

Jill Steinberg, president, Interlink Group Professional Services and secretary/fundraiser for the Cat Network Inc., Miami, FL

My black cat came from the shelter with a rather standard and boring name—Chestnut. I fixed that—Chestnut now has many nicknames, including C-Nut H. McGillicuddy—a fun and fancy name with a corresponding tune that my husband, Jason, and I sing to her each morning while sharing our scrambled eggs with cheddar cheese breakfast with her.

Tara Phillips O'Mara, founder of PDX Pet Design and cat entertainment slave

The story began with "I'm not feeding you," when a stray black cat made herself at home on the ratty old couch I had on the front porch of the college apartment I was sharing with several other housemates. Followed by "and there's no way I'm buying any kitty litter!" By day 4, despite the landlord not allowing pets, the little black cat had decided she had found her home. Once my housemates confirmed she was going to be a permanent resident, her name became a subject of great debate, one usually discussed after many bottles of liquor. One of the girls became fond of calling her by seven names all at once. "Why hello, Xerxes Hamilton Alexandra Salt and Pepper Trojan Beatrix Sersons the Third," she would proclaim after downing a shot of something. The name would change, except it always ended with "Sersons the Third." Eventually, all prefixes were dropped and our little black cat officially became Sersons the Third. Even though Sersons had a home, I stood behind my promise of not getting a litter box. I kept the front window of my studio apartment open, allowing her to come and go as she wanted, with our backyard being one big litter box for her. The open window did have its drawbacks—Sersons often left me gifts, such as dead lizards, and once, I was awoken by a loud cat fight in the kitchen, as another cat had come into the kitchen to steal a meal.

Chris Barnes, chief operating officer, Doorstep Delivery, Plantation, FL

My cat, Oliver, has a bad habit of jumping on the kitchen counter. When he gets caught (which is almost every time because he's not exactly discreet), I tell him to get down. Each time, he runs behind the kitchen faucet and "hides." He will look in a different direction when his name is called to make sure he does not make eye contact. When he does accidentally make eye contact, he quickly hunches down a little bit further and looks down into the sink. This can go one for quite some time. I've even tried turning the faucet on (it's the lever style, so it pushes into him gently when I turn the water on) but he doesn't move. Eventually I end up picking him up and putting him on the floor. Each time he gets caught, he always gives a look as if to say "How did you know I was there?" before wandering off in defeat.

Stacey Herrle, Alberta, Canada

~PURR POINTS TO PONDER~

It's pretty simple logic why your cat might not come when you call him to meet company—there's now a strange being, with strange new smells, who appeared seemingly out of nowhere, now plunked front and center in your living room. To be more precise, a strange person that has appeared seemingly out of nowhere and is in *your cat's* living room—*his* territory. Your cat's delicate equilibrium has been upset and he just needs time to adjust to the intrusion. Some cats warm up to company right away; for others it might take some time before they feel comfortable enough to come out when you call them.

A cat carrier—that's a whole other issue. For them, seeing the carrier is often the first sign that something bad is about to happen (i.e., a trip to the vet). In a multi-cat family such as mine, if one cat reacts, it's a chain reaction of tension in all the cats. The first step to reducing the stress associated with cat carriers and vet visits (or travel in general) is to create positive associations for your cat with the carrier.

If you can, start when your cat is young. Kittens usually adjust to new experiences more easily than adults, so begin the carrier-training process as early as possible. Try keeping the carrier in plain view during everyday life. Many cats only see the carrier when it's time to go somewhere, so they begin to feel anxious as soon as the carrier appears. If you prefer to keep your carrier in storage, don't abruptly bring it out and chase your cat when you need him to go in. Notwithstanding emergency situations, if you know you have a planned trip to the vet, or other travels, try to bring the carrier out several hours or days in advance.

Many manufactures now make carriers that are both stylish and practical that you can keep out every day, rather than the traditional hard-plastic models. I have one from a company called Sleepypod® that my cat's love—it's shaped like a round hatbox with a removable mesh domed lid, lined with a plush faux fur interior. The nylon material and all the components are held together with sturdy nylon zippers that come apart to suit whatever need you have at the moment. It's also practical—all the parts can easily be wiped down or washed when needed.

You can also practice techniques via food, treats, and playing. Feed your cat inside the carrier by putting his food dish a few feet away and move it an inch or two closer to the carrier each day. Or teach him to go inside with treats or toys and praise him for staying in the carrier.

A Door Is a Door Is a Door

Adoor is a door is a door, unless of course you're a cat, then it's so much more. My cats are **obsessed** with doors. The door to our guest bedroom is permanently shut and locked because it's the one room we have in the house that's carpeted. Carpet to my cats is another word for "here's a good place for a hairball." It's also the room where we store random stuff, like my sewing and crafting supplies, so it's just easier to keep it closed rather than deal with seven curious cats who are uncontrollably enticed by spools of thread, balls of yarn, sharp needles, sparkly beads, and sequins.

If it's a bathroom door and you dare to close it, it takes less than five seconds before you see a paw underneath the door, frantically digging to get in. My angel Jazz was so obsessed with closed doors he would open any of them that weren't locked (we had to buy several hook lock kits just so we could keep a door shut when we needed to). He'd stand up on his hind legs and jiggle the door handle until it opened. A cute habit, unless you're a modest teenage boy, or visiting company using the bathroom who is forced to get up from the toilet to close a door that seemingly was opened for no reason other than the sport of it.

One time Jazz helped his cat-buddy, Zee, out of a jam. When Zee was about two years old, he went through an obnoxious phase where he would play with Jazz too roughly—rabbit kicks, biting, and just general bullying. One night I had enough and abruptly picked Zee up and put him in my bedroom, shutting the door firmly for a "time-out." I wasn't paying attention, and two minutes later, Jazz opened the door to let Zee out—they both looked so proud of themselves that I didn't have the heart to put Zee back. And naturally, right back to rabbit-kicking Jazz he went!

Jazmine is fascinated with the doors to the pots and pans cupboard and the door to the pantry in our kitchen—she can be sound asleep, but if I open one of those doors (which don't even make a noise that I can detect to my human ears), she'll come zooming into the kitchen to climb inside. She likes to make a game out of it—I'll shut the door and say, "Where's Jazmine?" After a few seconds I'll open it—if she's in the pots and pan cupboard, I'll find her tucked in between the frying pans—if she's in the pantry, she's hidden amid cans of soup and jars of spaghetti sauce. I have to play the game with her every single time I open one of those doors—if I don't, she stares dejectedly at me, so what choice do I have?

Soup anyone?

Zoey can also hear doors that seem to silently open—in particular, the closet door in my bedroom. I literally check before I open the door to see if she's around, which she isn't, and then by the time I get into the closet—trying to quickly shut it without slamming my fingers before she magically appears, she's right next to me. I honestly don't mind her company—she's so happy once she's inside that she'll do a sing-song meow to me and prance about on her tippy-toes—but she also uses Dan's hanging shirts as a ladder to climb up to the top of the closet. All of his left-side sleeves have pock marks from her claws, and for some reason, he's not a fan of that.

Sometimes I'll open the door and think to myself, I'm just going to be in here for a second to quickly grab something, so I don't need to shut it. Obviously I should know better than that. Not only does Zoey zoom in—I swear so many cats suddenly appear, that I often wonder if the entire neighborhood's cats are in my closet as well!

Zoey's also the only cat I've had that shuts doors. During random times of the day I'll hear a door slam. 10, 9, 8...then comes the wailing meow. It will be her letting me know she's locked herself in somewhere. When I find her and open the door, she glares at me like I'm an idiot—obviously she meant to trap herself in the room. To make sure there are no unwanted incidents, I've taken to placing full soda box cartons (the 12 packs) against any open doors we have so she can't shut herself in somewhere that might not have a litter box.

~MEWS FROM OTHERS~

Perhaps it's because my cat, Gizzie, was initially found wandering the streets of Atlanta, Georgia, and understands the dangers that can lurk outside closed doors, but even I was surprised at how astute my loving and loyal Maine Coon was. I had fallen asleep one evening with him by my side and woke to his trademark loud meows and trills. I asked him, "What is it, Gizzie, do want a treat?" He then jumped on my bed, tapped my face with his large paws, head butted me, and frantically turned around, looking at me as if to say, "Get off the bed, I need to show you something." Knowing it best not to ignore him, I stumbled out of bed. He led me through the kitchen, looking at me every other step as if to say "Hurry up!" He then walked past his food bowl (unheard of) and stopped and sat in his regal posture, turning to the front door—the front door that was wide open because I had forgotten to shut it!

I also recall a time when I lived with my dad in South Carolina. I worked odd hours, and no matter the shift, Gizzie would keep vigil at the door, waiting for my return. One evening my dad had fallen asleep on the sofa. The back door was locked, and I didn't have a key to get inside. Gizzie paced frantically from the door to the den where my dad was sleeping, loudly meowing. It took some doing, but after sitting on my dad's head with his large body and meowing in his ears, Gizzie was finally able to wake him and get his attention. He then jumped down from the sofa, walked to the back door, meowed loudly, turned around, and looked at my dad who then finally heard my frantic knocks and let me in, much to the relief of a very worried Gizzie.

Cassie J. Fox, Soul of the Blues, *Our Generation Radio.com* and *Spice Radio.com*

My cat, Monty, is not your typical cat. He has a chromosomal abnormality that already makes him different looking, but he also has his own ideas when it comes to windows and doors. When Monty goes out the door, he insists on getting in through the window as if the door has ceased to exist, even though it's just next to him. During the night, something will snap inside him and he'll fight like crazy to get out the window next to the bed in which he sleeps with me and my fiancé, Mikala. I'll wake up and open the window—Monty will stand still and quietly sniff the night wind and then, completely anticlimactic, go back to bed and I can then close the window again.

Michael B. Nielsen, owner of Monty Boy, Copenhagen

My cat, Isis (named after the Bob Dylan song), is sweet, beautiful, and loving. However, when it comes to doors, she becomes a wild lunatic, throwing herself at them like a lemming. If she wants to enter a room and the door is closed, she'll throw herself at it at breakneck 60 mph speed. If the door doesn't open, she will take further and further run ups until she is running at full speed from the other side of the room, and if she catches the handle, she will dangle until someone opens the door.

Bobby Long, British singer, songwriter, and poet

Phantom is a black and white cat, with a black tear drop starting at the crown of his head that my family and I got when he was a six-week-old kitten. When he was several months old, it was snowing out one day. I opened the front door to see how much snow we had gotten and then closed the door. One of my other cats, Aisha, began to urgently meow that something was terribly wrong! Meow, meow,

meow—she wouldn't let up. Concerned, my family and I started looking for Phantom and his other cat-mate, Shadow. We found Shadow, and I could hear Phantom, but I couldn't find him anywhere. I opened the side garage door and heard him clear as a bell, but I still didn't know where he was. I closed the door, and Aisha was still beside herself trying to let me know something was wrong! Finally, to Aisha's great relief, I opened the front door. Who came sauntering out, but Phantom! Apparently after I had opened the door to look outside, he got stuck between the front door and the screen door!

Deadra "Dede" Ghostlaw, New Windsor, NY

Despite my best efforts to keep a doorstop in place in my powder room, my orange tabby, Waffles, still manages to shut himself inside the room on an almost daily basis. One night he locked himself in five times. He just loves standing up on his back legs with his front paws outstretched on the door and pushing it shut. He doesn't cry to be let out, quite the opposite—I often hear him chortling away, entertaining himself! Then when I open up the door, he's sitting on the toilet seat, perfectly posed, head tilted to the side. A little meow-trill and he jumps down and trots out the door...only to repeat...

Debbie Glovatsky, award-winning blogger and photographer, *Glogirly.com*

It's not necessarily unusual for a cat to open a door, but when you're the person behind the door and not expecting it, unless you see it with your own eyes, it's hard to believe! That's how I felt when my son, Nikko, and I were in his bedroom with the door closed. All of a sudden, the door opened and in sauntered my cat, Stella, like it was no big deal. Nikko exclaimed, "Stella just opened my door!" to which I said, "No, she didn't." Nikko then said, "I'm going to prove it." So he set up his phone to video the outside of his door and we went inside his room. Within a minute, the door opened again and in walked Stella! This time we had proof because he recorded the whole thing!

Vanna White, hostess, *Wheel of Fortune*

~PURR POINTS TO PONDER~

Why are cats so intrigued with what's behind a door? Probably because they're insatiably curious and can't stand not knowing the unknown. Even a room they've been in and out of for years—it only takes the door being closed once or twice before they get the idea the closed door could mean some sort of change. Add in the fact we're often in the room behind the closed door, doing things they want to know about, which heightens the fascination.

That's why when a cat hears the forbidden door open, they will virtually appear out of nowhere to satisfy their curiosity about the room. I know for me, it's actually a trick I sometimes use to find them if they seem to be missing. I also use doors as a positive reward system—as indoor cats, they can get bored easily, and I like to provide them with interesting stimulation out of the blue when I can.

I will randomly open the guest bedroom door—there is a certain time of the day when the sun is just perfect for cat napping (I call that time hair light—that glorious twilight moment when every bit of cat hair in the house enchantingly dances about in the air, and on all the furniture, counters, and appliances, like a beautiful first fallen snow), and I like to let them explore the room for a few minutes before they jump up onto the bed for a nice slumber. I always make sure my crafting projects are put away and I have a follow-up magic trick to get them back out so I can close the door again—it's called pop open a can of cat food or shake a bag of cat treats and see how many cats come running!

Home for the Holidays

I've had cats in my life for a long time, so the list of crazy things they've done around holiday time or special occasions runs the full gambit. From peeing on Christmas gifts under the tree that hadn't yet been opened to taking ornaments off the tree and hiding them under the couch for me to find months later to playing with the water in the kitchen sink that the Christmas turkey was defrosting in, they've done it.

You distract them by doing something cute and I'll grab the turkey!

I was the kind of person who was wired to years of treasured traditions—especially at Christmas—from adorning the house with precious family heirlooms passed down from generations, to lavishly decorating a real Christmas tree with a spectacular array of fragile ornaments, lights, and more. Christmas 2009—a time when we had four adult cats and three energized kittens—changed all that after hearing glass hitting the floor for the umpteenth time in the span of an hour and seeing one of the kittens swinging from the tree like they were training to be an acrobat circus act.

You'll be mine soon
Christmas ornament,
just you wait and see...

I came to the conclusion it wasn't worth the aggravation or stress. Cats are instinctively curious, so what's the point of all those decorations if you can't enjoy them? And all doesn't need to be lost. I found the perfect way to channel my Christmas spirit— we now have an artificial tree that the cats can't destroy—it's securely tied to a heavy floor lamp and decorated in my favorite theme—leopard! I made dozens of homemade ornaments out of leopard print fabric to complement the store-bought, unbreakable ones, and it's actually nice to have a new tradition based on the love of my cats.

~MEWS FROM OTHERS~

Heading from Schenectady, New York to South Sutton, New Hampshire for the Thanksgiving holiday to visit a friend, a 150-mile journey, I had no idea what was about to be unveiled. Driving cautiously through a raging snowstorm, I was white knuckled upon arrival. Greeting me in a joyous chorus of barks was my friend's dog, recognizing my familiar car. The barking soon became annoying— he focused his attention on the car engine, and soon the barks turned into whimpers of distress. Taking his cue, we opened the hood of the car, and to our astonishment, saw a bundle of fur wrapped precariously around parts of the motor. With delicate hands, we extracted a filthy, shaking bundle, now accompanied by its screams of terror and the dog's ecstatic "I told you so" barking. It was a kitten—a kitten that had most certainly climbed into the engine of the car for warmth so many miles ago and unexpectedly found himself going for the ride of his life. He was immediately taken to the vet and declared, incredibly, to be free of any broken bones or burns. He was, however, completely deaf and would never recover the loss of hearing suffered from the constant roar of the engine. We named him Hobo, and he became a cherished part of the family for 17 years, close companion to the dog, and the only creature who wasn't offended by the constant honking of the geese who also lived on the property!

Pamela Bushnell, commissioner, City of Tamarac, FL

After my beloved cat, Lucy, died I made a vow not to leave my other cats, Cinder and Rainy, home alone if I didn't have to. Loving them so much, I wanted to spend as much time with them as I could, as I know how fleeting time can be with our precious pets. So now when my husband Andy and I go to visit Andy's parents every week (they live six blocks away), rather than keep Cinder and Rainy at home, we crate them up and bring them, too! They are put on flexi-leashes to give them unrestricted freedom, and they really like being included in the excursions. Andy and I also bring them for special holiday visits, and if it's Christmas, Cinder and Rainy will get gifts too!

Allison Hunter-Frederick, part-time teacher and blogger

Freckles is a gorgeous black and white domestic long-haired cat that I got when he was 5 weeks old. He's now twelve and I discovered one Thanksgiving that he had an affinity for a very surprising food product. My mom and I were making stuffing for the turkey—it was your traditional stuffing with celery in the recipe. After chopping up the celery, we threw the ends of it into a garbage bag. Freckles took note, went up to the bag, and started rubbing up against it. Apparently it had the same effect on him that catnip does with most cats. Now when I cut up celery, I'll throw several pieces of it on the floor—Freckles will roll around all over it, exposing his full belly, and act intoxicated from the smell for about 15 minutes! The same thing happens if he catches wind of peppermint. One day he kept trying to get at my mom's purse where she kept her peppermint gum. Since I knew he liked the peppermint scent, I gave him a peppermint tea bag to sniff, and it caused the same reaction as the celery!

Lisa Herrick, accounting assistant, Grand Rapids, MI

Gibson and Oliver are two male cats adopted as a wedding gift for me from my husband, Brad. It was sort of a mutual choosing by all parties—I had initially picked out a medium haired tortoiseshell from our local shelter which housed its cats at my nearest PetSmart. We went to pick her up two days after our wedding, but it turned out she did not like men (something that was unknown at the shelter at the time) and she attacked Brad when he went to officially meet her. When we had first walked into the store, Brad had seen the boys in their cage and commented to me on how gorgeous the orange one (Oliver) was. After the little tortie went crazy on Brad, he asked the lady in charge of the rescue about the boys. They just seemed like a

great fit, and Brad and I wanted to get to know them better. We took them from their cage to play with them and adopted them that very afternoon! It's been happily ever after, ever since!
  Stacey Herrle, Alberta, Canada

Grigri (pronounced gre gre) showed up one day at my house, came in, and decided to stay. (My mother never met a cat she didn't love.) He was a huge gray tabby and very exotic looking. Not exactly domesticated, he often ran after me to scratch my legs in the early years. But with time, his aggression vanished and he became very gentle, accepting all the new cats that followed, lovingly caring for them like a doting grandfather. My family's favorite memory of him was a Thanksgiving Day. The guests had arrived but, to our horror and surprise, the turkey had vanished from the kitchen counter! Grigri had dragged it through the house and under the bed. I won't say exactly what ensued, but we all had a lovely turkey dinner.
  Jacqueline McKannay, owner of ThirstyCat Fountains

~PURR POINTS TO PONDER~

While holidays and special occasions can be magical and we love to deck the halls, bestow gifts, eat, drink, and be merry, when it comes our kitties, we have to be mindful of their safety because cats can be extremely curious and many of the foods, plants, and decorations that are part of the festivities can be dangerous or even lethal to our feline friends.

Rather than constantly worry about what your cat might be doing that could hurt him, some preventative measures can help. To begin with, a cat is a cat is a cat, and that needs to be in the forefront of your mind. For example—that tree that suddenly appeared in your living room out of nowhere with all kinds of enticing smells and tempting branches—clearly it's an invitation to be climbed. And those shimmering ornaments dangling from hooks—certainly that must be slinky and slivery prey to catch.

Thinking in those terms, it's nearly impossible for your cat not to be intrigued.

To avoid potential mishaps, consider decorating your tree with shatterproof ornaments. If they're knocked to the floor for a game of hockey, it's not a big deal and there won't be dangerous shards of glass that could hurt your cat. And an artificial tree might be less appealing to your cat to climb than a real one. If you do decide to go with a real tree, cover up the base of it with something like foil that will startle your cat and keep her away.

Many of the fertilizers and preservatives used to keep real trees fresher longer could make your cat sick. When you bring your tree home and put it in water, toxic chemicals could seep into the water and harm her if she decides to drink it (including the aspirin tablets many of us put in the water to keep pine needles from dropping). Nibbling on pine needles could also cause sickness, and regardless of what type of tree you use, always be mindful of the lights and never leave them on unattended while you're out of the house. A couple of chews on the cord are all that's needed for a tragedy to occur.

You should also avoid draping your tree with tinsel—most cats are mesmerized by the shiny decoration, and if ingested, it could become entangled in their intestines, causing them to twist and close off, requiring expensive and dangerous surgery. If you want something shiny for the tree, try non-breakable icicle ornaments. The same holds true with fancy ribbons, strings, and yarns that are tied onto gifts. They can be irresistible to cats, so consider larger grosgrain ribbons, decorative gift tags, or big bows as an alternative.

Plastic bags you bring into the house to carry gifts, food, and whatnot can also be a hazard—cats startle easily and can quickly find a bag handle around their neck. Either cut the handles or immediately put the bags away somewhere they can't get to them. And live holiday plants such as mistletoe, poinsettia, holly berries, hibiscus, and amaryllis blooms can be toxic to one degree or another if ingested by your cat. Lilies (including traditional Easter lilies) are also problematic—many varieties, including Tiger, Asian, Japanese Show, Stargazer and the Casa Blanca can cause kidney failure.

Typically, your cat will not ingest enough to cause harm and it's usually not necessary to treat them, but to be safe, it's highly recommended you visit your veterinarian no matter how much you think your cat has eaten. You can also call the Pet Poison Helpline for advice at 855-764-7661.

Decorate with silk plants, and if you use candles, try flameless ones—they still give a nice glow but you don't have to worry about kitty burning a curious paw or knocking them over and setting the house on fire!

And all those yummy foods that makes the holidays so special—be aware that many of them are dangerous to cats: chocolate, grapes, raisins, nuts (especially macadamias), rich and fatty foods such as gravy or grease, onions, garlic, alcohol, uncooked doughs with yeast and raw eggs, bones, candied sweet potatoes or yams, desserts, and more. If you must give your cat a titbit of something, such as fully cooked turkey, do it in moderation, and avoid anything excessively spicy or drenched in rich sauces.

It's just best to respect your cat's nature rather than spend the holidays stressing out. They will need their private time in the midst of all the hustle and bustle, and if you have company coming that's especially true. Make sure they have access to a private room with food, water, and litter to feel safe and secure, and if you're thinking the holidays are a good time to bring a new pet into the house, despite your good intentions, it's probably not a good idea. Getting a new pet is best when you have the proper time to devote to a new family member, and the holidays can be very traumatic to an animal even in the best of times.

For those who live in colder climates, be mindful that outdoor cats will often seek out any warm space they can find, and the cozy confines of a warm car engine is a tempting lure for them. It's best to keep your cat indoors to avoid any potential incidents, but even with your cat safely inside, neighborhood and feral cats could still be hiding under your car. Before you start your engine and drive away, it's a good idea to check underneath your car to see if any cats are hiding and to make some noise, like honking your horn, banging on the hood, and slamming your car door to wake any cats that might be sleeping. Give them time to run off and then you can start your engine.

To Catch a Thief

Turn your head, and Jazmine or Peanut will steal the straw from your glass. Jazmine will also steal anything off your dinner plate—a piece of spinach, a chickpea, a noodle, a cube of cheese—whatever strikes her fancy. She's the cat version of Oliver Twist's Artful Dodger. I've had my dirty underwear stolen from the floor and found it in the hallway. I've since learned to always make sure I immediately put it in the hamper, as one time Mia actually got her head stuck in my underwear and gave Dan and me quite the scare as she tried to find her way out.

I also remember a time when I was staying the night with a girlfriend many moons ago—she also had a feline underwear stealing thief in the house. I know this because her husband found my underwear on the hallway steps before I came downstairs for breakfast. Talk about awkward.

I've found the usual things under the couch—pens, plastic milk rings, Christmas ornaments, socks, and more. We had an incident once with a guest who had an expensive make-up brush not only stolen but thoroughly chewed up and ruined. But to be fair to whichever cat did the injustice, I'm certain it was done in the spirit of defending the house. Those makeup brushes can be awful threatening looking, what with all that hair and all.

I also remember once I thought I had lost one of my flip-flop sandals, but it turns out it was Zee—he had brought it into my office for me and left it underneath my computer chair. I had a habit of taking a morning walk back then, and I believe it was his way of channeling me back home.

Your pen? Doesn't it belong under the couch with my toys?

~MEWS FROM OTHERS~

Petie was an enterprising thief when it came stealing his beloved snacks that I kept stored in a cabinet above the refrigerator. Despite being a rather hefty and sedentary cat, he was still able to manage to leap from the countertop to the top of the fridge and finagle the cabinet doors that opened towards him, meaning he had to somehow get around them or duck under them to get to his loot! I caught him red handed one morning as he was in the process of opening the doors of the cabinet, about to knock some treats on the floor. He also figured out how to break the seal on the refrigerator where I stored his dry food (to keep it away from him, mind you). I'd been hearing odd noises at night that I couldn't place, and one morning I awoke to unravel the mystery—after several tries, Petie had succeeded in opening the door as evidenced by kibble scatted all over the floor! Thanks to his antics, I had to toddler proof my kitchen, and anyone who came into my home would have thought I had children, since I had to open a safety lock just to get into any of my cabinets or refrigerator!

Tamar Arslanian, author of *Shop Cats of New York* and publisher of *IHaveCat.com*

My black cat, Ebony (aka Crazy Cat), loves to steal Q-tips from my vanity if I forget to put them away in the drawer. Also on her list of stolen goods are panties and socks out of the dirty laundry basket, as well as earrings and other assorted loot she finds around the house. She has stash spots behind the furniture and under the stairs so anytime I can't find something, the first place I'll look is her hiding spots! She'll steal the Q-tips any chance she can get, sometimes in front of me (and sometimes the used ones she finds in the trash), but with the jewelry and other smaller items, she usually sneaks around at night, often waking me up to the noise of her trying to get into my jewelry box!
  Cheri R. Gable

My cat, Little Man, and I shared an instant connection when we first met. Little Man was born in a barn somewhere in rural Nebraska and was promptly stepped on by a horse. He was miraculously uninjured, and I got him about 5 weeks later while I was still an officer in the United States Air Force, stationed at Offutt Air Force Base in Omaha. He was a cat with no fear—he flew on assignments with me worldwide and was even named mascot of my military unit. But he wasn't just a military cat—when on home base, he chased an actual thief away from my house! I got the call at work one day from the security company, and when I got home, Little Man met me at the destroyed door as though he was standing guard. Most incredibly, after the burglar broke through two doors, not a single thing in the house appeared to have been touched!
  Jonathon Scott Payne, Lt Col, USAF (Ret.), engineer, author, screenwriter, Madison, AL

Working in my studio one evening, I heard my refrigerator door open—I didn't think much of it until it dawned on me that I lived alone and didn't open the door myself! I looked to see what was going on, and sure enough, the door was wide open, with my black cat, Kublai, standing in front of it, looking over the contents, with my other cats standing behind him waiting, with his clearly annoyed message, "Humph, there's nothing good in here to eat." *Despite being funny, it was also a worry to me, as it could be fatal if the door swung shut with him or one of the others inside. A new refrigerator was out of the question, so I tilted it slightly forward so the door wouldn't swing shut if opened and added a bungee cord wrapped around from the side to hold the door shut. This went on for years. Sometimes I would forget the bungee cord, and the door would always be open the next time I entered the room. I swear Kublai gave it several tries a day just for the heck of it. Kublai eventually passed, and a few months later, I finally decided to rebalance the refrigerator, replace the seal, and remove the bungee cord. None of my other cats cared enough to open it, so I was quite surprised when I came home one day to a wide-open refrigerator. Missing Kublai terribly, it gave me the first good laugh I'd had, knowing he'd gotten one over on me. I don't know if instead one of the other cats had opened it or it had simply fallen open on its own, but I trusted my intuition—Kublai had been there for a visit as he knew how hard it still was for me to face my home without him in it.*

Bernadette E. Kazmarski, award-winning artist and writer, publisher of *The Creative Cat*

~PURR POINTS TO PONDER~

Why do cats steal our stuff? Depending on the item, there could be several factors. Cats that steal food from your plate might do it as a result of constantly being rewarded with a tasty morsel when she begs during meals, so she just feels she can help herself rather than waiting for you to give her something. That's fine, but be careful— your little cat burglar might be the cutest thief on earth, but many human foods aren't good for her, so it's best not to encourage the behavior.

Cats are also predatory by nature. If your cat is stealing your food, she's not necessarily hungry. Serving food to her nice and easy several times a day doesn't really satisfy her natural hunting instinct. Make feeding time more challenging for her by using a puzzle feeder on occasion to encourage her to use her wits to get to the food inside. Consider learning about raw feeding as well—not only is it an optimally healthy diet for her, but raw feeding appeals to her natural instinct to catch and kill her prey.

For household items, it might be attention-seeking behavior—good or bad, most of us will react to our cat's antics, and that's a form of attention for them. If you don't want her engaging in thievery, don't fuss over her when you take back the stolen item. And be very careful of small objects that are easy for your cat to grab such as paperclips, hairbands, rubber bands, and more. These items can potentially cause great harm to her if swallowed, so you should keep them out of the reach of your pet.

Your thieving cat might simply be telling you she is bored with the same old routine day in and day out. By stealing, your cat is finding her own way to entertain herself. Make sure to provide her with lots of interactive toys, attention, and stimulus throughout the day to help keep her mind off any tempting items, not to mention, it's a great way for you to bond with her.

Things That Go Bump in the Night

I suppose in retrospect since my cats nap most of my waking hours, it shouldn't be a surprise when I go to bed they are **really well rested** to do whatever it is cats do while their humans sleep. I'm not completely certain, but I do know much of it includes being exceedingly noisy.

There's the thunderous noise of their otherwise delicate and graceful feet that sound like a herd of elephants when they run across the hardwood floors chasing one another. And what was a sweet and melodic meow during daylight becomes a blood-curdling, ear-piercing scream in the night when they decide they are no longer best friends and napping buddies, but mortal enemies defending the corner couch cushion, which is worthy of a fur-flying fight.

And then there's Zee. Zee with his strangely garbled, Marlon Brando/The Godfather, cotton in his mouth sounding meows that stem from a habit that began in 2009 that continues to this day—a very methodical procedure that starts when we go to bed. Actually, it starts several minutes before we go to bed.

We typically call it a night at 11:00 p.m., so about 10:45 Zee starts to get extremely antsy—he'll pace back and forth around the couch, he'll wander toward the bedroom and back, and he'll chatter incessantly, meow huffing and puffing, kind of like he's telling us to wrap it up and get up off the couch. As soon as we get off the couch, he runs to the bedroom, excitedly chattering, and when I finally get myself tucked in after washing my face and brushing my teeth, he immediately jumps up to snuggle next to me. And then Dan. And then me. This lasts for several minutes until he jumps off the bed and leaves for round one.

It varies—sometimes it's only a few times, other nights he might do it more than a dozen—I think fourteen is his current record, but regardless of the number, he brings assorted plush toys into the bedroom by carrying them in his mouth. He loudly announces his arrival each time, hence the garbled meow, and insists we say "Thank you, Zee." He then drops the toy on the floor and heads out again for more.

All in a night's work.

This can be a quick ordeal, or it can last all night long. Sometimes he'll grab a toy and then come back on the bed to snuggle next to Dan or me for an hour or so before he takes off again in pursuit of plush. What's most interesting about this habit is that he seems to have an arsenal of favorite toys, and regardless of where they are (we have numerous toy baskets throughout the house), he's able to discern how to find them to bring them into the bedroom. When I get up in the morning, there's literally a minefield of toys for me to step over before I can leave the room to make it to the kitchen!

All of Zee's nightly conquests have been of the plush variety; it was my Shami who hunted the real deal. Shami was a black and white tuxedo cat I found while at work when living in Upstate New York. It was mutually decided by both of us that I would immediately adopt her, which I did. She was a sweet girl unless it came to mice, and then it was serious business. She used to climb into the pantry cupboard at night, sentry guard to any mouse foolish enough to enter looking for a midnight snack. If she caught one, I'd stumble upon it on the kitchen floor, prompting me to jump and scream, and then I'd call my next door neighbor to come and get it as I was petrified to pick the poor thing up. Normally I would have my ex-husband do it, but many times he was at work, so my neighbor would come to my (and the mouse's) rescue!

~MEWS FROM OTHERS~

Every morning I have to pick up the piles of toys my cat, Joan Victoria, leaves for me in the bedroom. One day I was vacuuming and said to my husband, Tommy, "We have rats in the bedroom." He bellowed back, "What?!" I then showed him a big pink stuffed rat—one of Joan Victoria's toys that she had hidden under the dresser!
Karen M. Worden, St. Cloud, FL

Normally my tortoiseshell, Amarula, is an excellent sleeper. She pretty much goes to bed when I do and wakes up at the same time. But one night in the dead of winter I was awoken at about 3 a.m. by the sound of heavy thumping. I was the only human at home, and the house was entirely dark. Thump...thump...thump...The noise started to get closer and louder—someone was coming upstairs! With my heart in my throat, I turned on the light and grabbed the phone to call the police. I stopped dialing when I looked over to find my other two cats, Frodo and Zulu, standing at the top of the stairs placidly watching what I was convinced was a murderous stranger, coming up the stairs towards them. Calmed ever so slightly by their equanimity, I decided to take a look. To my surprise, I saw Amarula trying to drag one of my winter boots up the stairs!

Sandra MacGregor, cat blogger at *hairballsandhissyfits.com*

Without fail, every night, my angel cat, Jasper, would find a creative way to, ahem...amuse himself. My husband, Johnny, and I would get into bed, and no more than 20 minutes later Jasper would start making a God-awful, very loud sound. When it first started happening, it was quite alarming. As it turns out, he was only having what I came to call "sock love." He would find a sock anywhere he could and "hump" it—continuously in a circle—repeatedly. It got so bad, we had to make sure there were no socks lying around before bedtime. But even that didn't work because he figured out how to get into the hamper. He could even open drawers to help himself to socks—I remember getting up one morning to find a trail of infant socks from my baby's room going down the hallway!

Terri Tye, medical billing specialist, Corbin, KY

About twenty years ago my husband and I lived in an apartment that had cable TV. One day we discovered we were billed for ordering an adult movie on a premium channel. According to the bill, it happened at 3 a.m. My only guess was that one of our cats hit the wrong button on the remote while the TV was off. I had to call the cable company and explain there was no way we'd ever order an adult movie, let alone even be up at 3:00 a.m. to watch it. I explained it must have been one of the cats and suggested they charge it to the cat's credit card. The cable company ended up dropping the charge, and we've made sure to keep the remote out of the kitties' reach ever since.

Anne Moss, owner and forums admin at *TheCatSite.com*

My guest bathroom is situated right outside the guest bedroom. In the wee hours while my husband's cousin, Arnold, was visiting and staying the night, he awoke to a strange "boing...boing...boing" sound. It was 3 a.m. and he scoured the bedroom trying to figure out what was making the noise. Was something plugged in? Something shorting out? A cell phone alert? In frustration, he gave up and headed to the bathroom. The door was shut. When he opened it up, one very concerned tuxedo cat, Katie, who'd obviously been pulling at the boingy doorstop on the bottom of the door, looked at him with wide and wild eyes and then tore out of the bathroom. Meanwhile, her orange tabbied cat-mate, Waffles, was hanging out in the sink like he was waiting for someone to take his drink order.

Debbie Glovatsky, award-winning blogger and photographer, *Glogirly.com*

~PURR POINTS TO PONDER~

First and foremost—your cat evolved from wild blood and no amount of domestication has eradicated his desire to hunt and kill. Even well-fed indoor kitties feel the urge to hunt, so when your cat brings you a gift, or two, or seven, or fourteen, he's offering you the ultimate compliment when he presents you with the results of his hunting prowess. He's telling you he loves and cares about you, and you should praise him for his exceptional skills.

For those less appealing gifts deposited at your feet or your bed that aren't the store-bought plush variety, such as bugs, mice, or live prey, your fearless hunter should still be praised. He's proud of his spoils and wants to share his victories with you. He considers your home a safe and secure den, worthy of being his lair, and his actions should not be reprimanded.

When he's not looking, appropriately dispose of the victim and move on. Ideally, you should keep your cat indoors anyway. Cats face far too many dangers when they are outdoors, such as fighting with other cats and dogs, getting hit by a car, or being exposed to diseases. If your cat must be outdoors, make certain he or she is spayed or neutered, microchipped, and up to date on vaccinations. If your cat is really adept at hunting, you could attach a bell to his collar (removable/detachable style) so the prey will hear when your cat is stalking.

As far as cats finding particular toys in the dark, that's due to their strong sensory abilities. The toys give off a discernable odor that their noses can quickly sniff out and their eyes have several anatomic features that are designed to enhance their night vision, which is important to their natural nocturnal hunting behavior. They also have heightened senses in their whiskers which allow them to detect and respond to even the slightest change in their surroundings.

Good Help Is So Hard to Find

If nothing else, my cats are helpful—whether I need (or want) it. For example, close a dresser drawer—Rolz will open it. The habit started when my Jazz was still with us. He had an obsession with the drawer that held my bathing suits. I didn't make the connection at first and always wondered why my bathing suits were strewn about on the floor—first off, even though I live in South Florida and I'm blessed to have a pool, I rarely go swimming—and secondly, I might be a bit messy at times, but not *that* messy. But since I caught him in the act, it really wasn't much of a mystery any longer.

Rolz doesn't take any clothes out of the drawer; he just likes the power of being able to open them. Any drawer or door actually—bathroom cabinet doors, the pantry door, closet doors. Mia doesn't care about drawers and doors—her addiction is clean laundry fresh out of the dryer. She can be sound asleep and somehow, no matter where she is, she knows I have left a folded pile of warm clothes on the bed, still waiting to be put away. She instantly fabricates before my very eyes and quite gracefully climbs to the top of the pile, managing the delicate feat of being able to sit on this precarious mountain of clothes without it tipping over.

When I wash the sheets and make up a fresh bed, not only is Mia obsessed—all the cats are. It can take me over half an hour to make the bed as it seems imperative each and every cat pounce on every square inch of the sheets to make sure they are safe from whatever monsters lurk within thread counts!

Wrapping Christmas gifts, unwrapping Christmas gifts, putting up Christmas decorations, taking down Christmas decorations—all an ordeal with a cat in the house. What else? Reading a book or magazine, typing on the computer, crocheting, sewing, cooking, paying the bills, putting away groceries, exercising—all of these activities and more are done with the "help" of one or more of my cats.

To this day, I still have puzzles I can't finish because one kitty or another has stolen a piece and run off with it, never to be found again. Or if it is found, it's so riddled with bite marks it's completely useless. Board games are play at your own risk—Zoey's so obsessed with dice that we can't play Yahtzee because she zooms up onto the table—zip—and bats the dice around like a game of hockey before we can tally the point score. She will also steal your game token or knock over a block of hotels, so it's only a matter of time before a game of Monopoly will be disrupted (although when the game has dragged on for endless hours, I sometimes think it's a Godsend she provides a diversion).

And then there's the kind of help that's nearly disastrous, like the time I came home from work to what Dan and I can now laugh about, but at the time wasn't funny at all. We had literally thousands of pictures saved electronically—a lot of the pictures were invaluable to our livelihoods and some were precious photos of certain priceless moments in our life that could never be recaptured again—and on the floor, clinging to life with a dull, whirring sound was Dan's backup external hard drive where he stored all these images.

Because the memory space for these pictures was so significant, he stored them on the external drive rather than his computer, and that was our security plan. We didn't take into account curious cats or cats that might have been spooked by something, so there it was, sitting on the floor, knocked to semi-unconsciousness, and no matter what Dan did, he couldn't recover the images.

We never did figure out who knocked it to the floor or why, but it didn't matter. Obviously it was an accident, and no matter how hard you try to reason with a cat, they don't understand what it means when you say, "Bad kitty, do you realize what you just did? Our whole life is ruined and it's your fault." (This is where your cat looks at you, blinks, and daintily washes his paws).

After breathing in a bag to prevent hyperventilation, we contacted a recovery team, and thankfully they were able to restore the images. And we learned some very important lessons about backing up data in more than one place.

~MEWS FROM OTHERS~

My son, Matt, has a cat with many quirks. Her name is Goober, and it turns out she's a seasoned pool shark, as in billiards! One of her favorite activities is helping the guys play pool and hanging out in, yes, in the pool table. It all started when she was a kitten—she figured out she was small enough to crawl into the pockets of the pool table and would move around inside like she was part of some secret tunnel club! As she got older, not realizing she was bigger, she still tried, but with a lot less luck!

Karen L. Malena, inspirational author and blogger

The life of a writer is often a solitary one, but not for me. My cat, Seren(dipity), a high-energy Siamese wannabe, has been my "right-paw" for 20 years. When she was a kitten, I conducted my business the old-fashioned way—by phone and fax. She would cleverly relieve her boredom (and get my attention) by "playing" with buttons on the fax to make them beep. This would consequently take the machine offline, causing me to miss important faxes. On top of that, she learned to answer my phone, knocking the landline receiver off the cradle when it rang when I wasn't there to answer. She meant well, but because she never learned to take messages, I missed several calls. She even made a few calls of her own now and again. Once I figured out the culprit, a box took residence on top of the fax, and she wasn't allowed in my office except when I was there. Ultimately, she learned to open the office door by hanging off the lever handle.

Amy Shojai, CABC, author of 30 pet care books and a founder of the Cat Writers' Association

Sometimes good help is hard to find, but not for me when it comes to my cat, Calvin, who is more than willing to provide a helping paw and a little entertainment to boot. One time my old computer was failing and I had no choice but to buy a new one. Knowing the process of migrating data from one computer to the other could take days, as I had thousands of photos to transfer, I left the computers alone. Later that evening, I heard the melodic voice of Carole King floating down the stairs. "Tonight the light of love is in your eyes...But will you love me tomorrow..." The only other person in the house was my 20-year-old son, and I was sure he hadn't discovered my old Tapestry album. I ran up the stairs and there was Calvin, sitting on my old laptop. Whatever combination of keys he pressed had pulled up my iTunes, thus the Carole King music. He sat on the keyboard with a "Whatcha lookin' at?" expression directed at me. Luckily no harm was done—I shooed him off the laptop and shut both computers behind closed doors with "Will You Love Me Tomorrow" stuck in my head for hours. In another helpful Calvin moment, he decided to take a nap—on my keyboard. This caused some sort of anomaly that I'd never seen before on my screen that I had no idea how to fix. After clicking on checkboxes, turning things on and off and on again, I finally figured it out—but what I'll never understand is how he was able to cause chaos in one quick fell swoop that took me 300 hundred precisely crafted steps to undo!

Susan C. Willett, writer and humorist, *LifeWithDogsAndCats.com*

Anytime I get on my phone, my black and white rescue cat, Zoey, is positive I'm calling her, so she wakes up from napping on the couch and comes over to "talk" with me, thinking I'm holding an important conversation with her! She wiggles into my lap and head butts my face, all the while meowing at me while I'm talking to whoever is on the other end of the phone. When I hang up, she departs from my lap to go back to napping on the couch in peace, a job well done.

Joe Barnes, Stamford, NY

My cat, Bear, is so helpful that I had to go to extremes just to finish a simple sewing project. A large body pillow—something that probably could have been made in a couple of days, took me ten times longer than that because Bear wouldn't leave the spools of thread alone. He's obsessed with string—all of my electrical cords are taped to the wall, and he can't have any cat toys with string because he'll chew it and I worry about him swallowing pieces. I had *the great idea that I'd wait until he was asleep, go in the bathroom, close the door, and start the shower because usually he wants nothing to do with the bathroom if the shower's running. But somehow he always knew what I was doing and would wake up and come running, howling and banging at the door because he's not only obsessed with thread, he hates closed doors. I remember a time I was only gone for the day and had shut my bedroom door (it was the one room in the house where I hadn't taped the electrical cords to the wall). I put a very large ceramic bowl full of water in front of the door to keep him away; otherwise he would tear at the carpet to get inside. I got home to find the bowl completely empty and moved away from the door. I still have no idea how he managed it—the carpet wasn't wet and it didn't look like he drank the water based on what I found in the litter box.*

Katherine Kern, writer/blogger at *Momma Kat and Her Bear Cat*

~PURR POINTS TO PONDER~

Why do cats feel the need to help us with just about everything we do? There's not one definitive answer but a variety of reasons. First, our cats enjoy our company, so of course they want to be involved in anything we're doing. Add in the fact they're naturally curious, as well as hunters by nature, and it explains a lot.

It's not so much they're trying to interfere with what we're doing, but for instance, to them, a sheet rippling in the wind might be simulating prey underneath the sheet and they feel compelled to catch it. It's okay to let them have fun and help you out; just keep safety in mind so the curiosity doesn't become dangerous to them.

For example, when it comes to wrapping gifts and decorations don't tempt them with ribbons and strings—these are dangerous items, which if ingested could wrap around your cat's intestines and kill them. I also don't use gift bags with rigid handles because they can get caught around kitty's neck. I learned my lesson the hard way when Zoey accidently got her head caught in the handle of a bag. She panicked and ran all around the house. Luckily I was able to finally catch her and remove the bag without her hurting herself, and I honestly don't know who was more terrified—me or her. I also don't put any gifts under the Christmas tree anymore that could entice them—if you feel the need to get your cat treats and toys, put them out Christmas morning so they aren't tearing at the packaging in advance.

With games, be aware small pieces can be swallowed, causing your cat to choke. Don't leave games unattended and always put them away when you're done playing. If you want to make your bed in peace, just shut the door for a few minutes. Sure, it might drive your cat nuts, but he'll get over it. I actually like to have my cats help me, because it's a fun change of pace in their daily routine and I know they enjoy attacking sheet monsters!

For cats that like to open drawers and doors, make sure there is nothing that could cause them harm, such as toxic cleaning products or poisons. If need be, invest in childproof locks to keep prying paws from danger. If your cat does get into something suspect, reference the Pet Poison Helpline at www.petpoisonhelpline.com for a comprehensive list of what common household plants, foods, chemicals, and more are dangerous to them.

If You Scoop It, They Will Come

Fine. I admit it. When it comes to scooping cat litter I'm compulsively obsessive. They go, I scoop. But honestly, with seven cats, sometimes it gets out of hand. For example, I will have just scooped before I finally sit down at the end of the day to relax and watch some TV. I can't relax if the boxes have even one iota of soiled litter in them, and inevitably the second I settle on the couch, I'll hear the distracting scratch, scratch, scratch sound of claws on plastic that drives me batty. Try as I might, I can't just leave it be, so I get up and scoop. And then another cat will go. And then I get up. I think you get the idea.

They do the same thing before I go to work in the morning. I can't leave the house if I know something is in the litter box. I scoop and bag it up, confident I'm done and can head out, knowing the boxes are clean enough to pass my rigid standards. Then another one will go. And then sometimes the same cat will go again. And sometimes one of them will jump in the box as I'm scooping. This can literally go on five or six times in a row as they go from litter box to litter box, and it drives me bonkers.

I really truly believe they think providing me with a nonstop supply of litter gifts to scoop is quite probably the kindest thing they could do for me. I'm sure in their minds they're completely baffled as to why I keep taking away the "gifts" they leave me. And as if those gifts aren't enough, sometimes I'll find litter remnants on top of the toilet seat in our master bathroom, a result of some serious litter flinging by which ever cat is burying their business. And another thing I've noticed is that they seem to think it's highly appropriate to use the litter box as soon as company arrives so when I give a tour of the house, there's always something waiting in the litter box to greet the guest.

~MEWS FROM OTHERS~

My cat, Suki, might have been small at 7 pounds, but she was big enough to ruin a large, automatic litter box! She was fascinated by the rake's doings and would come running to watch it whenever she heard it starting up to mysteriously comb the waste into unknown worlds. Eventually, she parked herself close to the box, just in case it might decide to rake and she'd miss it. One day she had the bright idea that she could watch better if she sat on the rail of the rake, so that changed the score to 1 for Suki, 0 for the rake—and I no longer use an automated litter box!

Ingrid Rickmar, Battle Creek, MI

Many years ago, I owned a 24-hour convenience store. I installed a Pac-Man game for my customers, and a young girl came in regularly to play the game. But one day rather than come in to play, she came in with her mother, holding a basket of four kittens. They were only a day old, and it was made clear it was a dire situation that the kittens be adopted. I decided to take one, and since the kitten clearly didn't have a mother to nurse on, I went to a toy store and found a baby bottle to fill with milk for her round-the-clock feedings. I named her Boo Boo—she was a beautiful tortoiseshell—and she became the store mascot. When she was about six or seven weeks old, she started to climb up my legs to be with me—I sat on a tall pedestal behind a window where customers would pay me. One day when someone handed me a dollar, Boo Boo swiped it with her paws, put it in her mouth, and ran off to bury it in her litter box! She began doing that several times a day, and it quickly became a sensation with customers lining up to give her a dollar to swipe and bury! I, of course, would take the money out of the litter box as soon as she put it in, and some days she'd bury nearly ten dollars in stolen loot! I ended up selling the store when she was about 8 months old—I took her home to live with me and she lived a long and happy life, passing away at 23 years of age.

    Chuck Boccio, call-center director, Pompano Beach, FL

In an effort to "catify" my home, i.e., keep it visually appealing for my discriminating human tastes but practical for my cats, I have a litter box stashed away from sight in the space under my staircase. It has a cat-sized opening so my cats can access the litter box in a discrete manner. Well, apparently my cat Petie didn't get the memo. Being on the chunkier side, he would get on his hind legs, grab hold of the door knob, and open the door completely—exposing the litter box for all to see—rather than stooping to enter through the cat hole!

    Tamar Arslanian, author of *Shop Cats of New York* and publisher of *IHaveCat.com*

For the past eleven years, every morning when I go downstairs to scoop and clean the three litter boxes in my household, my cat Gibson follows me. He waits for me to go to the first box, and as soon as I scoop the litter, he runs into the box and does a small amount of his business. When I move to the second box, he does the same thing. Again, when I go to the third box. I've tried everything to break him of the habit, but nothing has deterred his valiant efforts. One day I even tried fooling him—running to a different box quickly while he was in the first, but all he did was speed out of the first and scatter litter everywhere while speeding to the box where I was at! It's gotten to the point where I just scoop around him, because it's the only way I can get the boxes clean.

    Stacey Herrle, Alberta, Canada

For many of us, scooping litter is seen as nothing more than a chore, but not for my parents. They had a large, black and white domestic shorthair tuxedo cat named Mr. Nuts whose litter "gifts" were so special they were clairvoyant, being used to predict the loser of certain sporting events, elections, and baby births. Using a highly sophisticated method, Mr. Nuts would be presented with two separate litter boxes, manufactured by Five Pet Place, each representing a competing entity. Whichever box got his "deposit" was the predicted loser. Mr. Nuts correctly predicted the Super Bowl loser in 2010 (Pittsburgh Steelers) and 2011 (New England Patriots); he also selected Mitt Romney to lose the 2012 presidential election to incumbent Barack Obama, and correctly predicted Prince William and Kate would have a son (which was revealed on July 22, 2013). Mr. Nuts was named for his pre-fixed manhood and died of intestinal cancer on March 13, 2014. He remains an Internet legacy and even has his own Wikipedia page!

Michael Ostrofsky, founder of Five Pet Place

My cat, Carmine, is the litter box quality control inspector. He parks himself in the kitchen, on guard, and anytime cat-mate, Milita goes into the bathroom to do her thing, he'll wait until she's done, then he goes in to bury her business. In his opinion, she never does a sufficient enough job covering up her stuff!

Sierra Koester, cat blogger, *Fur Everywhere*, Denver, CO

My neighbors had a cat named Loo (Little Orange One), but my husband, Chris, and I called him Eddie Haskell because the look on his face was always so innocent. When we'd catch him doing bad things, we always imagined him saying, "That's a lovely dress you're wearing, Mrs. Cleaver!" like he was trying to distract us from noticing what a naughty boy he was! Loo was an indoor/outdoor cat, and my own four cats had an elaborate cattery for their "outdoor" time. The cattery was, in part, made of welded wire fencing with a 4"x4" opening. Loo, at 17 pounds, in one of his aforementioned naughty moments, would break into the cattery by squeezing himself through one of the tiny squares. He would then enter my house through the cat door under the deck that allowed my cats' access to the cattery. Once inside my house, he would poop in my cats' litter boxes, eat any and all food of theirs he could find, and then curl up on my bed upstairs and take a nap. This happened at *least once a week for almost a year and only stopped because we moved.*

Adrienne Usher, researcher, Kearneysville, WV

~PURR POINTS TO PONDER~

The truth is, while cats are fastidious by nature and don't like a dirty litter box, they're also territorial, so as soon as you clean, they like to reestablish their territory and mark it. They're not trying to create extra work for you; it's just a cat thing. The concern should be the times when a cat pees or poops outside the box because when a cat is acting inappropriately they're actually communicating that something could be wrong—they're not deliberately trying to frustrate you.

If your cat is exhibiting any unusual litter box habits (both inside and outside the litter box), you should consult your veterinarian first to find out if your cat has any medical issues that need attention. Pee or poop outside the box is an easy indication something is amiss, but if your cat is using the litter box more frequently or is straining to go or has blood in his pee or stool—these are immediate causes for concern. This is particularly true of male cats—they are prone to the development of microscopic crystals in their urine, and these crystals, which are like very fine grains of sand, irritate the bladder, and may plug the urethra, possibly becoming life-threatening.

If there are no medical issues, the problem is probably behavioral and will require you to identify what is triggering the inappropriate litter habits. Start with the basics—perhaps you need to add more litter boxes to your household or change the location of where you keep the litter box or change the type of litter you are using or even change the litter box itself. Not all litter boxes are created equal, so it can be trial and error to find one that works best for your cat's needs.

Keep the boxes clean, scoop frequently, and do a deep cleaning every week or so to disinfect and remove odors. Keeping boxes clean is especially important in a multi-cat home because cats have a tendency to spray to mark territory. Making sure your cats are spayed or neutered can also help reduce potential problems. If it's more complicated, it's a bit like being a detective—has something changed in your environment to cause stress?

What's nothing to us can be everything to a cat, and despite how it might seem, cats don't urinate or poop outside the litter box to spite us. Having company over, moving, changing furniture around, having changes in your own personal life or routine, seeing other cats outside the house—all of this and more can cause a cat to react in a negative manner—their way of communicating to us they're unhappy with the status quo.

Some of it's the age of the cat, too. As a cat nears the end of life, using the litter box can become extremely difficult for them. It's important to keep the litter box as accessible as possible for a cat in these circumstances—a litter box with high sides in a room far away might need to become a litter box with low sides, placed closer to the cat that might be having difficulty walking with ease. At this point, it's not so much worrying about why kitty is peeing or pooping outside of the box but making sure kitty is comfortable. In cases like that, carefully placed pee pads around the house may be the kindest solution.

I've actually been lucky with my cats—very rarely do I have problems. The biggest issue I had was with Rolz—he's a "stand up and perch as high as he can to lift his tail and pee kind of cat." He makes no qualms about it—he's proud of his litter habits and will announce it to the world with a conversation of very loud meows that can be heard throughout the house that he's doing his business.

With his stand tall and proud habits, without the right litter box, it often resulted in pee on the floor and walls. He actually would spray with wild abandon in the litter box we keep in our master bathroom at the same time I was using the toilet, as if we were part of some highly selective, secret peeing club. I tried numerous litter boxes to fix the problem—nothing worked and I was forced to tape pee pads on the wall around the litter box with duct tape to catch his mishaps. I finally had enough of the pee pad art nouveau look and had Dan make a custom litter box from an over-sized plastic Rubbermaid container we found at Home Depot. The sides are super high and we haven't had an incident since.

Watering Holes and Bathroom Breaks

Look—it's not like I want to mention it, but there's no way around it if we're going to talk about weird cat habits—my Zee insists our special bonding time is when I sit down on the toilet in the master bathroom. I don't even know how he knows I'm in the bathroom. I walk into the bathroom and it's empty. The next thing I know, he's on my lap. The bathroom doesn't even have a door, so it's not like he hears me opening or shutting anything.

Actually, it's not that simple. Zee's a big cat, and jumping with ease is not his thing. To get on my lap, he has to use the plastic cat litter container next to the toilet as a step stool. It's adorably awkward, and I inevitably have to help him, as smooth plastic is a slippery step at best. So there we sit. And sit. And sit. He curls into my laps as pleased as can be (I can feel his body give me that contented sigh that signifies he's fully relaxed), and we'd be there all day if I let him.

Work? Surely they won't mind if I'm late. Someone else needs to use the bathroom? We have others—go somewhere else. But all good things must come to an end and eventually I have to remove him from my lap. I feel guilty, but at some point life does have to move on. And I do realize we'll meet again. I have a very tiny bladder, so it's inevitable.

It's not just Zee—somehow my bathroom is like the Starbucks of the house—a hot spot with beverages (i.e., dripping or running water), litter box facilities, and socializing areas for them to converge. I go. They go. How lovely is it that we can share a litter moment together? And seriously, I honestly believe sometimes they hold it in, waiting for me to come home from work so they can relieve themselves the same time I do. It's disturbingly considerate. They also like to nap in the sink while I'm showering. And Rolz likes to sit on the counter, intently watching me put on my makeup, cheering me on with some "meow" conversation. Rolz also likes to poop in the guest bathroom tub, but that's a whole other story.

Zoey doesn't mind the bathroom *now*—she and Zee can frequently be found napping together on the hamper we keep in there—but years ago when she was a mama cat, the bathroom represented all that was evil in the world to her. It started when her kittens were five weeks old. Dan and I let them out of the bedroom closet they were living in to explore more of the room, and all heck proceeded to break loose in her very orderly, parental world.

They were inexplicably drawn to the shower stall, which was about 20 feet away from the closet. It was an effort for them to get to the shower, as their legs were still wobbly at that young age, so once they got there, it was an achievement. There was nothing really out of the ordinary to see once they arrived, but Zoey instantly reacted and would grab them, one by one, by the scruff of their neck, to bring each one back to the safety of the closet (and bless her heart, the second she would bring one back, another would move forward). In her defense, I can only imagine the eminent danger she suspected was just around the corner to harm her offspring. In her mind, the loud torrent of water that randomly gushed out of the faucets every day must have seemed terrifying.

~MEWS FROM OTHERS~

My cat, Forest, was rescued as a kitten from the streets of Chicago trying to wiggle his way through the iron grate of a storm sewer and he's been fascinated with water ever since. When I'm showering, he grabs hold of my ankles from under the shower curtain, and when I get out, he licks the water drops from my legs. He also watches me from the counter when I wash dishes (occasionally dipping his front paw into the soapy water) and when it rains, he sits in an open window letting the mist coat his fur. Every toy that he owns or any stray straw, wad of paper, plastic milk jug ring or insect he kills seems to end up in water. That water could be in the dog's bowl, a sink, bathtub or birdbath. One morning I came into the kitchen to find a large furry object floating in the dog's water bowl. It startled me, appearing to be a dead rat or squirrel. Forest had carried his mink tail toy to the bowl and dropped it in during the night. But the craziest had to be the first time I took him to the vet's office. He was around four months old and I sat him on the exam table. He instantly hopped around like a monkey and his first spot to explore was the small sink in the room. As soon as he saw the drain stopper, he pulled it out with his front paw and tossed it onto the floor!

Tracy Ahrens, *www.tracyahrens.weebly.com*

For my cats, Shorty and Moo Moo, it's all about location! Shorty insists his morning treats must be served in the bathtub, and Moo Moo insists she must drink her water from the bathroom sink! Since I have a one-bath apartment, between Shorty's treats and Moo Moo's drinks, there's very little room for me to get ready in the morning!

Jennifer A. Robinson, Hoover, AL

My mom has a cat, Binks, that's so obsessed with the upstairs bathroom that he thinks every time I even slightly move on the couch that I'm going to get up to go to the bathroom, so he immediately dashes up the stairs to meet me! Sometimes I pretend to go up the stairs just to see him react—he's a big ole boy, so to see him running up the stairs is quite the sight!

Eliza Mc

My husband, Tim, and I adopted Baby, a Siamese Lynx, not too long after we were married. She was a very loving cat, always wanting to be carried and snuggled, and she stuck by me like glue. We would share conversations all the time, but the funniest thing she would do was when I would get ready for work in the morning and get out my makeup supplies. Baby would get up on the counter and just stare at me while I was putting on my eye makeup. I would then have to pretend I was putting makeup on her, too!
    Lonna S. Perkins, Southport, NC

I have an interesting routine with my cat, Slappy. He sits on the bathroom counter every morning waiting for me to get up. I hit the snooze button on the alarm a few times before I get out of bed, so he probably goes in there when it first goes off. He patiently waits for me to come in and turn the sink on with a dribble of water for him to drink. And when I come home from work, he runs in front of me to the bathroom because he knows I'll change my clothes, and again, he'll get fresh water out of the faucet!
    Lynette Noykos, Freeland, MI

I have several cats with some weird water habits. My Tuna is a healthy water drinker, but if he senses I'm watching him drink, he stops immediately and refuses to drink any more until I'm out of his range of vision. My angel, Sauce, used his water bowl as a means of artistic expression—sometimes he would drink out of it, sometimes he would stick his paw in it, leaving bits of litter to float around, and other times, if I tapped the side of the bowl, making the water ripple, he'd sit and watch it for half an hour. But probably the weirdest is my parents' cat, Daisy, who is now 13 years old. To this day, no one has seen her at the water bowl, ever!
    Da Tabbies O Trout Towne

Catsby was a feral cat that hung out at the high school where I taught. I had been feeding him, and when I finally trapped him to be neutered, I discovered he was HIV positive. I consequently adopted him, and he turned into quite the loveable guy—anytime I come home, he'll greet me like a dog and jump into my arms. But he has an odd habit with water—I have water bowls and fountains all over the house for him, but I never see him drinking out of them. But, if I turn on a faucet in the kitchen or the bathtub, he'll come running and stick his head under the faucet to drink. In addition, if I leave a glass anywhere in the house with liquid and ice in it, he'll immediately find it for a drink. Inspired by his behavior, I gave him his own mug and filled it with water. He ignored it—until I put ice in it. Now it's become his thing—I'll fill up his mug with water and gives him two ice cubes. Any more than that, he ignores it. He'll rub his face on the mug, test it with his paw, and then take a drink!

Rosemary Lewis, retired teacher, Orlando, FL

~PURR POINTS TO PONDER~

Why do some cats decide your lap is most desirable when you're sitting on the toilet? I'll be honest, Zee rarely sits on my lap in other spots of the house (although he does sleep on my head at night), and the answer might simply be because he got my undivided attention the first time he sat on my lap while I was on the toilet and was rewarded with petting and loving conversation. He associated that as a positive experience, and it became a habit. Bathrooms are typically a small room—from a cat's perspective, you're a captive audience, with little opportunity to escape, so they give it a shot.

As far as cats in sinks, it's a relatively common behavior—whether it's the cool surface or the contoured shape that's suited for a cat's body—they're just drawn to them. It could also be a fascination with water—some cats find drinking from a dripping faucet thoroughly entertaining.

It might be instinctual as well. I know after Mia and Peanut were spayed and I brought them home from the vet, I set up cozy bedding on the floor in my bedroom for them to recover. I didn't want them jumping up onto the bed while still woozy from the operation, but both bee-lined to the bathroom sinks (we have double sinks), somewhere they normally didn't go , so perhaps the sink simulated a cave, den, or lair to them—a place to safely hide from predators and danger while in a weakened state.

What? A sink isn't a cat bed?

For cats that poop in tubs, this can be a sign they are letting their human know something is wrong. It may be time to clean the litter box or switch to a different type of litter. It might also be the result of a new situation that's causing your cat stress. In the case of Rolz, the only time he poops in the tub is when we have company come visit. It's not that he doesn't like the company, but it's a change in his world and he likes to send a very clear, albeit unappealing, message.

It's 5 O'clock Somewhere

Daylight savings, weekday, weekend—it doesn't matter—my cats, in particular, Peanut, know when it's time for dinner—5:00 p.m. sharp, *thank you very much*. It's the same thing every day. If I'm on my computer, fully aware of what time it is, Peanut will start with her moan of starvation about 15 minutes before dinner time to remind me I need to feed them (her) soon.

It's 5:00 p.m. Please kindly step away from the computer. NOW.

Her panic signal on the weekend is triggered by me getting my evening glass of wine—once I do that, she knows dinner is *supposed* to be right around the corner. I'll get my wine and wander back to my office to do some last minute computer work before I start winding down for the day. She gets so overcome with the notion I might not remember to feed her that she jumps up on my lap and taps my cheek with her paw to indicate I need to get up. I'll admit sometimes I do get distracted with what I'm doing, but I can assure you I've never, ever, ever, ever forgotten to feed them (or her) let alone be more than a few minutes late with it.

On weekdays, I work, and when I get home to the front door, I have seven cats impatiently waiting for me. I try to weave in and out of 28 furry legs to get to the kitchen without tripping and falling flat on my face, while listening to them sing me a howling chorus of "Hurry up, feed me!" Once there, the fun really begins as I do my best to prepare dinner for seven cats with a variety of eating needs.

The task involves an enormous amount of skill, as not only am I preparing meals to put in seven separate bowls, but I'm also simultaneously picking one cat up off the counter who has jumped up, only to put him or her down to be replaced by another cat who has jumped up. This happens **every single night**. Never once has it occurred to any of them that I don't feed them any quicker by the urgency (or frequency) of their meows or jumping up on the counter.

-121-

In between all that will be the wrestling and swatting matches. One cat hits another, and then like a chain reaction, the cat that got swatted swats a different cat. They randomly tousle around, they hiss, they have hostile stare downs, and more. It's like a pre-dinner show at some sort of gladiator event. And then, after all that pomp and circumstance, when I finally set the food dishes down with a resounding clang, each cat eats from any bowl other than their own, and like a Thanksgiving dinner that has taken all day to prepare, dinner is promptly done approximately two minutes after serving it. The event will then conclude with Rolz "burying" any scraps of food left in the bowls into the tile floor with his front paws.

This has been the Bible of Ritual for as long as I can remember, and as a side note, it's been duly noted by my cats that unless the meal comes from *me* and *me* alone, the feeding doesn't count. On those rare occasions when Dan has to feed them, I will be thoroughly reminded they haven't eaten, even though they obviously have.

The only break in pattern happened several years ago—long before we were the family we are today that includes Zoey and her kittens and long before I started feeding my gang a diet that consists of a mixture of raw and canned cat foods, Zee went through a stage where he was losing weight. He was also becoming a bully with our other cats, so we determined he needed some quality alone time with us, as well as some uninterrupted time to eat some kibble, to put some meat on his bones.

We decided to lock him in our bedroom at night so he could sleep with us and so I could give him a bowl of his very own kibble that didn't have to be shared with the others. And that's how Zee and his OCCD (obsessive-compulsive-cat-disorder) behavior began. After I brushed my teeth, I would put the bowl of food down for him. He would eat a few bites and then jump into bed with us. The trick was, he was adamant I lie on my back so he could purr and knead my stomach for a few minutes.

I have no idea why this behavior started with him, but if I was spooning with Dan, he got agitated and would make a Cowardly Lion from the Wizard of Oz "R-R-Ruff" noise, and he wouldn't settle until I rolled over so he could knead my stomach. This ritual would last for a few minutes, and then he would jump down and go eat some food. Then he would jump back on the bed, prowl the bed for a minute, and then plop, back down to finish his food. Then, finally, he would jump back up on the bed and settle for the night.

If I were so sleepy that I inadvertently forgot his bowl of kibble, he would meow and scold me that I had forgotten something important, and I would have to hop out of bed to accommodate his needs. This went on for several months until Zoey became part of our life—he fell instantly in love with her and the days of closed doors consequently stopped and Dan and I were temporarily tossed to the wayside as he courted his new, true love.

~MEWS FROM OTHERS~

My cat, Lola, expects breakfast every morning, but she insists it never be in the same spot each day! I frequently find myself following her around my apartment, with food bowl in hand, which I put down when she decides on the perfect breakfast spot.
Dawn White, *Lola The Rescued Cat*

My cat, Thor, is very methodical when it comes to eating his dinner. He'll pick a single piece of food out of his dish, bat it around the floor for a while, and then finally eat it. He then proceeds to pick out another piece of food and does the same thing. He also likes to play with his water, batting at it and making a general mess everywhere.
Amber Ramey, Elgin, South Carolina

I don't have a meal schedule for my cats, they have one for me! My tortoiseshell, Gretel—a true diva—and Jean Pierre, my handsome ginger boy who acts like my "husband," demand they get breakfast in bed whenever they want. I literally carry a tray with their bowls to serve them—color coordinated to boot—and Her Highness, Gretel gets a pretty pink and orange kitty cat placemat that matches my fuchsia blankets.

Christine Michaels, award-winning blogger, *Riverfront Cats*, and founder and president of Pawsitively Humane, Inc.

While some might prefer wine with their dinner, my sixteen-year-old blue-eyed white Oriental Shorthair, Sir Hubble Pinkerton, prefers a bit of the nip from his banana toy. He has several banana toys stuffed with catnip, but the one he favors is really old and ratty. He takes a bite of dinner and then he takes a moment to suck and chew on the banana, holding it down with his paw so it won't move. Hubble had some nerve damage from an extraction years ago, and my vet and I think the catnip has soothing properties that are helping him with mild pain control. The banana ends are squished in and blackened, but I'm afraid to wash the thing for fear it won't attract him anymore and he needs it somehow.

Jo Singer, MSW, CSW, LCSW (Ret), professional blogger, Orange City, FL

My cat, Merle (aka Merlin and Merle the Pearl), who eventually became "The FBI Cat," was an orange tabby found abandoned and famished near some railroad tracks. He was very smart, quickly learning to open doors, and he had a keen interest in everything that went on outside, often following the action from window to window and opening the next room door if he needed to get to the next window. He wasn't a lap cat, but there was one exception—my dad liked to watch the FBI show on Sunday nights and as soon as the music for the show started, Merle leaped into my dad's lap and lay there contentedly for the duration, leaving only when the show ended. But what was really curious about Merle was, despite his early hungry years, or maybe because of them, when my other cats were being fed, he would take a bite and then distractingly stare into space as though solving a mathematical puzzle, allowing the other cats to finish his food. He eventually had to be fed separately or he would have been starving again.

Jacqueline McKannay, owner of ThirstyCat Fountains

~PURR POINTS TO PONDER~

How do our cats know when it's time for dinner? Can they tell time? It's not so much that they can tell time but that they have our routines figured out. They're aware of when we eat, sleep, get up, go out, and come back. For those who return from work around the same time every day, not only does your cat become accustomed to the time you get home, but she has a keen sense of hearing, so she knows when you're about to walk through the door—hence her waiting to greet you.

Sometimes our clocks don't always align with our cat and that can be frustrating—especially if you've got a cat that insists 4:00 a.m. is breakfast time and you want to sleep. This can be for a variety of reasons—one is because cats have shorter sleep cycles than humans. Short of banning kitty from the room, shutting the door, and not letting her sleep with you (What? Do people actually do that?), there are ways to train your cat to be more accommodating to your sleep schedule.

One of the primary reasons your cat may attempt to wake you up early (ear piercing meows, deadly biscuit making on your chest, and relentlessly pawing your face all qualify as attempts) is to secure her morning meal. If you succumb to her wishes, you've already set the pattern of behavior in motion for her to turn this into a daily routine.

If you want to break the cycle, hard as it may be, the most effective solution is to ignore her. It will require patience and perseverance on your part, keeping in mind that even a frustrated yell or pushing her off the bed is considered attention to her. When she eventually realizes she isn't acknowledged for her behavior, she will likely stop because it serves no purpose.

Be aware, however, that when you first begin ignoring a behavior that worked in the past, it often gets more intense before it will get better in what is known as "extinction burst." This means your cat will try the previously rewarded behavior with increased intensity when it's suddenly ignored. By consistently ignoring your cat's early morning antics, it's very likely she will either devise her own entertainment or simply settle in to sleep longer with you.

You could also try several techniques prior to morning— engage her in playtime activities the night before to wear her out. Or establish a feeding pattern of several smaller meals a day, including one close to bedtime so she won't be as hungry early in the morning. You could also use blackout blinds to help block the early morning sun, which in some cases can help your cat to sleep later in the morning.

Rules of the House

On the rare occasions Dan and I travel together it becomes an official ordeal. My mom lives nearby and is our designated cat-sitter. Despite her being a cat person and having had them nearly all of her life and despite her knowing my cats quite well, I still present her with a list of rules and "do's" and "don'ts" as long as a new parent does for a babysitter when they go out for a night on the town for the first time.

I carefully outline the list with every conceivable detail I can think of and type it up. I then print the rules and leave them on the counter for her to read. I will verbally tell her the rules in person, and I will also call her several times before I go to remind her of the rules I already spoke to her about, in case she somehow forgot what I said or can't remember how to read any longer.

And mind you, I'm not just dictating rules for one or two cats; I'm typically asking her to watch at least seven cats at a time. Feeding instructions, litter instructions, not going outside instructions, reasons why she might need to call the vet, what doors not to open, what doors not to close, and so on. The list is endless. Some of it stems from the fact I'm just a neurotic person and I fear something happening. But some of it stems from reality.

If I say something like pay attention to any odd noises coming from behind the refrigerator, it's not because I'm overly paranoid, it's because at one point when Mia, Peanut, and Rolz were kittens, they figured out how to jump to the top of the refrigerator—and then would inexplicably fall behind it and become trapped until we heard their faint mews, alerting us they needed rescuing.

But my feeding instructions—yes, they're insanely detailed. This cat gets this. This cat gets that. This one eats here. This one eats there. This cat gets this bowl. No, not *that* bowl, *this* bowl. I label cat food containers and I draw pictures. In other words, I go overboard trying to be the best cat parent ever. Naturally, of course, when I'm gone it's a free for all, with them eating wherever, and whatever they feel like.

I'll also call a million times to check up on them and my mom will text me pictures to prove they're okay. I'll have her let me "talk" to them so they hear my voice and I'll bring home gifts so they love me (because yes, sometimes I do get that indignant "how dare you leave me" attitude from them when I get back) and I'll just generally be thinking of them the entire time I'm gone. Deep down I know they're in good hands, but I miss them so much that I truly can't relax until I get home!

And bless my mom. Since she knows how important they are to me, it probably puts undue pressure on her to make sure everything's okay. Well, actually, when I say "probably," what I really mean is that it *does* put undue pressure on her to make sure everything is okay, as evidenced by what happened on one particular cat-sitting experience.

Between watching our furry gang and handling her own personal commitments, my mom had a lot on her plate. Scooping out the litter boxes before she left for the day, she went into the garage where I had conveniently left the trash cans for her (rather than at the end of the driveway where they normally are) to throw away the scoopings. She had carefully shut the inside door so no curious cats would follow her, and when she turned around to head back inside, she found to her horror, the door had locked!

She franticly searched the garage for a spare key and couldn't find one. She had no phone with her and nothing on but a flimsy T-shirt. The garage was sweltering hot, but because she was too modest to open the door in her attire (not to mention, she's an elected official and didn't want the headlines), she thought of a Plan B and found a screwdriver and hammer and proceeded to remove the hinges from the door. The only problem was the door was about eight inches higher than the garage floor and she worried how she would get it there without crushing her feet.

Kitty litter to the rescue! She found several unused plastic containers of litter that she strategically placed so the door would have a resting place once it was freed (Dan and I had scored a "Buy One, Get One Free" deal on litter the week before, so the garage was full of litter). That worked until she realized the door was steel and much heavier than she anticipated. It came at her full force, and in a state of panic, she pushed with all her might to get it to fall forward rather than flattening her like a pancake. Bleeding, hurting, and exhausted, she was finally able to wiggle her way around the door to the safety of the house without even one curious cat getting into the garage!

She found every pillow, blanket, and towel she could to block any escape holes—she wasn't certain what dangers could be lurking in the garage and the cats' safety was paramount in her mind. Her next step was to call for help because getting the door back in place before Dan and I got home was not going to be a one-man job. She called my local son—he would have helped in a heartbeat, but he was hundreds of miles away for the weekend. I finally got the distress call and reassured her we were on our way home. We were several hours away, but being the considerate person she is, she got dressed and stationed herself outside the door, realizing very quickly that the cats *did* indeed want to do some garage exploring. She stayed until we got home and could get the door put back up. The next gift I got from her was a new doorknob with plenty of extra keys!

~MEWS FROM OTHERS~

If I'm going to be out of the house longer than half an hour, my cats have a babysitter (usually their "Grammie"). I worry if someone broke in, they would get outside and get run over by a car. The longest I've ever gone away is one night, and on those times, Grammie is instructed to sing bedtime songs to my cats, KaTwo and Millie. She has to sing Soft Kitty (the song made famous from the television show "Big Bang Theory") to KaTwo and Millie gets his own made-up song: "Time for sleeping, Time for sleeping, It's your bedtime, It's Millie's bedtime."
  Ellen Pilch, blogger at *15andmeowing.com*, Ware, MA

Heaven help anyone who tries to watch my cats, Sam and Zoe. They have a "treats" rule they are quite firm on. Although treats are welcome any time, the rule is that when I come home from work, they must get a treat. I'm greeted at the door, and Zoe will stretch and roll around the floor, posing as if to say, "see how pretty I am?" Sam curls around my legs, and then they both run to the pantry where I hide the treats because if I don't hide them, Sam will find them, tear open the package, and eat them all! I give them each exactly two treats, and the world is good. The same ritual then happens when my youngest son comes home from school, and again when my older son comes home from work. I was once in the hospital for a few days and when I got back, they were "mad" at me for being gone so long—I got the "look" and the silent treatment. However, I was not excused from passing out treats!
  Roberta MacKinnon, Bristol County, MA

My cat, Dark Chocolate (DC), and I live in Japan, but my family lives in the U.S. I travel back home every year, and when I do, I'm gone for at least 30 days. I could board DC at a pet hotel, but they're more like kitty jails. So, despite the cost and hassle of paperwork to take him on the plane, I bring him with me so he doesn't go to prison. I would also miss him too much leaving him in Japan—I rescued him from the streets, and between his respiratory infections, and being blind in one eye, we have developed a bond like no other.

Lee, Tokyo Prefecture, Japan

You can't imagine the look on my cat sitter's face when I explain to her the special feeding instructions for my cat, Frodo. Frodo loves to eat, and at feeding time he plunks his face deep in his bowl, only to lift his head again once all the food is gone—usually in less than two minutes. My other cats, Zulu and Amarula, are much slower. They'll only be a tenth into their food when Frodo wanders over to scoop their portions up before they even know what hit them! I tried feeding him in a separate room, but his crying and clawing at the door distracted the other two and they'd stop eating. After much trial and error, I finally found a way to slow him down—I throw his food up the stairs! I start by tossing a nugget of food up the stairs for him, whereupon it slowly bounces back down to land at his feet where it's promptly eaten (although sometimes he'll chase the food pellets and bat them around first before eating them). Essentially he is exercising and eating at the same time! By the time he's done with all his cat food, Zulu and Amarula are done eating.

Sandra MacGregor, cat blogger at *hairballsandhissyfits.com*

Having a good friend of ours cat-sit while my husband, Francois, and I were on vacation, we never thought we'd need a video camera to monitor our kitties while we were away, but our two boys, Zac and Harvey, proved otherwise by pulling a stunt during an unsupervised moment! We came back to our condo only to find out it had been flooded by one of the kitties! Apparently turning on the kitchen sink and rotating the faucet to face the ground was on Zac and Harvey's vacation "to-do" list. With both cats standing proud, paw-deep in water, we'll never know which one to blame, but we're pretty sure it was the water-loving Zac. Needless to say, along with the cat-sitter, we now have cameras to watch the boys while we're away.

Olivia Canlas, founder of meowbox

Some houses have rules for the cats, but for my husband Tom and me, it's the cat making the rules...for the dogs! Molly, a Maine Coon mix, came to us from a home with three big dogs, so it gave us reassurance when we adopted her that she'd be good with our three dogs: Chester, a coon hound (since passed); Emily, a treeing walker hound; and Olive, a brown Boston Terrier. Well—she did get along with them—but on her terms. On the surface, Molly's gentle, friendly, vocal and very approachable. She's always lying underfoot, but if one of the dogs ambles by, quite innocently, and gets too close, Molly will leap up, hiss and swat whoever dares get near her. If it's Emily, the bigger dog, she takes it in stride, Olive, on the other hand, who is probably smaller than Molly, yelps and scurries away! I'll exclaim, "Molly!" and then confront the offender with a frown. "Why did you do that?" Molly, with her best cat attitude fully intact, will rise, slowly walk away, and purposely follow Olive to brush by her before leaping onto her cat bed on a table, throwing Olive a wide-eyed backward glance. And then she'll follow this with a slow turn of her head, finally meeting my eyes as if to say, "I did it because I could."

Yvonne DiVita, co-founder of the BlogPaws Pet Community and publisher of *Scratchings and Sniffings*

~PURR POINTS TO PONDER~

Perhaps my cat-sitting "rules" might be a tad excessive, but when it comes to my precious gang, I'm of the "better safe than sorry" school. One of the biggest misnomers about cats is that it's okay to leave them alone for several days (let alone one day)—it's not. Yes, cats can be independent and self-sufficient, but putting a bowl of food and water out and leaving them to their own devices just isn't safe.

Cats are creatures of habit—while you might leave them every day to go to work or school or wherever, they become accustomed to your routine. If you—their loving guardian—suddenly leaves them unattended and breaks the routine, they become susceptible to emotional stress, anxieties and insecurities.

As your cat tries to adjust to a new schedule, he might look for places to hide and inadvertently hurt himself. Or your cat might become sick—if no one is around, he won't get the help he needs until you return. A litter box can also become objectionably dirty, especially in a multi-cat home, causing a cat to pee or poop in undesirable places.

A cat should also have access to fresh food and water on a daily basis. Dry kibble is not the best food for cats in the first place, and leaving canned or raw food out for several days would not work because it could spoil or bugs could get at it.

The best plan would be to have someone come to your place while you're away, such as a friend, relative, or neighbor who can stay the duration, or drop by at least once a day to check up on the cat and socialize with him (if the cat will allow it—many will be wary of a new person in the house), to scoop the litter, and to provide fresh food and water.

If you can't find someone to help out, there are plenty of pet-sitters available; just do your homework and check references. If you absolutely must board your cat, try to find an all-cats facility, as all-pet facilities with barking dogs and squawking birds can be highly stressful for cats.

But what about that cat that loves and misses you but almost seems angry when you get home? Why does he sometimes hide and run away instead of greeting you in excitement? It goes back to the need cats have for structure. Just about the time your cat becomes used to the "new routine" (you being gone), you return from wherever you went. Once again kitty's world is turned upside down, and to complicate matters, you no longer smell familiar because kitty hasn't been able to mark you with his scent while you were away (such as from head butts, rubbing against your legs, and sleeping on your head). As a result, some cats seem like they are "mad" by hiding or becoming defensive at our advances.

Rest assured it's *not* personal—your cat isn't "getting back at you"—it's just normal cat behavior and their way of relieving stress. To help accommodate the process, if you do get a pet-sitter or someone to stay at the house, try to make sure your cat has already been introduced to this person (several times, if possible). Have this person offer your cat treats or play a fun game with him to help associate the person with positive things. When they do come to cat sit, try to have them stay as close as possible to your normal feeding routines.

And when it's time for you to go, don't startle your cat with a suitcase the night before you leave. Bring it out several days in advance so she becomes used to it. Toss in treats or toys so it's a positive association for her. And leave behind a little bit of you for her, such as a T-shirt you've worn but not washed. Put it somewhere your cat likes to nap to help her feel less stressed while you're gone.

Before you leave, take an item of your clothing (such as a pair of socks) and rub it all over your cat—seal the clothing in a plastic bag and, when you return, slip on that item so your cat can immediately recognize you as part of the family. Some cats will be fine right away; for others it can take several days. Just be patient—don't force your cat for attention. Before you know it, all will be back to normal with you and your feline friend.

Trick or Treat

I remember a time when I had to give Zoey pills for a skin allergy she had developed. I think it was supposed to be three pills a day over two weeks' time. Zoey was already spooked as it was from going to the vet, so I rolled up my sleeves when it was time to administer pill number one and tried to be as nonchalant and calm about it as I could because even on a good day, Zoey's wary of *everything.* After finally securing her and casually trying to open her mouth to place a minuscule pill down her throat, I knew I had a battle in front of me.

She's a tiny thing, but she put up such a fight you'd think I was trying to strangle her, and I knew I'd need a different tactic for both of us to survive the ordeal. I did a quick Google search on tips to pill a cat and discovered an ingenious product manufactured by Greenies™ called a pill pocket that allows you to hide a pill inside a yummy kitty treat. They were available at my local Pet Supermarket, so I took a quick drive to pick some up to give it a try. Blessedly, it worked like a charm and she ate pill number one with gusto!

Victory! Problem solved! By pill number two, she had already figured out I had deceived her and wouldn't eat it, so I put the pill pocket in with her evening dinner and she ate it that way. Yeah! Problem really solved! Pill number three—she ate every morsel of her food with the exception of that one pill pocket, just sitting in the caverns of the empty bowl like a proud trophy, mocking me for thinking I had outwitted her.

No amount of cajoling, crying, begging, or pleading on my behalf worked with her and I was forced to pry her mouth open to pop the pill in because she wasn't falling for any of my tricks. It was a long two weeks for her, but I can assure you it was even longer for me. To this day, she still looks at me like I'm some sort of giant pill in walking form when I come toward her, even if I'm just randomly walking from one room to another without any intention whatsoever of going near her.

~MEWS FROM OTHERS~

There's a saying that a spoonful of sugar makes the medicine go down. For me, it's not a literal saying, but sometimes with medicine comes a sweet ending. I found this out after doing TNR in a very unsavory area. I came across a six-month-old black colored offspring of a one-eyed feral mom cat. She was a hissy, spitty little thing and my intention was to capture her, have her spayed, and then release her back to her colony. I dropped her off at the Humane Society, only to be called an hour later to be told the young cat was developing a urinary infection and they couldn't do the spay at the moment. I picked her up to bring her home for treatment, which can be a challenge for any cat, but even more so with a feral cat who doesn't want to be touched. It took three weeks for the virus to clear up, and during that time, I worked with her. Her guard came down and a sweet personality started to emerge. One day, she rolled over on her back to expose her belly and let me rub it. At that point, I realized this baby was going to have babies of her own. She then jumped at my face, not to attack, but to give me nose kisses. I never ended up releasing her back to her colony. I named her Misty, and both she and one of the five beautiful, healthy kittens she had are forever members of my family. The rest went on to great homes and Misty is one of the quirkiest, sweetest, most affectionate cats I've ever had.

Colette Kibbe, administrative assistant, Seneca, SC

My story is complicated, but it's all based on the love of making sure one little cat got well! I had a cat—Sunshine—that belonged to me and my wife until we divorced. Sunshine stayed with my ex for a while and then ended up with my son, Brandon. Brandon took Sunshine with him when he married and enlisted in the Air Force. Brandon, his wife, and Sunshine took up residence at Ellsworth AFB in South Dakota, and my second wife and I lived in Alabama. We drove up for our grandson's first birthday, and that's when I noticed something was wrong with Sunshine. After we left, Brandon took Sunshine to the vet where they diagnosed hyperthyroidism. As no vet in the entire state was qualified to administer the one-shot, one cure (radioiodine), I drove 2,800 miles round trip from South Dakota to Alabama to bring Sunshine for her shot. The total bill, not counting the gas and hotels on the trip, was over $1,400 for the shot and two weeks of boarding since she was considered radioactive for a period of time. She stayed with me and my wife during her recovery, and then she went back to Brandon in South Dakota.

Jonathon Scott Payne, Lt Col, USAF (Ret.), engineer, author, screenwriter, Madison, AL

Bob is our special needs cat. My husband, Chris, and I found him near death—every organ in his body was full of infection, and it took nearly a year to get him off steroids. Whenever he sneezes, it means another round of antibiotics and if I'm late with meds, he even comes to remind me! At one point, he was living in a bathroom with an air purifier and a humidifier but was still having trouble breathing. The vet recommended a nebulizer, but Bob didn't like the mask, so Chris built Bob an enclosed plastic "bong" container, and Bob spent a good part of a whole year in his bong, which thankfully did the trick! If Bob was particularly antsy and I knew an attack was coming on, I'd set up my iPad with bird videos for him to watch while in his special recovery container.

Adrienne Usher, researcher, Kearneysville, WV

My cat, Cheshire, was born to a wild mom, living with her for about a month before he let his guard down enough for me to gather him in my arms, take him to the vet, get rid of his fleas, and start him on the path to the life of a pampered housecat. He kept a lot of the feral in him and didn't let me touch him until a year later, the day his vet diagnosed him with fungal pneumonia (an infection that causes the lungs to become inflamed). I wasn't sure how he got it, but I think perhaps he breathed in the fungus while he was living in the crawl space under the house. He was very sick, and during that time, he let me hold him and even cuddled on my lap a couple of times. I had to give him pills every day for more than a year, with pill pockets probably saving his life. I was also able to occasionally touch his tail during the period of medication, but when he started to feel better, it was business as usual without touching. Cheshire has been with me for over eight years now—I've made some changes in the house that have helped to relax him. He now feels safe enough to climb on my back when I'm on the floor and even started cuddling on my lap— sometimes asking for more cuddles than I have time to give him!
Robin Bisha, PhD, Tellington TTouch®

~PURR POINTS TO PONDER~

Face it—pill is a four letter word, and most of us dread pilling our cat as much as they dread getting the pill. But at one point or another, chances are you'll be forced to give your cat a pill, so how do you do it without bloodshed? Every cat is different, and there are numerous techniques, but first and foremost, you need to carefully read the prescription's dosage instructions to come up with a game plan. Take note of how much medication should be given at one time, how frequently the dosage is given, and the duration of how long you need to administer the medication.

Check to see if the medication should to be taken with food or not. Some pills need to be given on an empty stomach, so hiding them in food could interfere with their effectiveness. And unless your vet recommends it, don't crush pills to put in food. Crushed medication can taste bitter, so your cat might not eat the food and won't get the full dosage.

While it might sound odd, you should actually get your cat used to pilling *before* the need even arises so she gets used to the activity and associates it with something positive. Gently handle her around her face and mouth, using treats to reward her for allowing you to touch her. As she gets more familiar with having her face handled, you can begin using your thumb and middle finger to gently lift up slightly on her mouth, forming a C-shape with your fingers. Place a very small treat that doesn't need to be chewed into her mouth and praise her for swallowing it.

When the time comes to administer medication, keeping calm is the key. Cats are sensitive to nervousness, and they may become agitated if you don't appear confident. Have a towel ready and wrap her into it like a swaddled baby, with her head protruding. This keeps her from clawing you and secures her for easier handling. If you have assistance, place your towel-wrapped cat on the counter or a tabletop. Ask your helper to hold your cat steady while you prepare to open her mouth and deposit the pill.

If you're alone, kneel on the floor to restrain your cat and place her (still wrapped in a towel) between your thighs with her head facing toward your knees. Make sure both your hands are free and able to administer the pill, place your thumb and middle finger at the hinge of her jaw, and gently pry open her mouth. Tilt her head back slightly so you can see the back of her mouth, where her tongue begins.

Drop the pill into the center of her mouth, and then quickly close it. Rub her throat and keep her mouth closed until the pill is swallowed. Cats can easily trick you into thinking they have swallowed the pill, only to spit it out. You'll know the pill has gone down her throat when she licks her lips.

If you can't handle the emotional duress of dropping a pill into your cat's mouth, sometimes a pill shooter can work. It looks like a straw with a soft rubbery tip that encases the pill, and it won't hurt your cat. It works like a syringe—push it in, and it pops the pill into your cat's mouth. You can also try pill pockets. Zoey caught on pretty quick that I was tricking her, but some of my others, like Peanut and Jazmine, gobble them up with medication inside like they're candy.

If your cat says no to pill pockets, he may say yes to the prospect of cheese. Place a small amount of cream cheese, soft butter, or a cheese slice around the pill, covering it from view. He might be so busy licking up the goodies he doesn't notice the pill. But no matter how you medicate your cat, always offer praise, pets, and a treat when the deed is done. This will help your cat associate something positive with an activity he would rather avoid.

No Room at the Inn

Raise of paws—how many of you have woken up to your cat sleeping on your head? Or on your feet? Or on your chest? Or meowing in your ear or patting your cheek with a paw? Or how many of you almost didn't wake up because your cat was sleeping on top of your alarm clock and invariably shut it off? Correct—about 99.9% of you.

If I had to guess, I'd say we have over a dozen places that are 100% specific to cat napping. Two giant cat condos with several assorted levels of sleeping shelves and cubbies. A padded hammock style seat that adheres to the dining room window. Four padded cat beds, three thermal heated cat mats, and countless folded towels and blankets placed strategically all over the house come to mind. Where do the cats sleep when it's time for Dan and me to go to bed? In our bed, of course.

Before you go and suggest something crazy—like closing our door or shooing them off the bed—please don't waste your time. That's not going to happen. Instead, we have to figure out a way to climb into the bed without disturbing them, and then we need to figure out how to configure our bodies into pretzel shapes so we can fit on the bed.

And honestly, we're so conditioned to have them with us, I don't know how we'd function otherwise. Zee even has his own pillow—he'll sleep on it temporarily, but inevitably he'll huff and puff, making a meow announcement that he's unsatisfied with where he is, and then he'll move to sleep on top of my head the rest of the night. Zoey likes to sleep snuggled next to my belly and makes no secret about it. She screams in her loud, ear piercing meow, announcing to the world that she's in the bedroom and then she'll jump up onto the bed, screaming a loud meow again to let me know she's going to circle around me for a few minutes before she contentedly settles down, all the while purring up a mad storm.

Mia, Peanut, Rolz, and Kizmet rotate all over the bed—sometimes I'll feel one or more of them on various parts of my body throughout the night, and sometimes one or more of them will be on Dan. Jazmine is typically in the bathroom, semi-sleeping on the hamper, as she is on guard duty and can't fall completely asleep. She found a lizard in the shower stall once and has made it her mission, ever since, to make sure our bedroom is a lizard-free zone, allowing Dan and me to sleep in peace, knowing we will never be under attack from these tiny, unassuming creatures!

There's plenty of room for you...

As far as needing an alarm clock to get up for work, those days are long gone. I set it for 6:00 a.m. just to be safe, but regardless of the circumstances, I'm wide awake by 5:30 a.m. Part of it's me—I just can't sleep in any more—and part of it's because my gang make it nearly impossible to even remotely think of sleeping past 5:31 a.m. It generally happens anywhere between 4:00 a.m. and 5:00 a.m., gradually getting worse as it hits the 5:30 a.m. mark.

It begins with the shredding sound of claws using the bed skirt as a race track to zoom around the base of the bed at breakneck speed. This would be Zoey and Jazmine—Zoey howling while zooming, competing for whatever record it is they're trying to break. Rolz is in the background, cheering them on with a loud and prolonged meow that has a really deep, echoing tone to it. Sometimes Kizmet will participate by digging into the top of either my head or Dan's, like he's looking for buried treasure, but Peanut wins the prize for being the most insistent and tenacious (i.e., annoying).

She starts with a plaintiff meow to get our attention. This turns to a louder, more insistent meow, pat to the cheek combination. After I push her paw away, it immediately comes back to pat me, this time, either near my eyes or mouth. The more I push her paw away, the more she does it again. And if I cover my face with my hands, she pries my hands away with her strong paws. She does this back and forth, to both Dan and me, and as you can imagine, I am fully awake by this point and I get up.

~MEWS FROM OTHERS~

As a widow, I know the potent healing power of purrs to mend a broken heart. My three rescue cats—Abby, Bubba, and Chase—all sleep with me at night to keep me company. I love them all dearly, but my ginger and white boy, Chase, is especially close to my heart. He was only a few weeks old when rescued, and we share a deep bond. He's also got an unusual sleeping habit—during the day, he'll climb into my laundry basket and sniff around in search of unwashed undies. He tosses them out and drags them to another place, as if he's making a nest, and then curls up to sleep on the pile. I have to be careful when removing his undie bed—if he catches me, he'll follow me to the laundry basket to drag them back out! But at night, it's all about me. He sleeps on my right side so I can cuddle him, and he purrs us both to sleep. If I try to move, he grabs my arm back to him. Bubba sleeps nearly on my face, and then about a half hour later, he moves to sleep between my feet. Abby jumps on the left side of the bed for some cuddling, and then she moves to the foot of the bed to stand guard.

Lisa Martin-England Stowe, West Columbia, SC

I have room to sleep on my bed, but that doesn't necessarily mean I get a full night of uninterrupted sleep! My kitten Nemo is a smart guy and has figured out how to turn the pull lamp in my bedroom on and off—and naturally he does it at night when I'm in bed!

Shawnee Lincoln

My husband Tom and I have a Maine Coon cat, Molly, who loves to be with the whole family. She adores sitting with Tom in the family room, with our dogs in their beds by the fireplace and the human's in our respective chairs. The ceiling fan will be on during the warm summer months, and Molly will glance at it as it provides a gentle breeze to the room. It's clear she's not sure of this moving creature on the ceiling, and her mistrust grows when we retire to our master bedroom to watch a little TV before bedtime. Molly struggles with the decision—does she join us or not—the ceiling fan in that room is much lower and much scarier! She'll then pause on the top step at the foot of our bed (the steps for our little Boston Terrier to get up and down) and stare wide-eyed at the fan! Then she'll tentatively come up on the bed, nudge us for scratches, step over (or often on) the dogs for more scratches, and then, in a sudden, crazy moment, she'll bolt from the bed and from the room, giving that dreaded fan a nasty look over her shoulder. About a half hour later, she'll repeat the process until she feels it's time for sleep. At that point, she'll sit in the doorway meowing. She's done with us, done with the fan, done with the dogs, and she wants her bedtime treat so she can curl up in her bed and do what cats do best—sleep the time away!

Yvonne DiVita, co-founder of the BlogPaws Pet Community and publisher of *Scratchings and Sniffings*

I'm not a morning person. I knew before the first kitten ever crossed my threshold that there could be none of that "cat-waking-owner-at-the-crack-of-dawn-for-breakfast" business. Several cats under my belt, that policy has been strictly adhered to—all of my cats have been fed after I've showered and dressed—not a second earlier. Spencer, a kitten who joined my clowder in 2008 apparently didn't get the memo and needed a little extra "schooling" when it came to bedroom boundaries. Shortly after he arrived, he began waking me in the middle of the night for chin scritches by pawing at my face and mouth with his claws slightly extended. For several nights, I tried to deal with the situation by hissing at him and turning my back to him—sort of cat-speak for "leave me be!" It didn't work. One night, when I was in desperate need of sleep, he woke me by hooking a single claw solidly into the corner of my lower lip and pulling. Between the shock of the abrupt awakening, the hurt, and my intense aggravation, I reacted in the spur of the moment—instead of hissing, I jerked awake with a snarling growl and literally "snapped" at his face. He leaped backwards with a startled hiss and fled the room. I don't recommend this method of "training" a cat, and I don't really know what was going through my mind other than this has to stop, but that single snap worked. It's been years since, and he has yet to repeat his midnight offense with me!

Tracy Dion, writer, feline nutrition consultant, and founder of *CatCentric.org*

~PURR POINTS TO PONDER~

Even though it's hard for me to personally imagine, not everyone lets their cat(s) sleep with them, and some experts even argue you shouldn't let them at all. Clearly I'm biased on the subject and not the best one to give objective advice, but for those who appreciate an uninterrupted sleep, they do make some valid points.

Because cats are nocturnal and on a different clock than us, they can disturb our sleep with their random bursts of energy in the early morning hours. Using the bed as a trampoline or the floor as if they're running in the Kentucky Derby can be normal behavior for them. Patting your face with a furry paw, chewing on your hair, making biscuits on your belly, incessant meowing, and a parade of toys brought into the room is also common. Cute, yes— restful, not so much.

And for those with asthma and allergies, bringing a cat into the bedroom could cause you to suffer even more, and in drastic circumstances, cats can pass on infectious diseases such as rabies, ringworm, hookworms, toxoplasmosis, roundworm, and giardia.

The decision is yours. If you prefer to sleep a full eight hours and want your cat part of that sleep, try to wear her out with exercise and playtime before you go to bed. Feed her several small meals a day so she isn't as likely to be hungry early in the morning, and if you do have allergies, how serious they are will determine if she can be in the room with you. Often allergy medication and an ionizer in the room to purify the air can help, but if your allergies are severe, it might be best to keep her out of the room.

To avoid any potential infections or medical issues, schedule regular veterinary checkups to make sure your cat is in good health. This should include keeping up to date with vaccinations and shots, treating illnesses with medications, and using flea and tick preventives, since fleas and ticks carry bacteria and diseases that can also be transmitted to people.

An Angry Bird Is Worth a Thousand Words

I've already shared with you that Zee likes to bring stuffed toys into the bedroom for Dan and me during the night while we're sleeping (or, I should say, trying to sleep). I initially thought that would be the extent of it, but I was wrong. Zee also likes to use plush toys—in particular, an old and ratty Angry Bird brand toy that is several years old (it's literally the head of the bird and nothing else), that he uses it to communicate to us in one form or another.

You'd be angry if you were carried all around the house by a cat too...

Angry Bird has been found all over the house—in empty food dishes, floating in full water dishes (making him look even angrier, if that's possible), next to the backdoor, next to the dining room window, in my shoe, in my purse, on our bed, and other assorted places. He's also frequently dropped directly at either my feet or Dan's, depending on who's home, and when Zee isn't trotting him all over the house, Jazmine uses him to play endless games of drop, have human throw, fetch, drop, have human throw, fetch.

I'm always impressed by Zee's creative nature with Angry Bird, but his most valiant effort for carrying a toy has to be a particular teddy bear I have in my office. It's a brown bear, extremely big and heavy—at least twice his size—and one day I caught him dragging it in his mouth from my office to the bedroom. My best guess is that it was his not-so-subtle way of saying to me, "I associate this bear with you, you're in your office too much, get up from the computer and come spend time with me."

Zee's greatest catch.

Angry Bird (or any plush victim for that matter) is carried with great ceremony. No matter where you are in the house and whether it's Zee or Jazmine, the announcement of the victory kill echoes through the house. They both speak in garbled, low moans, and once you hear the sound, you know you are about to be bestowed with an angry gift sometime soon.

~MEWS FROM OTHERS~

My rescue cat, Emmy, a Ragdoll/Snowshoe mix, has an unusual habit with one particular brand of toys. Called Zanies® Honeysuckle Love Cat Toys, each round-shaped toy is infused with honeysuckle—an irresistible alternative to traditional catnip that can make some cats too aggressive. Emmy likes to carry the toys around (accompanied by loud, meowing that sounds like a baby crying) and drop them into specific geometric patterns, like a very straight line, a triangle, or a diamond. She'll typically have them arranged at the foot of the stairs, and I usually find the toys either when I come home from work or when I come downstairs after watching TV. Emmy came to me as a very frail and emaciated cat, but despite that, she was quite wild, and I think she was probably feral. She calmed down thanks to my black cat, Piper, who "raised" her. But I did learn that catnip was the one thing that caused a rift between the two—anytime Piper caught a whiff of it, he would torture Emmy like she was a kitty kicking bag—hence the honeysuckle toys—a Godsend that restored peace between the two. I do admit Emmy is no angel—all the time I was blaming Piper for being a bad boy, it turns out Emmy often started the fight! She'd whack Piper on the head and then run off. Then when he went after her, Emmy would innocently look up at me with a "please save me look!"

Shayne Cohen, Houston, TX

My Siamese cat, Rosie, came from the adoption agency with "Duck," a stuffed squeaky toy that was her best-friend companion. It was nearly as big as she was at the time, more likely a toy for a small dog than a cat, and it was very apparent that Duck provided her a great deal of comfort, so obviously it has stayed with her. She comes running and gets very excited when someone squeaks Duck and throws it for her to fetch. If you aren't paying attention, she'll drop Duck in her water dish, despite the fact I've told her time and again, "That duck doesn't swim!"

Lynna Reese Walter, South Florida

Out of the blue one day, my cat, Waffles, trotted over to where I was sitting on the sofa with a small toy in his mouth. He dropped it at my feet and looked right into my eyes. I tossed the toy across the room, and a Fetch Fanatic was born; now he brings me all sorts of things to play fetch with. His favorite is the little mesh nip nibbler pet sticks. He has about 42 of them underneath the piano. When he ran out of those, he found a random soda bottle cap. It was a game changer for him—it dances across the hardwood floor and is a perfect fit in his mouth to bring it back home.

Debbie Glovatsky, award-winning blogger and photographer, *Glogirly.com*

I shared a unique relationship with Tux—a tuxedo cat in my apartment building who determined on his own he wanted to live with both his owner and me. His owner and I came to a mutual custody arrangement, and many times I would wake up at 6 a.m. to the sounds of him meowing his head off at my door—he wanted in. What really clued me in were the mice. He had two blue toy mice, and sometimes I would find them in front of my door when I left in the morning or when I got home. No doubt he was saying, "Here are my toys—please let me in." On the other hand, if he was home alone and was waiting for his owner to return to bring him to my place, he would stand inside his door, mouse in mouth, screaming to be let out. On one occasion a neighbor said she thought the owner was deathly sick and crying for help, while another thought a baby was crying!

John Brindisi, cat care giver from New York

~PURR POINTS TO PONDER~

Cats dropping a toy at their human's feet or into a food or water dish, or bed, or whatever else is not that unusual. Much of it's because a cat is predatory by nature. The toy is "stalked" and after it's "caught," the cat tries to find a safe nest area to hid it from predators. Since indoor cats don't really have a nest or lair, they may consider their food and water dishes, beds, and more the safest areas within their indoor habitat.

Cats also have excellent memories. For example, in my household, our cats are not allowed outside (despite what they'll tell you as they wait patiently by the backdoor), but there have been rare occasions when we've brought them out for a morning excursion, supervised, in our fenced-in backyard. A toy brought to the door is an association that something positives happens when the door opens. Almost like a gift to the "Open the door to outside for me" gods.

Cats are also paying you back for giving them food, shelter, food, toys, love, etc. A gift dropped at your feet is the ultimate compliment, and your cat should be praised for the behavior. They also enjoy the interaction of playtime. You throw the toy, they chase after it, as in the thrill of the hunt, and then they catch it and bring it back to you. For some cats, it's a stuffed toy; for others, like Kizmet, it's a glittery pompom ball. To each cat his own.

Thinking Outside the Box

My cats are typical when it comes to boxes—there's not a single one they can resist. Big, small, too small, long, tall—they will attempt to sniff, sit on, squeeze into, or nap on any or all of them. Normally the fuss is temporary—usually because I throw said box away after they've climbed in and out of it or put it away because the box actually has a practical purpose (such as holding Christmas decorations).

There is one exception—a rather large box, couch cushion shaped in dimension that came to the house in 2015 when I did a product review for a cat scratching post. We put it on the floor next to the TV armoire with the intention of throwing it away after we assembled the scratching post. Although a great product, the scratching post wasn't a big hit, but the empty box was—it's been residing on our living room floor ever since.

Okay everyone! It's safe to come out now! I caught the mouse!

Jazmine was the first to lay claim to it by declaring it her hunting lair. She stalked and captured some of the fake mice that apparently were taunting her from the toy basket in the hallway and brought them into the box. Crouched back as far back as she could, she waited for any of the other cats to walk by so she could swat them away from her catch.

Once she determined she had taught the mice a lesson, the box became a piece of furniture for her. She loves to nap on top of it—the box has buckled in the center from her weight but it's her favorite place to be. We tried bringing it to the garage once with the intention of throwing it away, but she became so forlorn we had to bring it back. And now it has a folded blanket on top of it to boot. Score: Jazmine and box, 1; Deb and an uncluttered and seemly living room, 0.

~MEWS FROM OTHERS~

My cat, Mister Meow, appeared to be lonely, so my roommate and I went on a quest to find Mister a forever sister! We found the perfect her—Minnie Purrl (for her Pearly Whites plus Minnie Pearl and the Grand Ole Opry) at Metro Animal control in Nashville, Tennessee.

She was a real beauty—playful and exquisitely patterned in cow style. I wondered how anyone could surrender such a darling, and one spay and several days later all was revealed—Purrl lived up to her Pearly Whites—she was a biter! She loved to bite all things, first starting with toilet paper art and then moving on to human flesh. While impressed with her creativity, I wasn't thrilled with the paper manipulation nor the human biting. After several months of research and training, and a whole lot of love, the biting of humans ceased. Purrl found the perfect medium for her habit—a cardboard box! Now, like a hungry termite, she chomps away on any box she can find. Purrl is happy, the humans are happy, and together we live in peace and creative, pain-free harmony!

Anna Grupke, creator of the "Cats Coming and Going" T-shirt design and owner of *Meow.com*

Benjamin Lil Bear was one of four surviving kittens of a white feral cat named Angel. She had seven kittens, three black and four white, and he was the only black kitten to make it. I found him and his littermates under a couch sitting curbside that my brother was going to throw away. We captured Angel and set up a kennel for her and her kittens to stay in, and she was a good mama, spending most of her time with them. When the kittens were only three days old, Angel had to be rushed to the vet, possibly having another kitten still inside her. When the tech lifted the top off the carrier, Angel sprung out, causing the kittens to fly out and land on the floor. Miraculously, they were okay. Several weeks later, Lil Bear got his foot pinched by the kennel tray. After that, everything seemed to unnerve him, and he had difficulty calming himself. But I found a solution—boxes! Any time he would run around the house and play too rough, I would tell him "no." He would then stop and go to the empty box I had for him in the living room where he would lay down for a "time-out." Now when Lil Bear is stressed, he gives himself a "time out" and gets into the box on his own!

Kat-Renee Kittel, cat artist and blogger, Wichita, KS

Rufus the Red was found living in a feral colony and was scooped up in a TNR operation. After he awoke from his neutering and ear tipping, it was determined he was no feral cat! My husband and I adopted him when he was about two years old and he's charming, affectionate, and fearless. We've found him exploring everywhere from the recesses of file cabinets to pantry drawers. Any closed door is a challenge joyfully accepted but when it's time for us to prepare food or eat a meal; he drops everything to curl up in a box that's sitting on our kitchen island to observe. The box arrived one fall with a gift of fruit from friends, and since it's clearly beloved to him, it's been there ever since!

Maggie Swanson, children's book illustrator and volunteer at PAWS in Norwalk CT

~PURR POINTS TO PONDER~

What's up with cats and boxes? Why are boxes so darn irresistible to them? There are several explanations, but one of the most logical would seem to be for a sense of safety and security. Boxes can help a cat cope with whatever might be stressing them out, and its instinctual behavior for them to seek refuge. If your cat's feeling overwhelmed or in trouble, a box represents a safe, enclosed place where she can watch the world around her without being seen. Maybe there's a cat outside in the yard that's causing her duress, or maybe you moved the couch around in the living room. It might not seem like a big deal to you, but to a cat, these little things can rock their world.

Some of the love affair with boxes stems from their wild roots. For them, a boxed space, such as a cave, cubby hole, or den, represents the perfect environment to catch prey and retreat back to safety. Cats also love a box for warmth. A cat's normal body temperature can range from 100.5 to 102.5 degrees, which is higher than our human average of 98.6 degrees. We tend to keep our homes in the mid-70 range, and cats are most comfortable in settings anywhere from 86 to 97 degrees, so they gravitate toward cardboard boxes because these boxes provide warmth and insulation. Boxes also provide cats with a cozy, safe place to sleep, which is important since cats can sleep for up to 20 hours a day!

You eat ice cream when you're stressed. I sit in a box.

Paper or Plastic

We go grocery shopping once a week, and when we get home Jazmine gets over-the-moon excited because she knows it means she'll get some sort of food treat—usually a piece of rotisserie cooked chicken. Even though I'm a vegetarian, in theory I can understand her excitement. Peanut and Mia not so much—they get excited because they're obsessed with licking the plastic bags we carry the groceries in.

The same thing happens in the morning (and I mean *every* morning) when I make my first cup of coffee. Peanut will come tearing into the kitchen—all bright-eyed and bushy-tailed (and why shouldn't she—it's not like I'm pawing at her face all morning, interrupting her sleep to get up). Then she jumps up onto the counter and practically dives into the cupboard I keep the coffee filters in so she can lick the packaging. Miraculously, the same cupboard houses my ceramic coffee mugs, and to this day, she's yet to have knocked one over and broken it, despite it being clearly inevitable, the way the mugs are precariously stacked one on top of the other, that it will happen.

She also does the same thing when I feed them dinner. I'll open the pantry door to grab a can of food—but she doesn't care about that—she wants access to the top shelf where I keep the paper napkins so she can lick the packaging. She jumps up and stands on the counter that butts the pantry and then, on her tippy-toes, stretches her body like a slinky to form a bridge from the counter to the pantry shelf and proceeds to lick the packaging in that position. At Christmas—between the cellophane wrap that covers wrapping paper and gift tags to ribbons and bows—I have to wrap presents under lock and key to keep them away (collectively, all of them, like a swarm of bees seem to instantly converge on whatever I'm trying to wrap), otherwise it's a revolving pattern of me yelling at them to stop it and gently pushing them away.

~MEWS FROM OTHERS~

My cat, Jasper, was so grateful for his second chance at life that he helped me no matter where I was, or what I was doing. I got him when he was eight weeks old—a friend asked if I would please adopt him as her daughter, who was only a toddler, was too rough with him, and she was worried she would harm him. Jasper and I shared a close bond—he lived to be 17 years old—and one of my fondest memories was of him helping me in the kitchen. He especially liked to lie on my feet while I was baking, but one evening he really gave me a scare. I had gone to the grocery store, and he always wanted to investigate the bags (he'd look for shrimp, one of his all-time favorite foods) and somehow got one of the empty bags around his neck. He took off running like a super hero, with the bag billowing and parachuting behind him. He ran like wildfire all through the house— room to room—at lightning speed. I couldn't catch him, until finally he stopped under my bed, panting like a dog, and looked at me like "Okay, I give up, it's got me!" Needless to say, after that, I kept the bags away from him while I was putting away the groceries.
Terri Tye, medical billing specialist, Corbin, KY

My cat, Ernie, has a serious paper obsession. He loves to unroll the toilet paper in the bathroom and the paper towels in the kitchen. He also loves to mess up the napkins that are in a holder on my kitchen counter—he paws them all out and knocks them to the floor. He also likes to chew on hard plastic items, especially when I'm in the process of feeding him and my other cats. It's almost as if he's trying to tell me I'm not getting the food in the dishes fast enough. Some of his favorite chewing items are the coffee pot cord as well as the plastic cord cover I consequently bought and placed over the coffee pot cord I didn't want him chewing!

Sue Doute, blogger, *The Island Cats*

Coco the Couture Cat has a paper fetish befitting her stylish nature and moniker. She doesn't unravel the toilet paper roll to make one, big unruly mess but instead stands on top of the vanity and reaches down and bites chunks out of the roll, leaving lovely little pieces of debris for me to clean up. The mess is so pretty that it looks like the paper snowflakes I used to make in school when I was a kid!

Teresa (Teri) Thorsteinson, veterinary healthcare professional, Montclair, VA

My cat, Minko has chewed on so many plastic coated cords, I need a revolving account with Best Buy just to keep replacing them! Expensive power cords for my laptop, countless earbuds, recharging cords, and more—I've tried everything, even spraying the cords with bitter apple. His reaction— "Please gives me more, that tastes yummy." So now the power cord to my laptop is encased in an old sock and all earbuds and recharging cords are kept out of reach in an off-limits bedroom. One time he did sneak in and was just about to munch on a cord, but I spotted him in time before any damage could be done!

Ingrid Rickmar, Battle Creek, MI

I had a habit of filling the vegetable bin in my refrigerator to the brim, which often meant taking everything out to get at what was on the bottom so I could get what I needed to make dinner. I'd set the stuff I took out onto the floor next to the refrigerator, which my cat, Kitty, found fascinating. Well, actually not everything was fascinating; it was a bag of pre-cut salad fixings in a plastic bag that she became fixated on. The first time I set the bag on the floor, she started rubbing up all over it. For about a week after the first time, I would get the bag of salad out for her and let her enjoy the salad's company until I put it back in the bin. Eventually I had to throw the bag away, as it was rotting, but it was a lovely friendship between Kitty and Salad until then.

Katherine Kern, writer/blogger at *Momma Kat and Her Bear Cat*

~PURR POINTS TO PONDER~

Chewing on plastic might seem odd to us, but for some cats, it's an enticing and logical choice. Numerous theories attempt to explain why cats exhibit this strange behavior, and the rationale is probably different for each individual cat.

Plastic bags that come from a grocery store or take-out food establishments are more obvious in reasoning—cats have an incredible sense of smell and plastic bags (which are porous) can carry the lingering scent of the food contents, which makes chewing them too tempting a proposition to pass up. Bags can also be made of animal by-products, such as gelatin, or can be coated in substances such as cornstarch and stearates, which can explain why a bag from a non-food retailer could attract a cat.

Since chewing on bags can present a hazard to your cat's health, it's important you don't allow her access to them. Either dispose of them right away in a place your cat can't get to, or if you recycle them or keep them for other uses, make sure they are in a safe place your cat can't get into, such as a cabinet. Baby proof if necessary, as some crafty cats can easily open cabinets and drawers.

For other cats, the reasoning can be less obvious, and there is a term for it—Pica. Cats that exhibit Pica behavior might be chewing on plastic or other non-food items due to deficiencies in their diet or dental problems. A trip to the vet would be in order to determine if they are getting enough daily nutrients or if there are any other underlying medical problems.

Cats might also exhibit Pica behavior due to boredom or stress. Cats with anxieties might try to self-soothe by engaging in compulsive licking, and a bored cat who is not receiving adequate mental and/or physical stimulation might do the same to provide himself with entertainment. Provide your cat with increased enrichment and playtime to help tire him out and dissuade him from chewing. Look for interactive toys, such as bird/feather wands that encourage him to stalk and hunt.

It's also possible your cat just likes the sound, texture, smell, and taste of plastic. If that's the case, look for items your cat can safely play with that simulate those needs. Pet stores and online retailers sell a variety of products, such as crinkle balls and bags, that might just be enough to satisfy your little plastic addict.

Makin' Biscuits

I've yet to have a cat in my life that didn't know how to make biscuits—you know—that rhythmic kneading motion they make by alternating their paws, pushing in and out against a pliable, soft object such as a lap, soft blanket, or pillow, typically accompanied by loud, contented purring, and sometimes bonus drooling. My Jazz was so adept at it he took it to extraordinary levels, putting the Pillsbury Dough Boy to shame with the number of biscuits he made over the years!

It stemmed with bedtime—his favorite moment of the day when I would finally crawl into bed. I sleep on my side, and he liked to drape his body over my backside to snooze for the rest of the night. But before that could happen, he had a ritual he neurotically followed.

First was the circling—he would turn around and around—frantically, over and over, with intermittent mews, as he kneaded the bedspread. I believe it was his way of staking his territory because while he was making biscuits, so was Zee. The only difference was Zee would be kneading my belly and he would be in a deep trance while doing it. His eyes would glaze over, and his body would tremor while kneading me.

Jazmine is a biscuit maker too, and she'll make biscuits on anything—even the air. This happens anytime she is lying on the shelf above my computer. She likes to roll onto her back while she's up there and tilt her head to look down at me. If you call her name, she'll knead the air in a greeting of happy acknowledgement.

Happiness is...Makin' Biscuits...

~MEWS FROM OTHERS~

As a single woman who works a lot on her feet between my job as a walking tour guide in South Beach, and taking care of numerous neighborhood community cats, I'm in constant need of a foot massage and I found a clever solution! I have six cats and was able to leverage the morning friskiness of one of them—Helio (aka Thumper)—to provide me some much needed pampering. It's an interesting process—I slowly bring my foot towards Helio to pet him while he's lying at the foot of my bed. He then grabs hold of my foot with his front paws and starts thumping on the inside of my foot with his hind paws, and I angle my foot to ensure he hits the spot! I call it the "The G spot"—the giggle spot—where the balls of my feet are ticklish! So I start my day with foot rub and a laugh!

      Christine Michaels, award-winning blogger, *Riverfront Cats*, and founder and president of Pawsitively Humane, Inc.

My cat, Sir Hubble, has an ear fetish! But not human ears—those are of no interest to him—it's only cat ears! When he gets an opportunity to chew and suck on one of his cat-mates, it drives him to states of ecstasy! His eyes glass over, and he purrs loudly in joy. He has a new little brother, Aki, who is thrilled with Sir Hubble's habit—

Aki enjoys being the recipient of Sir Hubble's affections as much as Sir Hubble enjoys licking Aki!
 Jo Singer, MSW, CSW, LCSW (Ret), professional blogger, Orange City, FL

Feet, ears—to each his own—my cat, Buckaroo, is a boob man, which doesn't particularly surprise me; it's just his whole boob-biscuit making process that does. Buckaroo not only kneads my boobs, he drools while he does it. He also paces, back and forth, back and forth, across them the minute I go to bed. When he steps on them, he always hits the bullseye, causing me major discomfort. And when he jumps on the bed, he never jumps up on my side. He has to jump up to my hubby's side first and walks across him to get to me. He never makes biscuits on my husband either.
 Karen Nichols, editor, artist, and user interface engineer, Castro Valley, CA

Kevin and I got Bandit when he was an eight-week-old kitten. He's four years old now, and every single day, from about nine weeks on, he's been lying in Kevin's arms for some "paw time." Similar to a kitten nursing on his mother, while Kevin cradles him, Bandit suckles on his own arm. He does it several times a day, and I don't think it's a habit he'll ever give up.
 Mindy and Kevin Stone, Salt Lake City, UT

My cat, Ashton, sleeps on my head at night and kneads my hair. At first I thought it was cute, but sometimes it can hurt—since I don't have the heart to kick him out of bed, I've taken to wearing a turban twist on my head to sleep!
 Cindy Rein, co-founder of Catopia Cat Rescue

I got my cat, Reese, at nine weeks old when he came into the shelter I volunteered at. I was there for a meeting and wound up holding him and letting others do the same. He very sweetly began to knead at my neck/chin as he was licking my left cheek and then my right one.

He then nipped my nose, and I knew I had to keep him. He kept this habit of kneading my neck and kissing my left cheek as a nightly routine before I would fall asleep. He's 13 now and doesn't do it every night as he did for his first five or so years, but he still kisses me goodnight several times a month!

Robin K Rotherforth, graphic artist and volunteer at Protectors of Animals Shelter, Rocky Hill, CT

~PURR POINTS TO PONDER~

There are many theories why cats knead, but it's without doubt a trait that began at kitten hood. A nursing kitten instinctually kneads its mother to help stimulate milk production. Why they continue to knead past nursing age is probably because adult cats forever associate the motion of kneading with the rewarding comfort of nursing. So even if your cat is hurting you by happily digging his claws into your skin, you should feel honored he feels comfortable enough to let you share in that special moment of contented bliss!

There's also a more practical aspect to kneading which would explain Jazz's exaggerated behavior. Cats have scent glands in the soft pads on the bottoms of their paws. When they knead, some of their unique scent is released onto the surface being kneaded, and that scent serves as a kind of territorial marker for any cats that might come along and try to stake a claim. So when your cat is kneading your lap, he's not only telling you he feels comfortable and secure, he's claiming you as his own.

But let's be honest—all that love and territorial marking can be quite painful, since the happier your cat is, the harder he'll dig in with his sharp nails to let you know how much he loves you. Rather than discourage a wonderful bonding moment with him, there are ways to enjoy pain-free biscuits. Keeping his claws trimmed is one, or you can just put a thick blanket on your lap before the biscuit making marathon begins!

A Hair-Raising Experience

The Murphy's Law of Hairballs at my house is simple—even if one of my cats hacks up a hairball in the most innocuous of places, like behind a dresser, I'll find it and step in it. I don't know how or why the phenomenon happens, it just does, and it actually applies to any bodily function my cats can occasionally emit, such as vomit, urine, and diarrhea. I'll spare you the details, but one of the grossest times for me was stepping into a gushy hairball seconds after getting out of the shower. One of them also once vomited on the TV remote; interestingly enough, it still worked.

That's why I groom my cats every day. I've been doing it for years and for a variety of reasons: it helps to keep their fur tangle free, it helps to detect if they have fleas (something prevalent in South Florida), it reduces the tendency for hairballs to form, and it's a wonderful bonding opportunity for me with them.

Just a trim today, thanks...

They actually love it, but even so, sometimes they can be a handful to corral in. Some—like Zee—will come running to me the moment I get the comb out of the "cat drawer" and give me some "mer-ruff" noises and weave in and out my legs until I bend down to comb him. Others, like Mia and Zoey, are certifiably wacky—they don't mind the actual combing—it's the getting them to cooperate part that's difficult (I think they're actually why the term "corralling cats" was coined).

If I come up to Mia with a comb, she runs. But if I corner her next to the back door, she arches her back in contentment and I can comb her all I want. I don't know how I even found this out, but I did. Zoey absolutely refuses to cooperate. If I come near her with the comb, she gallops away from me like a wild Mustang, loudly meowing in the wind at the same time, and will hide under my dresser, thinking I don't know where she is.

However, if I manage to somehow catch her and pick her up (it requires enormous trickery and skill on my part—plus I'm a really patient person), she purrs like crazy and head butts me to keep combing her. If I happen to find her somewhere where she's napping, then I'm home free. For whatever reason, probably because she's fully relaxed, I can comb her. The only drawback—she's curled into a tiny ball and I can barely reach any part of her body adequately.

Rolz is another wacky one. When I first start brushing him, he looks at me like a deer in headlights. His eyes say to me, "Why are you doing this?" About two seconds later, his body relaxes so fully, it's almost like he's turned into liquid cat, and his eyes then look at me like a moonstruck teenager in love, and if I stop brushing him he head butts my arm as a signal I need to continue!

Kizmet enjoys being combed, but only on the top tier of the cat condo in the dining room. I either have to climb up the condo to reach him (it's a really sturdy piece of furniture and I'm a very tiny human) or grab a step stool to climb on as a ladder, and once I do, he flops over and exposes his belly, begging me to brush it.

Jazmine likes to be brushed—in limited doses, but not on her belly or hind area—and only because she associates it with positive rewards—typically after I brush them, I'll give them treats and some treasured playtime, so she puts up with me. Peanut loves, loves, loves to be brushed. She's a cat that enjoys any type of physical contact, but she has a really funny habit—when I brush her, I'm usually squatting on the kitchen floor—she is insistent that she must bury her body underneath me, almost like I'm a cave for her to hide in.

~MEWS FROM OTHERS~

My cat, Zoey, has a stuffed animal fetish—but it's only one stuffed animal in particular that gets her attention. The bed in my guestroom is covered in plush bears, along with one lone, stuffed cat. She likes to pull the kitty from the bunch, out to the middle of the bed, and groom it until its face is sopping wet. Even with all those stuffed bears to choose from, she'll only groom the cat.
Sue Doute, blogger, *The Island Cats*

I live in northern Michigan with Jane, who is part Maine Coon. Jane has thick, long hair and doesn't like it. The temperatures range from super cold to really warm, and she's not happy until she gets a tiger cut. She will lie on the floor, miserable as can be until she gets her hair cut. As soon as she has it done, she runs around and plays with her other cat-mates, Smokie, Alice, and Denver as free as a bird!
Jenn Weisman, health aide, Traverse City, MI

It's not so much unusual that my grey tabby cat, Teddy, loves to have his fur brushed, it's how I do it that is! I was sweeping the floor one day with a large bristle brush broom—it's about 18 inches wide and the bristles are quite stiff. Somehow I ended up brushing him with it and discovered he loves it—actually the harder I brush him, the

more he likes it! He's a nutty cat—he also enjoys climbing inside the reusable bag I use to go grocery shopping to have me carry him around while in it!
   Larry Sobelman

Every time I think my cat Gia has exhausted the possibilities of strange and/or difficult places to deposit a hairball (e.g., in the heater vent, in the track of the sliding closet door, or vomiting from great heights to do the most damage), she goes and outdoes herself. When I returned from a recent vacation, I nearly sat in her latest surprise—on the toilet seat. Not a drop landed in the bowl or on the floor. The entire mess, hairball and all, was perfectly placed on the wooden seat, just camouflaged enough to almost fool me into sitting on it.
   Colleen Funkhouser, librarian, Alexandria, VA

I was used to seeing my two cats, Merlin and Samwise, bond by affectionately grooming one another. Intrigued by their loving relationship, I decided to try it. I started with Merlin and gave him a lick. After quickly getting a mouthful of fur, I decided to leave the grooming to the two of them and didn't bother to continue with Samwise! It definitely wasn't the bonding experience I was expecting, but what I found most hilarious was after I confessed what I'd done to my family, my sister admitted that she had once done the same thing to one of her cats!
   Karen R., Texas

For years, my Siamese cat, Gus, ran from the vacuum cleaner. In his youth, he was somewhat aloof, but later in years he began to enjoy being groomed, likely because the chore had become increasingly difficult for him. One day as I was vacuuming around his bed, he didn't budge. He picked up his head as if to say "would that work on me?" so I gently began to vacuum him with the hose end of the vacuum. From that point on, every time I turned on the vacuum, he would come running and stand in front of the vacuum, begging to be *groomed. Apparently he didn't understand that I couldn't vacuum him with the base of the vacuum when I wasn't using the hose!*

Lynna Reese Walter, South Florida

My husband, Josh, and I watched the cats in our multi-cat household groom each other all the time. We observed that only those cats who have a good relationship with each other engaged in the grooming ritual, which included licking us. To show our cats just how much we loved them, we decided to design a licking device so we could lick our cats back without getting a mouthful of fur! Taking the idea to Kickstarter, we raised over $52,000 and the LICKI Brush was born, with the simple premise of bringing people and their cats closer. Many people think the LICKI brush is a joke, but I know true cat parents understand the mama-baby grooming dynamic.

Tara Phillips O'Mara, founder of PDX Pet Design and cat entertainment slave

~PURR POINTS TO PONDER~

Whether you have a longhaired cat prone to tangles and mats or a shorthaired cat with few issues, regular grooming is important for a variety of health reasons. Brushing your cat helps to distribute natural oils and improves the overall condition of her skin and coat. It also removes dead skin flakes, dirt, and grease. With frequent brushing, you can manage tangles before they turn into mats. Tangles and mats can be quite painful to a cat—they can pull on their delicate skin, making it difficult for them to walk, sometimes even tearing the skin.

Thick mats also block air flow which can cause skin irritation or wounds. Invasive fleas can also easily hide in the mats, making it difficult for you to find and remove them. With regular grooming once or twice a week, not only will it help your cat become accustomed to you handling her, when she ages and is no longer able to groom adequately on her own, you'll be able to help keep her clean.

If you have a cat that won't tolerate being groomed and there is some potential injury that could occur to your cat or yourself in the process, make an appointment with a professional groomer or your veterinarian.

The condition of your cat's skin is also an indication of her overall health—if she has a problem, she might react with excessive scratching, chewing, or licking. She might become covered in bumps or start losing hair, and any number of reasons could be causing it—allergic reactions to fleas and parasites (keep in mind, even if your cat is an indoor cat, fleas can be carried inside via humans and other methods), seasonal changes, stress, or even the food you are feeding her. It's often a process of trial and error to determine the culprit, so it would be wise to bring your cat to the vet to help diagnosis the problem.

Regular grooming also gives you a chance to be up close and personal with your cat to check for any abnormalities. Check her ears for wax, dirt, and infections. Look at her paws to make sure they're wound-free and check her nails—do they need to be trimmed? Your cat also needs clean teeth and healthy gums—damage to these areas can lead to serious health risks—damage that often can be prevented with regular check-ups and preventative measures, such as brushing their teeth. You should also check to see that your cat's eyes are free from any tearing, crustiness, or cloudiness, as that might be an indication of a health problem.

And those mushy hairballs that we've all probably stepped in at least once, while we sometimes joke about it, the truth is, hairballs actually can be a sign of something much more serious in your cat and are no laughing matter.

Hairballs develop as a result of a cat's common grooming routine. When a cat licks its fur, tiny hook-like structures on its tongue catch the loose and dead hair, which is then swallowed. The majority of this hair passes through the digestive tract with no problem, but if some hair stays in the stomach, a hairball can form. Typically, the cat will hack up the hairball, but if you notice symptoms such as vomiting or gagging without producing a hairball, lack of appetite, lethargy, constipation, or diarrhea, your veterinarian should be contacted, as this could indicate a hairball has caused a potentially life-threatening blockage or some other ailment.

Regularly grooming your cat is one of the best ways to prevent your cat from getting hairballs. Brushing/combing removes much of your cat's lose hair *before* it can be ingested, thus limiting the amount of hair your cat swallows. Using a product specifically made for grooming, such as the FURminator brand DeShedding tool can significantly reduce the amount of hair a cat ingests.

A number of different hairball products are on the market today, most of which are mild laxatives that help hairballs pass through the digestive tract. Proper diet will also help to reduce hairballs, and specialized cat foods formulated to reduce hairballs are available. Discuss your cat's situation with your veterinarian before you begin administering any of these products or changing your cat's diet.

For some cats, licking can be a compulsive behavior. In these instances, try encouraging play activity instead of licking when a cat seems to be excessively grooming. And while many cats vomit an occasional hairball, it should not be a common event. If your cat is vomiting frequently with or without hair in the vomit, there may be other health problems. Again, in these instances, you should seek advice from your veterinarian.

The Twilight Zone

It could just be me, but sometimes I think I have ghosts living in my house—or at the very least, my living room. On several occasions, Rolz has stopped dead in his tracks—completely spooked—staring with a glazed look into what appears to be nothing. Whatever it is scares him to the point he won't come back into the room, not even to walk through it to get to the kitchen when it's dinnertime—one of his most cherished parts of the day.

Other times aren't ghost related, but I'm completely flabbergasted at how well my cats can sense something undetectable to me. For example, Dan and I will be watching television—the volume is blaring and it's pitch dark outside. All of a sudden, a cat will dart past us—clearly on a mission.

Like a well-orchestrated machine, another cat will perk up and follow suit. Soon, each of my seven cats is on high alert and looking out whatever window that's attracting some sort of outdoor cat, raccoon, or possum. How do they wake from a sound nap to hear something several rooms away like that, with the television blaring to boot?

What lurks outside? Only the cat knows.

These are the same cats, mind you, that I can call over and over by name that will ignore me if they so choose, and the same cats that can spot a bird across the street during the day, sending them into a tail twitching, teeth chattering frenzy, but can't see a food treat I put right under their nose!

I've also had my own paranormal experience with one of my cats—my Jazz who came back to me in the afterlife. It's not really a surprise—he and I shared fifteen years together and he had been through nearly all the highs and lows of my life. The first time I "saw" him was in the hallway, standing next to the TV armoire where he stood a thousand times before when he was with me. He used to stare at me for a few minutes in that spot before he would come over to snuggle on the couch with me for the night.

I just assumed it was me missing him so desperately, that I willed his image to me. But then I began to feel the weight of his body on mine when I went to bed at night. I'm certain it wasn't any of my other cats, and it was in the *exact* spot he used to sleep on me. But it was the night he came to visit me in my office that was most startling. I was going through an emotionally difficult time, questioning a business trip I was supposed to take with Dan to a pet-related conference. I was on the verge of canceling the trip, but sensing something, I looked up from what I was doing and that's when *it* happened—I saw him standing in the doorway.

He had never visited me in my office before and when I saw him, our eyes locked. The long and short of it was him telling me the trip was important, so despite my reservations, we went. And that's where Dan and I first saw Jazmine. Found as a stray kitten, she was at the conference as part of an adoption event. The moment we met her, we fell helplessly in love, and she significantly changed our life for the better. I'm certain Jazz is responsible for the connection. That's why we named her Jazmine—in tribute to him.

The visits have since stopped, with one exception—when Harley unexpectedly died of complications due to a seizure almost a year after Jazz passed. Jazz came to me in my bedroom one morning when I was especially raw from grieving her loss. I saw him in the exact spot Harley laid with him during his last night with us—I believe he wanted to comfort me by letting me know she had arrived at the Rainbow Bridge and that he was with her.

~MEWS FROM OTHERS~

Ebony is a cat with quite an unexplained habit. I have a framed print hanging over my dresser drawer—it's a lovely Victorian piece done by English painter Charles Burton Barber of a little girl sleeping on her dog. When Ebony hears a dog bark outside or on TV, she runs over and jumps up to the painting and presses her face on the dog in the picture. She's about four years old and has always done this and I don't even have a dog.
   Cheri R. Gable

One April evening, while the ground was still frozen, a very pregnant cat politely asked me if she could come into my home to give birth to her kittens. I welcomed her warmly and witnessed the birth of four healthy kittens. The last one born, the runt, stayed with me after the others were adopted. I called her Fawn—my little torbie who was big on attitude. Ten years later, on my birthday, a friend sent me a balloon bouquet at work. I brought one home and tied it to a lamp in my studio. My birthday was also, sadly, the day I found out Fawn's previously diagnosed cancer had come out of remission and would not respond to treatment. I decided to have Fawn put to sleep in the familiar comfort of our home—my veterinarian brought her one-year-old daughter, and a friend agreed to babysit her in the studio while the vet and I were upstairs. They untied the balloon, letting it float free.

Eight days later, I woke up and out of habit looked over at the top of the bureau where Fawn typically slept. The balloon was hovering over that spot—either it had been carried upstairs by one of my other cats or it had made the journey on its own and was roughly above where it had been hovering on the first floor. If it were the latter, it had traveled a very complicated path to make it to a spot where nothing held it in place.

When I came home from work that evening, the balloon was still in its spot. I put the photograph of Fawn that I'd been carrying back and forth to work on the sewing machine across the room where I kept photos of family and all the cats I'd lost. I returned to the room later that evening to find the balloon had moved across the room and was hovering over Fawn's picture, with the ribbon touching it, where it stayed, on its own, for two weeks until it was completely out of air. Fawn chose to return to me in a form I'd understand—as a symbol of cheerful celebration via an object which freely floats as high up in its space as it can to be reassured the bond they had when she was there carried on to the next existence.

Bernadette E. Kazmarski, award-winning artist and writer, publisher of *The Creative Cat*

I found my soulmate cat, Bobo, as a stray in sub-zero temperatures when he was approximately six months old. We went through the highs and lows of life together, and he had a remarkable way of being attuned to every aspect of my being. When he passed at eighteen years old, I grieved intensely and put many of his belongings, such as his favorite toys and his feeding bowls, into storage, not being able to part with them. I have since adopted my sweet boy Cody, and while I love him dearly, I can't bring myself to let him use Bobo's bowls or play with his toys. Another item of Bobo's I couldn't part with was his carrier. I keep it in the closet of my office and everything in it is exactly as it was since the day he died. One day I couldn't find Cody—I searched everywhere, and when I finally found him, he was in the closet, in Bobo's carrier. Somehow he had opened the door and crept in. It has become one of his favorite sleeping spots, and I'll find him there nearly every day. I believe on some level he and Bobo are communicating, but it's still puzzling to me as to how and why Cody ever discovered the carrier in the first place. But since it brings him happiness and comfort to sleep there, I'm happy for the connection.

Caren Gittleman, publisher of *Cat Chat with Caren and Cody*

One afternoon I had my cats, Gilly and the Captain, outside on the front porch. I was trying to get them back inside and proceeded to carry Gilly in. I then had to catch the Captain to bring him in, but when I got in the door, not two minutes after I'd just left him, Gilly started screaming at the top of his lungs and threw himself at me with all four paws full of claws extended—his back feet hitting me on the upper thigh! I dropped the Captain, and he looked at me like, "what the heck is going on?" I mentally replied to him, "I don't know!" I kept calling Gilly's name and trying to calm him, but he was hissing and backing away from me, all fluffed up and cowering close to the floor like he was terrified. He did the same thing to the Captain when he'd try to get near him, and I wondered if maybe a wasp had stung Gilly when he was outside, but he'd been fine out there and didn't show any symptoms of a sting. I had to separate them and close a door between them so they wouldn't get into a fight, and it took Gilly at least three hours before he'd let me touch him again. I never did figure out what caused the upset as they were only apart for less than two minutes.

Lynn Maria Thompson, founder of *OldMaidCatLady.com*

When my husband, Tommy, and I lived in Connecticut, I worked at a junkyard in the office. It was the middle of winter, and one day a co-worker brought in a scraggly looking cat and dumped him on the floor. The guy said the cat was mean, always attacking his mother-in-law's ankles, but I knew the guy just didn't know the difference between a cat attacking and a cat playing. I scooped him up and brought him home. I named him J.C. for junkyard cat, and he made

himself right at home, with no fuss, immediately making friends with my other cats. He also made the 1,200 mile move when Tommy and I relocated to Florida. One day J.C. seemed to have trouble breathing, so I brought him to the vet. I was told he had the worst diaphragmatic hernia they'd ever seen. Surgery would kill him, so I did all I could to keep him comfortable. I had to take him to the vet every day for sub-Q fluids so he wouldn't get dehydrated, and eventually the vet told me I could do it at home to save the trip to the office. Out of the blue one day while giving J.C. his fluids, he died right in my arms. I stood up to get the kitty casket (i.e., the laundry basket) and every light in the house flashed on and off. I just knew it was J.C. flashing the lights. I had him cremated like I do all my animals, so he'll always be with me in spirit. He was sick for only a short time and the vet couldn't understand why he was alive with such a bad diaphragmatic hernia, but he would run and play and catch birds and mice right until his last days on earth.
    Karen M. Worden, St. Cloud, FL

I came upon Target, a sleek black cat, while volunteering at my local shelter. I was playing with him, and when I went to put him back in his cage, he wrapped his paws around my neck and wouldn't let go. He stole my heart, but with several cats at home, I wasn't looking to adopt. A month later, I gave in to the inevitable and took him home. He was a happy cat—intelligent, a talker, and a joy to be around. At 10 years old, he became ill and required risky surgery. I drove him to the vet and was overjoyed when I got the call—he had made it through the surgery and was in recovery! A few short hours later, I got another call—his heart was giving out and he wasn't going to make it. I drove back in time to be able to hold him and he passed in my arms.

His death was so sudden, and I grieved intensely. On the one-year anniversary of his death, I facilitated a writing workshop at a women's retreat at a camp in the wilderness of northern Minnesota.

When I walked into my cabin, I felt a change in energy. Not scary, just different. I chose a room that overlooked the lake and unrolled my sleeping bag to go to bed, but before I fell asleep, Target came into my mind—his humor, his love, his enjoyment of people—and I started to speak his entire life story out loud. My emotions full, I felt as if a presence in the room was listening and receiving my story, lovingly and without judgement. I fell asleep, feeling the beginnings of healing. The next morning, I did yoga in the living room of the cabin, looking out at the lake through a picture window. As I meditated, I heard the rustle of a skirt, or a broom, in the kitchen. When I left, I thanked the presence for receiving Target's story and helping me move through my grief.

Catherine Holm, life coach, yoga instructor, and author

~PURR POINTS TO PONDER~

This is a complicated subject with a variety of possible answers. First off, while it's the most difficult theory to prove, there's no denying a great many people believe in the paranormal, myself included because I've witnessed ghosts and spirits firsthand—both in feline and human form. Given that cats have a heightened sensitivity to the world around them, why wouldn't they be able to sense ghosts or spirits, too?

But if it wasn't a ghost, just what did cause your cat to randomly become so terrified of a particular room in your house that he's 100% familiar with? Chances are good something happened that triggered your cat. Maybe a strange smell you tracked in with your shoes from outside or a distant neighborhood noise. Or if you have a multi-pet home, maybe an altercation occurred that you weren't aware of. Or maybe a book or some other object dropped to the floor earlier in the day, and it spooked your cat.

The slightest change in environment can set off a cat, so the best thing to do is remain calm and try to slowly coax your cat back into the space in question. Treats, playtime—things associated with positive reinforcement. Be patient—don't chase after him and plunk him into the room that's scaring him. Let your cat settle his nerves on his own time.

In more unusual circumstances, some cats can develop a strange disorder called feline hyperesthesia which is a condition when a cat has an abnormally increased sensitivity of the skin. Your cat might suddenly turn toward her tail as if something is bothering her and take off running out of the blue as though something is scaring her. She might show sensitivity when any point along her spine or back is touched and she might also be agitated—biting or chasing her tail and hissing and vocalizing. She could even seem to be hallucinating, following the movement of things that aren't there.

In drastic cases, a cat might self-mutilate by biting, licking, chewing and pulling out hair. It's difficult to know what causes hyperesthesia, but one of the first things you should do if your kitty is showing symptoms is investigate what's causing the itching and biting.

Perhaps it's a flea allergy that's causing your cat to go bonkers. Get a specially designed fine-toothed flea comb and run it through her fur. Start at her ears and head and work toward her tail, paying close attention to both the underside and the top of her neck and the area around her rump. If there are fleas, you'll notice them as black dots moving around on the comb. Since the bite from a single flea can cause serious, long-term itching and skin irritation, you'll need a game plan to rid both your cat and house of these dangerous parasites. A bad case of fleas can cause your cat to lick and scratch so aggressively that she can lose patches of hair on her body.

Cats that are fed a dry kibble diet can also aggravate a hyperesthesia condition. Many cats are allergic to the grains in dry foods, so it's best to switch them to a balanced diet—preferably one that's raw food based, or a high-quality, grain-free canned food diet. It could also be a form of obsessive compulsive disorder, with the obsession being excessive grooming. Some breeds might also be predisposed to the mania, such as certain Oriental breeds that are triggered by stress. Certainly the best advice would be to bring your cat to the vet for a thorough physical exam to determine what can be done to keep her happy, stress-free, and healthy.

For a cat that seems to stare deep into space at what seems to be nothing at all, it could be because they actually *do* see something. A study by Ron Douglas, a biologist at City University London, England, indicates that cats (among other mammals) are thought to see in ultraviolet light.[1]

UV light is the wave length beyond the visible light from red to violet that humans can see. Humans have a lens that blocks UV from reaching the retina, but cats might have the ability to see UV light, which would help explain why they are so adept at hunting prey. While we might think they are looking at nothing, it's quite possible they can see something as minuscule as sunlight glinting off a fleck of dust.

As far as that cat that seems to have Superman-powered eyes but can't see a treat in the palm of your hand under his nose, interestingly, there's a blind spot in cat's vision right under his nose. That's why when you drop anything right under his nose, he'll have to sniff around before finding it.

[1]http://www.petmd.com/news/health-science/what-cats-and-dogs-can-see-humans-cant-you-wont-believe-it-31380

Cat in the Hat

When I was younger, *The Cat in the Hat* by Dr. Seuss was one of my favorite books. I was so shy back then and loved imagining myself being either Thing One or Thing Two—the wonderfully naughty characters who created such havoc in the book. Little did I know I would actually have a cat who would become a hat for me—my Kizmet. Kizmet's a special cat—even when I got him as a tiny kitten, he already had an old soul spirit and his coming into my life was a result of fate and destiny (hence the name, Kizmet).

It all started when I went to buy some cat food at Pet Supermarket on my way home from work several years ago—a Pet Supermarket that *wasn't my regular location!* Rather than walking directly to the aisle with cat food, I made the mistake of breaking my Pet Supermarket Rule Number One—walking past the cages holding cats for adoption, when I already had seven cats at home as it was.

I saw him and our eyes locked. I was prisoner to his darling little face, and in a moment of utter insanity, I grabbed a store clerk and my mouth opened and formed the words, "May I hold him?" He's been with me ever since, and I don't know if it's his way of thanking me for a warm, safe, happy, and loving forever home, but he shows his gratitude to me every night in the most precious of ways.

It's all part of my nightly routine—I finish up whatever work I have going on for the day and settle on the couch with Dan for a few hours of television to unwind before bed. Zoey and Mia typically snuggle on my outstretched legs and Kizmet sleeps behind me on the backrest of the couch where we have a specially placed blanket to make sure he's as comfortable as possible.

A cherished moment in time.

Eventually I'll feel a pull on my scalp—like someone is digging for buried treasure in my hair or building a nest to lay an egg. It's Kizmet—he does that for a second, then he situates his body so his head is resting on mine, as if it's a soft downy pillow, and then he wraps his paws around my head in a loving embrace. We both collectively sigh, I reach up to give him a quick pat and a "Hi buddy," and the routine never fails to melt my heart.

Dan also has "cat in the hat" moments with Kizmet, but it's much different than mine—Kizmet likes to jump up onto Dan's shoulders (or head) to walk around with him. He's kind enough not to use his claws, but Peanut, who's also a jumper, isn't nearly as considerate when she lands on Dan's shoulders, often using her claws to steady her balance. This is strictly something they do with Dan only—I've never once had either Kizmet or Peanut jump up onto me.

~MEWS FROM OTHERS~

My cat, Rex, likes to be up, up, up. He once scaled the plumber who came over to repair a leaky pipe in the ceiling, and later, while the plumber was outside, I heard a crash and found the ladder on its side and Rex peering out of the ceiling with a "did I do that?" look. He's also climbed me, my stepfather (who now calls him "the devil cat"), and every cat-sitter I've had for him, ever.

Marguerite Nutter, membership director, Society for Ecological Restoration, Washington, DC

My cat, Calvin, likes to ride on my shoulders. Not necessarily unusual, but if a family member stands next to me, shoulder-to-shoulder, he'll often walk onto the next set of shoulders and the next. His only rule—he always has to start on the right shoulder.

Susan C. Willett, writer and humorist, *LifeWithDogsAndCats.com*

Peaches is a cat with an actual Cat in the Hat ritual! She has an elaborate daily "Welcome Home Hat Ceremony" when I get home from work. It's her little way of letting me know how happy she is to see me. She runs, meowing and purring to the front door and then jumps up to the table in the entranceway where I take off whatever hat I'm wearing. She then puts her head inside the hat, rolling around like crazy! My other cat, Paprika, usually comes to greet me about halfway through the hat ceremony—Peaches will be on the table and Paprika on the floor. I try to sneak a few pets on Paprika while she and Peaches are schmoozing, but if Peaches sees that I'm petting Paprika during her ceremony, she jumps off the table and stalks off in a haughty huff. Oh, and just to clarify, Peaches likes all fabric hats—cotton or wool—but she does not like straw hats!

Carol Lowbeer, photographer and publisher of the blog, *Peaches & Paprika, Calico Cats of Distinction*

I'll be the first to tell you my cat, Lando, is not aloof. One day a friend was visiting. I stepped out of the room for a moment and heard a cry of surprise from my friend. When I came back, my friend was kneeling on the floor, petting an unexpected visitor. It seems that she had been standing, rather innocently in the living room when all of a sudden she was face to face with Lando mid-air, and when he landed, she took the opportunity to pet him!

Andrea Dorn, RVT, MLT (ASCP)

~PURR POINTS TO PONDER~

Why do cats find the top of our head so appealing? Is it because the hair on our head feels like fur to them and they can relate, or are there other reasons? The most practical answer is probably warmth—cats crave warmth and seek it. If you live in a multi-cat home, often you'll find your cats sleeping, tucked together into a perfect ball of fur. Or you'll see your cat absorbing whatever ray of sunlight they can find before the sun sets, or they'll steal your chair when you get up because you left it nice and toasty warm for them.

Since people lose most of their body heat through their head, your cat considers your head a built-in heater. If it's bedtime, add in a soft and comfortable pillow—it becomes an engraved invitation for your cat to come nestle between your head, pillow, and neck.

Cats are also sensory and territorial. Your cat might like the smell of your hair—some hair products can be quite intoxicating (many cats actually like to lick hair) and some cats like the feel of hair. But your cat also considers you his property—property that he loves and adores—so he shares his affection by sharing his scent on you. All the licking, head-butting, and rubbing are his way of putting his special au du feline perfume on you.

When you go to bed at night, typically the only body parts exposed are your face and neck. So when your cat curls up with your head, he's claiming you as his. This way, if any other cats come around, they'll know you're already taken.

If you have several cats, usually there's a pecking order. The most dominant cat will probably sleep at a higher level, while the lowest-ranking cat(s) will sleep closer to the ground. Sleeping on your head puts the dominant cat at the highest point on the bed— crowning him King or Queen to lord over everyone else. Your more submissive cat(s) will probably sleep at the foot of the bed, somewhere else in the bedroom, or even in a different room.

Lastly, because your cat is a warrior, having a safe zone where he doesn't have to worry about predators is important to him. His sleeping with you at night reassures him he is free from danger— chances are good your cat will retain that safe association and sleep on your pillow, even when you're not in bed.

For a cat that's a jumper, if you don't want her doing it, you're going to have to stop the behavior quickly or it will become an accepted habit. If you don't mind the jumping and enjoy having your furry companion ride around on your head, back, or shoulders, then it's a good idea to keep her nails trimmed so she won't accidently hurt you with her claws.

As with a cat that sleeps on your head, a cat that jumps on your head just wants to be close to you. Cats love high spots, they love you, and they love the attention you give them when they're next to you. To deter her, you'll need to stop cooing or fussing (or swearing) when she suddenly jumps up onto you because that's attention to her. Gently place her on something like a cat condo and praise her with treats for staying there. If you don't break the habit right away, she'll have no idea you consider what she's doing inappropriate. The choice is yours—if you don't mind the jumping, accept it as a compliment. If you do mind, then you need to discourage it from the get-go.

Hide and Seek or Lost and Found

We have sheer curtains in our bedroom, and Zoey is 100% certain on those occasions when she needs to hide (like when my grand dog, Rick, comes to visit or when I'm looking for her to comb her or when I'm just walking in her general direction to do something that doesn't remotely concern her, like to go to the bathroom) that she can't be seen. It's the gentle breeze of the curtain caused by the tell-tale tip of her swaying tail and her ears sticking out that gives it away, but I always give her the courtesy of pretending she's a great spotted-leopard in hiding and that I don't see her.

Ha! I'm invisible behind this curtain!

She also went through a phase, not so much hide and seek, as find and snatch. Zoey's an excellent jumper, and we've got a typical refrigerator—the kind that's cluttered with family photos, magnets, and clips of paper. I had tacked up an important document I was supposed to mail to my oldest son. I put it there as a reminder to take it to work with me, and when I went to grab it, it was gone.

I started to go crazy. Did I really put it there? I went through my purse, through old bags of garbage, through mountains of paperwork on the kitchen counter and more looking for it. Nothing. I went to work and emailed Dan to ask if he knew anything about it. After emailing back and forth with no luck, as a last ditch effort, I asked him to move the refrigerator to see if maybe by some chance of luck it was under there. He emailed me back: yes, it was! He put it back up and emailed me two minutes later—the paper was missing again, but this time he knew why— Zoey had already jumped up and knocked it down, sending it back under the refrigerator!

Jazmine also has her own version of hide and seek involving her toy mice. That's it—just her toy mice (the fake ones with real fur)—no other toys and no other style mouse. What these mice have done to her in the past, I don't know, but apparently they belong under the bottom drawer of the stove where we keep the broiler pans. I found this out when I pulled it out to do some heavy duty spring cleaning. Nine little critters, scattered in a fluffy cloud of old cat hair and covered in a layer of dust and grime, were on the floor.

Jazmine came running when she saw I had discovered her prey and was visibly taken aback when I scooped them up, dusted them off, and put them back into the toy basket where I foolishly assumed they lived. Her exasperation was clear—*great, now I have to put them back under the stove*. But then sometimes I'll catch her just sitting by the stove, staring at the drawer, as if she's willing it to open to see what's underneath.

As a courtesy, I'll open it for her, and sure enough, there will be a mouse or two on the floor. I take them out, shake off the cat hair, and toss them for her to catch. I assume she doesn't want them under there any longer, but she does. She instantly, and purposely, bats them back under the stove. Then she stares at the drawer. Then at me. I then remove the drawer, then the mice, and we repeat this game until I become too exhausted to play any further. To this day, no matter how many times I clean under the stove (admittedly, it's not many), there will be mice under there.

There was also an incident of lost and found many years ago with my angel cat, Whitney. Whitney was a funny little thing—it's not that she didn't like me, she did, but she was such a low-key, low-maintenance kind of cat that you barely knew she was around. She didn't snuggle, she didn't meow, and she didn't play. It's not that she wasn't content, it was just her way. One night when I was feeding the gang dinner, she didn't come out. I called her over and over and looked far and wide for her—even to the point of driving around outside in the pitch dark and getting lost in my very confusing neighborhood of dead-end streets.

I came home a defeated wreck, standing in the living room, wondering how I would possibly be able to sleep that night, worrying about her whereabouts. And then I looked down, and there she was, right in front of me! We had some built-in bookcases in our living room, and it seems she had found a hole with a crawl space and had snuggled behind the bookcase for the day. I also came to the conclusion she had become hard of hearing in her old age and was in such a deep sleep that she hadn't heard me calling her. I patched up the hole and from that point on, I always looked for her to carry her into the kitchen so she wouldn't miss a meal.

~MEWS FROM OTHERS~

Gregarious ginger cat Marmalade of the famous cat duo, Cole and Marmalade, is known for his humorous antics, but when he went missing one day, it was anything but funny for me and my wife, Jessica. With assistance from Cole who was following us all around the apartment, we looked everywhere—the bathrooms, the dirty laundry hamper, closets, in their special kitty boxes, under the bed, and in the laundry room in case we had closed him in there by mistake. Nothing. We started to get worried—what if he had somehow gotten outside? We were standing in the hallway, trying to think of other weird places Marm might be when we noticed Cole over by Jessica's handbag collection. Jessica has an actual retail rack to hang things, and she had a couple dozen purses hanging from it. Cole was particularly interested in the Union Jack purse my mom had sent Jessica for Christmas and was sniffing all around it. We walked closer, and that's when we saw the glimpse of ginger inside the purse—and then, out popped Marm's head! He had cleverly discovered he could climb into the purse, which was hanging from a hook, and curl up inside for a catnap in a very fashionable kitty nest! He loved the purse so much we would find him sleeping in it several times a week. Jessica eventually gave up the purse so he could have it as another cat bed, and she even lined it with faux fur for extra warmth. As time went on, Marm grew bigger and discovered he could no longer fit in the Union Jack purse, so he's upgraded to a larger one for more comfort!

Chris Poole, cat servant to Cole and Marmalade

Genghis came to us with the name "I.Q." He was a black cat that no one wanted, and the foster home he was staying at in North Carolina was part of a cat transport effort. As the fosterer was loading up all the cats who were chosen by various rescue groups up north, Genghis snuck into the back of one of the crates. He made it all the way from Rutherford, North Carolina to Fredericksburg, Virginia before anyone noticed! And then the poor baby got sent back to North

Carolina! Long story short, as I often helped with the transfer runs when I lived in Virginia, I was asked if I would take him to my farm, as he kept escaping his foster home. I did, and while his name was apt—after all, he was smart enough to find the perfect forever home—the name didn't roll off the tongue easily. My husband, Chris, and I tried a few names, and when Chris said "Genghis!" I.Q. chirped loudly and happily rolled around, so it stuck. Genghis no longer has to play hide and seek and has since moved with us to our new home in West Virginia.

Adrienne Usher, researcher, Kearneysville, WV

Our Flamepoint Siamese, Reno, might have been a plumber in his previous life. He's got a fixation with the drain stopper in the seldom-used upstairs guest bathroom. Somehow, he figured out how to remove it, and once freed from the drain, he runs around the house with it, like a dog and his bone. This was a puzzler for a while. My husband and I would find the stopper in various spots around the house—even once finding it in the kitchen sink downstairs. Now, most mornings, after Reno's finished playing in the fireplace and tracking soot all over the white carpet, he runs upstairs to get his drain stopper and bats it around the hardwood floor downstairs.

Karen Nichols, editor, artist, and user interface engineer, Castro Valley, CA

My childhood cat, Patch, didn't like offensive odors so she hid them! My aunt and uncle lived on the dairy farm that my dad grew up on and they came over for a visit. My mom put each of their coats on her bed, and when the visit was over, she went to retrieve them. Only one problem—my aunt's coat was missing! It seems Patch didn't like the...um, manure odor on the coat, so he pushed it off the bed and then pushed it under the bed!

Melissa Lapierre, award-winning blogger, *Mochas, Mysteries, and Meows*

I remember rolling over in bed one night and feeling something odd. It was a fork of all things! It happened several more times— sometimes it would be a fork or a spoon or some other weird item that I clearly didn't put there. I finally figured out the culprit—my Siamese rescue cat, Echo, who was a kitten at the time. He had a fascination with metal objects and would fish them out of the kitchen sink in the middle of the night and bring them to me as gifts. It was just a temporary phase and he has long since stopped doing it, but it certainly was one his more unique habits!

    Kris Wilson Potter, wine specialist, Plano, TX

My cats, Sam and Zoe, have a very unusual mealtime habit that involves hide and seek. They like to hide their food by covering it up with either a dish towel, or my son's artwork that's tacked on the fridge! Zoe is the one that steals the dish towels—she either finds a nice clean one hanging off the kitchen drawer or the back of a chair. Or if the linen drawer is left open, she'll hop up and fish one out that she likes. If she can't find a dish towel, Sam will pull one of my son's art papers off the fridge for her to use to cover up their bowls. Zoe likes her dinner bowls (she thinks she owns both) covered all the way, and Sam likes to see his. Now they've compromised and leave just enough space exposed for nibbling without having to pull off any towel. As the bowls become empty, the towel is moved little by little until it's crumpled up next to them. I've also learned to keep their water away from their food dishes, as they are splashing maniacs! Zoe's the worst—she splashes water into the food and then gets mad at me for it. Sometimes she covers the water bowl with a towel, too, but that never works out well. The towel is soggy, water is everywhere, and again it's all my fault. Zoe gives me that "why did you do that, fix it now" attitude.

    Roberta MacKinnon, Bristol County, MA

With my cats, Ella and Angel, it's not things they try to hide; it's how they react when I have to sneeze. Holding nothing back, I have a booming sneeze, so before I can even get the sneeze out, they sense what's going to happen and run for cover! Ella will just look and stare at me, and then once I release the sneeze, she bolts and runs to hide behind her cat tree and will slowly emerge a minute or two later to see if it's okay to come out. When Angel hears the sneeze, he crouches low to the ground and finds the furthest spot away he can to hide and also comes back out when he thinks it's finally safe!

Jackie Hawkins, Port St. Lucie, FL

My cat, Sahra, is an 18-year-old tawny tabby with green eyes and one loppy ear, the result of a hematoma. She was born with chronic respiratory issues to a semi-feral mom in one of the outdoor community cat neighborhoods I was taking care of. As she got older, she remained nearly kitten size and had a frail appearance. That was a ruse, however, because she was famous for her appetite for wild prey, earning her the nickname "Fierce Barn Predator." Eventually I had to move from my rural location to an urban one that stipulated the number of cats a household could have. Sahra was the only one of my outdoor cats that I absolutely couldn't part from—especially because of her health issues—so she moved with me to an indoor life. Years later, she still has the strength of a teenager, often yowling at the top of her lungs. I think it might just be a "senior thing," but it could also very well be because she is turning deaf and feels lost in her own house. So now it's a life of lost and found for her—when she yowls, I'll go and find her, to reassure her that her loyal servant is still there and will not leave her alone in the vastness of the house.

Jamaka Petzak, metro/freelance writer and cat wrangler, Los Angeles

My cat, Lola, has done the hide-and-seek routine with me—she'd disappear and I would unsuccessfully try to find her, with her reappearing hours late without me knowing where she magically came from. But when my other cat, Lexy hides, she's much more obvious about it. All I have to do is look for the tell-tale clues to find

her. For example, a pile of clothes on the floor means she's removed
them to make room for herself in my bedroom armoire!
Dawn White, *Lola The Rescued Cat*

~PURR POINTS TO PONDER~

It's all about the wild side. Your cat might not realize you can see
him through the sheerness of the curtain, so for him, the fabric
provides a safe and concealed spot to hide while still being able to
keep tabs on his surroundings—a camouflage bush come to life
from the jungle of your bedroom if you will. The same would be
true of other scenarios, such as hiding under blankets, in boxes, in
purses, or behind a potted plant.

As for those toys you find in your shoe, in a drawer,
underneath the couch, or whatever other clever hiding spot—think
about it—your cat basically lives within the walls of your home.
They get bored, so to create an environment suited to their natural
hunt and prey instincts, they have to improvise with items around
the house.

Your cat is just doing his best to be a cat with the tools at his
disposal. Quite ingenious, actually. To help keep his mind and body
sharp, consider providing him with new and interesting toys to
play with. Surprise him by tucking something near his scratching
post or sleeping spot so he can "find" it. You can get some great
puzzle toys to put treats into to help keep his mind engaged, with a
yummy snack as a reward, too! Or give him an empty box out of
the blue to play with. Imagine how you'd feel if you had to live in
the same space 24/7/365 with nothing changing; you'd invent
ways to keep things more interesting, too!

Interior Decorating

When you walk into my house, even if there's not a cat in sight (highly unlikely), there's no mistaking I'm a person who not only has cats, but who wants to make sure her cats are properly enriched and thoroughly pampered. Two large cat condos (one of them designed and rebuilt by Dan and me, complete with leopard fabric and cut out windows in the shape of my Zee/Zoey logo), dozens of cat mats, a cat condo that looks like a real tree, cat beds, and cat cubbies are just a handful of the cat-related items that grace our home.

Of course he doesn't mind me sharing the hamper with him, why do you ask?

That said, naturally it's not enough. Where do my cats like to sleep? Zee loves to sleep on top of the hamper in our bathroom that we've padded with a towel for his comfort. Zoey loves being near Zee, so much so that she wedges herself between Zee and the wall while he's on the hamper. It doesn't look remotely comfortable for her, and he gets all surly and cranky about sharing (despite him once being overwhelmingly attracted to her), but she wants to be with him nonetheless.

Peanut likes the top of the file cabinet we keep in our bedroom—the cabinet is dreadfully out of place, but there it sits, year after year. We covered it with a plush blanket, so I suppose it's meant to be there exclusively for her comfort. Mia and Rolz are traditionalists—they like our bed; Kizmet likes the hard, unforgiving kitchen counter; and Jazmine likes to sleep on a shelf above my computer (also padded with a towel for her comfort).

We have a small side table in the hallway with a beautiful silk floral arrangement on it. I made the mistake of briefly removing the flowers to put a cat mat on the top of it for a photo shoot for a product review I was doing. First Jazmine, then all the other cats decided it was *the* place to be (often we would find several of them piled together, trying to comfortably fit on this narrow piece of furniture).

Don't mind me... I'll just squeeze in here... See... There's plenty of room...

The cat mat doesn't match my decorating scheme—not even the tiniest bit—but oh well, if they like the cat mat on the table in the hallway, then the cat mat stays on the table in the hallway and the floral arrangement is now in the garage. I also have pillows underneath any windows that allow for prime bird and squirrel TV watching, and there's a puffy cushion, blanket, or afghan on any ottoman or settee we have in the house.

And it goes without saying when Dan and I converge to the couch at night to watch TV, that all of the above-mentioned sleeping options remain vacant, as well as the entire couch, except for the end cushion Dan and I sit on. That's where you'll find all of us—some cats on my legs or lap, some on Dan's. Some on the head rest above us, and some next to us. It's a 3' x 3' area of squeezed comfort, and I wouldn't want it any other way.

Zoey has also added her own designer flair to the house. Several years ago we renovated our dining room and I found curtains with a handkerchief style swag that had tassels sewn on the ends that complemented the room. There were a total of four tassels and I think they lasted about three minutes before Zoey jumped up to snatch a tassel, rip it from the curtain, drop it to the floor, and jump up for the next one.

She managed to disengage all four tassels and hid them. When I finally found them, they were wet and mangled and completely unusable. Rather than despair, I figured out a way to make my own tassels to replace the damaged ones—approximately 43 seconds later, she had pulled them all down and I promptly gave up. Who needs tassels?

~MEWS FROM OTHERS~

There's an old couch sitting on the floor in the kitchen of a home in Boston. It was meant for either trash collection or Goodwill, but as soon as Zeuss Catt claimed it as his personal pad/bed/jungle gym, it's remained in that same exact spot for seven plus years. Known fondly as the "Sideways Couch," it sits near a window, perched on its side, standing upright. Zeuss Catt came to know the couch at ten weeks of age after moving from his native state of Florida to Massachusetts. Zeuss is also a famous cat in his own right—he was born to Zee and Zoey of this very book and his now human flew all the way from Boston to pick him up and fly him back home!

Zeuss Catt, West Roxbury, MA

There's decorating your house to make sure your cats are comfortable, then there's really *decorating your house to make sure your cats are comfortable. Or, in this case, remodeling your entire home by turning it into a mega-amazing feline playground. That's what I did for my eighteen rescue cats. It started in 1988 when I bought a 1600 square foot house—a home that came with two stray outdoor cats. After one was killed by a car and the other was injured, my partner, Manuel, and I made the surviving feline an indoor cat and adopted a companion for her. We never intended to have eighteen cats, but there were so many who needed homes, so we started adopting one or two every year or so.*

Wanting a home that allowed both humans and felines to share the same space in high-style and functionality, I was inspired by Bob Walker's book, The Cat House. *Since I was a general contractor, I figured I could do the same and started by building catwalks. Understanding a cat's instinctual need for hunting, play, high spaces, and scratching areas, the walks evolved based on how the cats used them. For example, some of the initial walks led to cats fighting or getting "trapped" and peeing. Thus, we learned to give them at least two ways to go so they didn't feel cornered. It cost approximately $35,000 for the remodel that also included a spiral staircase and sisal scratching pole leading to upper deck shelves, a superhighway of shelves in several of the rooms, and built-in hiding cubbies. Despite the high cost, almost everything I built could be installed on a budget to give the same effect. And most interestingly, in spite of the* *luxurious digs, give them a plain box, and my cats will always climb inside!*

Peter Cohen, co-founder of the general contracting company, Trillium Enterprises of Santa Barbara, CA

I'm a considerate cat lover—rather than buy just any old couch, when I went furniture shopping for a new one, I bought it based on whether or not it had wide arms and a wide back so my cats could comfortably nap if they so desired.

Tracy of *Pawesome Cats*, a cat-centric lifestyle blog in Australia

For me and my wife, Mary Kay, our story began with two cats: Tuscy—small, wiry, and nimble—and Luna—gentle, sweet and big boned. We wanted them both to be happy and active living in our home, and it didn't seem fair that Tuscy could climb up to our loft and look down on Luna, while Luna could only stare longingly up at him. So we made a simple ladder that allowed Luna to join him up there. She loved it, and it brought a happy balance to our home. We began to realize the benefits of "catification" and moved the ladder from place to place. Tuscy and Luna loved the changes and couldn't wait to explore somewhere new. When we saw how much fun they were having, we knew we had something to share with other cat lovers and turned our idea into a line of feline furniture at Catladder.com.

Joe Koziol, owner/designer *Catladder.com*

When our cat, Lucky, became slightly incontinent following bladder surgery, my husband John and I realized he could no longer enjoy his favorite perch and feeding spot in the house—the kitchen counter. We were sad about the forced change in Lucky's routine and tried to think of an alternative that would make everyone happy. The solution—Lucky's very own cat kitchen! We relocated some of our heirloom furniture to a different spot in our house, and, in its place, built a small kitchen adjacent to the kitchen, complete with a dedicated countertop that Lucky can enjoy, occasional drips and all.

He's happy with his new perch, and as a bonus, we now have cabinets for storing pet foods and medications!

Paris Permenter, author of 33 books on pets and travel and blogger at *CatTipper.com*

~PURR POINTS TO PONDER~

It's not so much that your cat wants to take over your furniture, but because they are territorial, they have a natural instinct to seek out personal spaces that cater to their needs of climbing, perching, resting, hunting, playing, and ownership. That's why they're right at home on top of your filing cabinet or bookcase. To help your cat satisfy his natural urge for vertical space (especially in a multi-cat household where access to vertical space is a necessity to peaceful cohabitation), it's important to create an environment for them that reduces stress and encourages personal confidence.

You don't have to break the bank, and you don't have to fill your house with items that don't appeal to your sense of style to keep you and your kitty happy. Well-placed pieces of furniture you already have that allow her the freedom to go around the room without touching the floor is all you need to do. Think of it as connecting the dots—let her jump from a shelf to a bookcase to cat trees/condos, etc. You just need to keep in mind that you should create multiple escape routes so there are no dead ends that back her into a corner, which will make her feel threatened.

If you want to get more creative, numerous companies make products specifically for your cat—from wall steps to perches to bridges and more. Or you can even make your own cat shelves to suit your budget. Jackson Galaxy, bestselling author and star of Animal Planet's *My Cat From Hell*, and Kate Benjamin, of the popular cat design website *Hauspanther.com* have a fantastic book available called *Catification* that guides readers through a step-by-step process of designing an attractive home for humans (with affordable options) that's also an optimal environment for cats.

Keep in mind, while most cats do love high spaces, not all cats are cut from the same cloth. My angel Harley, for example, was what I referred to as a "couch potato cat" because I don't think she ever jumped higher than our couch. That's because cats can be "tree dwellers," "bush dwellers," or a combination of both. It's all about the circumstances and what makes them feel the safest and most confident at the moment. Get to know your cat and make her feel comfortable with the signs she is giving you. If she prefers to hang out on a lower level, provide her an assortment of baskets, boxes, mats, and beds to nap in that are placed on the floor or other low areas.

Variety is important, too. Since kitty is relatively hostage to the walls of your house or apartment, consider putting a fluffy pillow or chair next to a window for her to watch the great outdoors. And don't forget how important scratching posts are for her health and well-being. Experiment to see what she likes best—from cardboard style boxes to elaborate furniture with built-in scratching posts, there is something available to suit every cat, every budget, and every decorating scheme. You can even make scratching posts out of old cardboard boxes to save money and to be environmentally responsible.

The Unexpected in Life

I'm not much of a talker—when it comes to communicating, being somewhat shy, I prefer writing to express myself. I actually think I'm part cat—rather than jump into new situations, I'd rather hide under the bed and slowly emerge to familiarize myself with what's going on. The exception is my cats—them I could talk to all day. Over the years I've come to hear every meow possible from them—from the loud, ear piercing yowls of Zoey telling me to wake up at 4:00 a.m. to the soft, sweet, and polite mews of Kizmet telling me he'd like to go outside, even though he's not allowed.

Not only do each of my cats have a distinctly different meow, the meow is different based on the circumstances—feed me, don't touch me, touch me, throw my toy, get off the couch and come to bed—and all have a different tone and urgency. The sound I heard from my angel, Jazz, after Dan and I did a knock-down, start from scratch renovation of our house several years ago was something I was not prepared for. I'd never heard anything like it before and I've never heard anything like it since.

Back then, Dan was a new member to my household. We'd been dating for a while and he eventually moved in. First on his agenda—updating my (now our) kitchen. Somehow that translated to the kitchen, living room, dining room, den, and office because all the rooms were interconnected like some intricate game of dominos—knock one wall down, the rest came tumbling after!

Our house was in complete disarray and the renovation took months to complete, but despite the whole invasive, filthy, and exhausting ordeal, the transformation was amazing. During the renovation, each of my pets reacted differently (I had a house full of cats and dogs at the time). For instance, Zee was curious and in the thick of it all. No matter what we were doing, he was a part of it—jackhammers, saws, drills, nothing fazed him. But Jazz was a different story.

One night, after we had knocked down nearly all the walls in what was then the dining room, we cleaned up as best we could. The lights were dimmed and we were sitting on the bare floor for a few minutes, basking on what we had accomplished before we set off for bed. The silence was deafening after the hours of loud and intrusive construction work. Jazz came out from our bedroom and stopped dead in his tracks in the center of the room. He then let out the most eerie, primal, and mournful sound I've ever heard from an animal. He was in shock at the loss of what he knew as his house—he couldn't comprehend what had happened, and he was pacing back and forth, looking up and down, trying to figure out where his walls went.

He kept meowing in frustration, trying to calm himself. We knelt down to his level to talk to him and to reassure him it was okay—that we'd somehow fix it so he could exist again in peace and harmony. It took some time, but eventually he was fine. He even became our "Inspector General" surveying each project we had finished at night's end. He would look everything over from top to bottom as if to say, "Yes, good work, this came out very well."

~MEWS FROM OTHERS~

When I moved to a new apartment, my cat, Carmine, was about three years old. This was the first move he had ever been involved in, and he seemed to be having a blast with all the boxes in the house that kept piling up during the packing process. However, when the day arrived and I needed to gather him and fellow cat-mate, Milita up to take them to our new apartment, I couldn't find him. I was in a state of panic—I had to get going, but I couldn't possibly leave without him. I finally found him in the craziest of spots—in a small hole underneath the stove! It took some doing to get him to come out, but he eventually did and once we moved and settled in, he thankfully adjusted well to his new apartment.

Sierra M. Koester, freelance writer/blogger, *Fur Everywhere*, Denver, CO

Mr. Meowgi, an orange and white kitten, was born at the Baghdad International Airport in Iraq under a shipping container. It was July 2015, and that's when I, a Navy reservist from Murrieta, Georgia, who was working as a government contractor, found him. I didn't know how many kittens were born, but he was the only one to survive. Several of the team cared for him and his mom, feeding them grilled fish, chicken, canned tuna, and Mr. Meowgi's favorite—BBQ beef! The mom eventually wandered off and abandoned her kitten, but I couldn't do the same. When it was time for me to return home for a reprieve, the kitten stayed on my mind. I worried if I didn't bring him back to the States the chances of him being alive when I got back were slim. I was informed the SPCA International ran a program called Operation Baghdad Pups, allowing soldiers, sailors, marines, and contractors to be reunited with the animals they cared for during deployments. That's all I needed to hear—Mr. Meowgi left Baghdad on March 27, 2016, to head to his new forever home to be with me and my family. His journey started in Erbil, Northern Iraq, where he spent time in foster care while his export paperwork was completed. Next was Frankfurt, Germany. Then New York City and Los Angeles, before arriving at his final destination of Murrieta. He settled in well with us and was a celebrity for a while too—from major coverage on the CBS network to being invited to a city council meeting by the Mayor of Murrieta, he's a cat that proves even in war, there can be love.

Brad VanCleave, navy reservist, Murrieta, GA

My cat, John Doe(JD), knows only too well the stresses of moving and change. He was abandoned at just a few months of age and found by a couple who fed him for a few months. They moved and were not able to take him, so once again he was abandoned. New buyers came—they were not nearly as concerned for the young cat's care and called the listing agent, demanding someone come and get him off their property. He was brought to the real estate office where I worked and I decided to take him. After he was vetted, I discovered he was FIV positive. JD now lives at NAWS, an organization I founded, devoted to aggressive spay/neuter to help families who meet income guidelines to alter their pets. JD likes being an only pet, as he doesn't play well with others. On the days surgeries are scheduled, he's typically in his Suite—an area fully furnished with an easy chair, couch, scratching posts, toys, country music piped in, and a big view of the bird feeders outside his windows. He now rules and lives like a king, no longer having to worry about being abandoned ever again.

Goldie Arnold, founder and president, Northland Animal Welfare Society

A classroom full of animated children ranks as one of the least desired places to visit among most cats. But my Pet Safety Cat, Casey, is no ordinary feline. When I open his crate door, he dashes out, kicks into purr mode, and delivers high paw hellos on cue during my pet behavior talks. He's a two-year-old orange tabby that I adopted from the San Diego Humane Society when he was four months old. Under my care, he thrives as arguably the country's only active (and willing) pet first aid cat. He teams up with Pet Safety Dog, Kona, and me when we conduct veterinarian-endorsed, hands-on classes through my Pet First Aid 4U program. He allows students to wrap him in a towel, check his pulse, test his capillary refill, and put on a face restraint muzzle without a hiss. When beckoned, he comes, leaps on the demo table, pops into a sit, and raises his left paw to greet each student. He easily and sweetly adapts to each new place and to each new person, not to mention, he lives with five dogs that he's got wrapped around his paws. I feel blessed to have such a great four-legged teaching partner—one that is making the planet safer for cats and dogs.

Arden Moore, The Pet Health and Safety Coach, founder *www.petfirstaid4u.com* **and** *www.fourleggedlife.com*

I currently live in Canada, but several years ago I lived in Cape Town, South Africa with my two cats—Zulu and Amarula. It was relatively easy to get them to Canada, because all they needed to become Canadian Cat Citizens, was proof of a rabies shot. It was the actual move that was tense, especially for me, as my kitties had to travel in cargo on a different day than me. One of the happiest days of my life was when I arrived to pick them up at the Toronto airport and went to customs to discover they had made it safely, relatively unscathed. Though I will never know what they went through on that 24-hour trek across the world, it's not through their lack of trying! On the one-hour ride home from the airport, they regaled me with incessant caterwauling, exposing the indignities of feline air travel and the cruelty of taking them from sun-soaked Africa to the cold, barren landscape of an early November winter in Canada. I'll never forget how the next day, anxious to survey her new realm, Amarula ran out onto the porch—and straight into five inches of snow! To this day, several years later, she still lets loose the most plaintive mewling at the sight of the first snowfall. But I still believe she wouldn't trade her well-fed, carefree, moments-by-the-fireplace-filled, Canadian life for anything!

Sandra MacGregor, cat blogger at *hairballsandhissyfits.com*

I first came upon Trey, a lynx Siamese tripod, at an outdoor colony I cared for. He was missing much of his back right leg, and I instantly knew he was special. He trusted me and after just a short time would allow me close, eventually letting me handle him. He would wait for me every morning and it broke my heart seeing him outside with such a hard time getting around. I found a seemingly nice family to foster him (I already had a house full and couldn't take him) and inspected their place. Not even 24 hours later when I called to follow up on him, they told me he had gotten out through the patio door and escaped. Despite me specifically telling them to keep him in the bedroom, they left the door open because they thought he "could use some fresh air." Even though the screen was secure, he was so terrified in a new environment that he broke out and was lost in an unfamiliar place. I spent nearly every minute I could searching for him—he was spotted on multiple occasions (often after crossing major traffic intersections), and when I got the calls, I would leave food for him. After three agonizing months, I finally got the call that led to his capture. I was overjoyed and found a friend to foster him. The whole time he was with my friend, I couldn't stop thinking about him—I knew after all the tears, worry, and heartache that he was meant to be mine, so I brought him to my house. After some decompression time, introductions to my other cats began, and oddly enough, once fully integrated, he no longer allowed me to come close to him. I can't pet, hold, or walk too close to him, but my love for him remains deeper than nearly any other I have ever felt.

Cindy Rein, co-founder of Catopia Cat Rescue

~PURR POINTS TO PONDER~

While we made every effort to make sure our cats were kept out of the thick of the renovation process (Zee being the exception) by providing them with a safe and secure room during the day where they had food, water, litter, and napping areas, even the slightest of change can cause stress in a cat, so major events, such as home renovations, moving, or introducing a new baby or pet into the household require certain precautions and steps to be taken to ensure a smooth and safe transition for all involved.

The key to reducing any potential problems and keeping your cat as stress-free as possible is planning, patience, and perseverance. Cats don't like change—they rarely react well to it—so you need to think like a cat to understand what they're going through. Imagine how you would feel if the house you've been living in for years, is unexpectedly replaced by a new one. Or all of a sudden there is a tiny being that seemingly appeared out of nowhere, crying, smelling all funny, and taking the full attention of your beloved human. Or a new furry family member shows up, potentially taking over your coveted turf, also taking the attention of your beloved human. All of this can greatly upset your cat's equilibrium. You know the change is going to happen, but your cat doesn't, and as a result, he may exhibit negative behavior, such as hiding or running away, peeing in inappropriate places, eating problems, and aggression issues.

You need to ease into each situation by gradually involving your cat in the process of change while maintaining as much of his existing routine as possible. For example, if you're moving to a new home, bring his carrier out a few weeks in advance so he gets used to it. You don't want him running away in fear of the carrier and hide (or escape outside) on the day of your move and you should also start putting moving boxes out a few weeks in advance so he gets used to you packing.

When you get to your new home, ease into the living arrangement by having a safe room ready that you can shut off with his food and water dishes, toys, bedding, litter box, and scratching post *before* you open his carrier to let him out. Keep him there for several days before you let him begin exploring further areas of the house. This will allow him to gradually get used to the sights, sounds and smells of his new home without feeling overwhelmed.

Make certain you have cat-proofed everything too—check that all windows are securely locked, with no rips in screens, tuck away any dangerous electrical cords, and block any areas where your cat could get lost or stuck. Then gradually give your cat access to the rest of the house, one room at a time (you may even want to gently rub a sock around your cat's mouth to absorb his pheromones—transfer his scent to pieces of furniture at his eye level to make him feel like he has already "been" there).

If the change is a new baby, set up the nursery and encourage your cat to explore the room to become familiar with the furniture, baby clothes, toys, etc., before you select surfaces to declare off limits closer to baby's arrival—such as the changing table and crib. Play videos of baby sounds to acclimate your cat to the new noises he's about to hear and start wearing baby powder and baby lotion while engaging in activities with him (such as feeding and playtime) to create positive associations with baby odors.

When you bring your baby home from the hospital, be respectful that your cat may be nervous, jealous, or inquisitive. Greet him calmly and give him something to sniff, such as a used receiving blanket to familiarize himself with the baby. Don't get all panicky and start yelling at him or shoo him away if he attempts to sniff the baby, and try to maintain a normal schedule with him to let him know you haven't forgotten him. Engage in interactive play sessions in the presence of the baby to help form a positive association—if you find you're too busy, try something like a puzzle feeder that dispenses treats while you're feeding the baby.

To safely introduce a new pet to your household with a resident cat, it will require that the new pet has a safe room or area to stay in for several weeks that can be shut off from the resident cat. The situation is stressful for all pets involved, so the introductions need to be made gradually—first initiated by "swapping" scents so the pets can get familiar with one another. Use a clean sock and gently rub it on the new pet's cheek to transfer his pheromones onto the sock. Do the same to your resident cat and place each sock where the other pet hangs out. Continue this exchange several times a day so each pet becomes familiar with the differing scents.

Gradually begin to let them sniff one another. If you have a dog, he must be properly leashed during the introductions so if the meeting goes awry or the dog acts aggressively, your cat can be protected from harm and the dog will be restrained. If it's a cat, gradually incorporate positive reinforcements to the equation by feeding your cat and the new cat treats or meals simultaneously, separated by the closed door. If they won't eat or they display aggression towards each other, back the food away from the closed door to a more comfortable eating distance and over the course of time, slowly move the feeding stations closer to the door until they are eating next to each other (still separated by the closed door) without displaying aggression.

In all instances, be sure to provide your cat with lots of love and attention. Maintain a regular feeding, grooming, and playtime schedule that she's accustomed to so she feels a sense of stability. Keep her litter box as clean as possible because even the smallest change in environment can result in mishaps. Provide her with access to high/vertical space (such as a tall cat tower) because it's important she have a safe-haven to declare her own. Be patient— it's a big adjustment for her and she'll need your love and support to make the transition as smooth and stress-free as possible.

It's also important to be prepared—moving, babies, and new pets are planned events. Sometimes situations out of our control can happen, such as a natural disaster or a medical emergency that requires instant action. You should always make certain your cat's records are kept in a safe and accessible place. Have your vet's phone number programmed into your phone and have a current picture of your cat available in case she goes missing.

Keep her carrier easily accessible and have a pet first aid kit on hand in case an emergency crops up that requires immediate attention before you can get to your vet. Kits can be purchased, or you can make your own[1] and it's wise to have two—one for your house and one to keep in your car. Keep a book on pet first aid handy and download a pet first aid app to your mobile phone to quickly consult if need be.

[1]For a comprehensive list of what supplies should be in a pet first aid kit, visit http://www.humanesociety.org/animals/resources/tips/pet_first_aid_kit.html

"X" Marks the Spot

Okay—not the most glamorous chapter or the most endearing habit, but sometimes with cats comes pee. Not so much now—let's just say I've learned a lot of invaluable lessons over time—but years ago I found cat pee just about anywhere you can think of in my house(s). Dirty clothes on the floor, open suitcases, bath mats, carpeting, rugs, newspapers, magazines, plastic bags, books, couch cushions, under the Christmas tree, on Christmas gifts, record albums, mail on the counter, homework, bed spreads, shoes, a stove top—all have fallen victim to a sprinkle here and there.

I've actually had to replace a couple of couches—I remember I would do my best to get up early in the morning before my ex-husband did to do a "couch-check" to see if there were any accidents that I could discreetly clean up without him finding out one of the cats had misbehaved again. He wasn't mean about it; I just felt guilty that I couldn't keep things under control. But honestly, it was a losing battle; once a cat pees on a cushion or sprays it, it's nearly impossible to get rid of the smell, hence the inevitable new couch (and when I say new, that translated to either a hand-me-down from someone else, or the cheapest piece of poorly made furniture we could find).

I tried everything—from buying bottle after bottle of stuff with enticing marketing words lulling me into believing my cats would magically stop spraying and that the pungent urine odors would miraculously disappear with just one squirt of the bottle to taping clear plastic wrap or aluminum foil on the couch in strategic areas to prevent them from peeing in the same spot. Nothing worked—I even tried spraying pepper sauce so the smell would distract them, but everything was for naught.

I also had to finagle a setup on my bed when Jazz was nearing the end of his life. He began to have incontinency issues, and sometimes I would find pee on my bedspread that would inevitably seep into the mattress. I cleaned the mattress as best I could with a steam cleaner and then taped several large plastic garbage bags to the mattress, and covered them with bath towels before putting the sheets back on the bed. That way, if he had an accident, all I had to do was wash the bedspread and sheets. Eventually that wore me out—I got a waterproof duvet to place over the bedspread and that worked wonders. Never once did I get upset with Jazz—he was my baby and I knew it wasn't his fault.

~MEWS FROM OTHERS~

My husband and I do what most cat people do—a "cat head count" before we go to bed. This is to ensure all is well and that no kitty is destined to spend the night trapped in a closest, room, or wherever. So, as usual, we performed our count and went to bed, content everyone was accounted for. We woke up the next morning to find one of our cats, Caster, had somehow shut himself in the downstairs bathroom at some point during the night. I don't know how long he was trapped in there, but it was long enough for him to have to go to the bathroom. When I opened the door, he ran out, and I found he had removed all of the trash from the trash can and had peed in said trash can—all without knocking the can over!
Emily Hall, blogger, *Kitty Cat Chronicles*, Macon, GA

As my thirtieth class reunion approached, I agonized: should I wear a frumpy suit that looked sadly similar to what I wore in high school or—the antithesis of conservative—a trendy, sexier outfit, the type I wear to hawk my novels at science fiction conventions? I packed both, deciding I would figure it out when I arrived. I also had to pack for my sixteen-year-old smoke and white kitty, Chani who suffered from chronic kidney disease. She required fluid injections under the skin every few days, and although the trip would be stressful, it was still better than leaving her with the pet sitter without her fluids. At the hotel, I opened my suitcase and eyed the boring beige suit. Still undecided, I fed Chani, set up her litter box, and took a quick shower. Drying off, I resigned myself to the Old Mother Hubbard's business suit. I picked up the folded blazer and felt something odd—a wet spot had soaked through several layers of the folded jacket! Likewise, the folded white blouse was adorned with some yellow moist spots. Panicked, I dug down to the bottom of the suitcase where my tank top and fitted jeans lay, unsoiled. By default, my little kitty had decided the evening's outfit. She wasn't angry, spiteful, or getting even; she was stressed by being yanked out of her safe and comfortable home and taken to a strange (and possibly dangerous, in her eyes) hotel room filled with the smells of the hundreds of people and pets who had occupied the room in the past. Marking my clothes with her own scent was the only way she could express her fear and confusion. When the evening was over, I snuggled her in bed and thanked her because my classmates told me how hot I looked!

Dusty Rainbolt, ACCBC, award-winning author of 12 books including *Kittens for Dummies* and *Cat Scene Investigator: Solve Your Cat's Litter Box Mystery*

My cat, Frankie, refuses to use her litter box, preferring to relieve herself on pee pads that I place in her favorite spots around the house. After she goes, she diligently works to cover it up as though the pad is kitty litter. She spends several minutes working the pad with her paws until she's successfully gathered it into a pile. It might not be for everyone, but I'm happy my hardwood floors have been saved by my considerate kitty!

Lynn K, retiree, of Northern VA

Dennis, my black and white tuxedo cat, has issues so extreme, he's nearly marked my whole house! Rescued from the streets when he was four weeks old, about two years after his rescue, he decided to relieve himself on the kitchen counter rather than his litter box. I took him to the vet to check him out, and nothing came up. I tried everything—I turned a spare bedroom into a cat's paradise for him, complete with six litter boxes and carpeted shelves on the walls so he and his other cat-mates could climb, jump, and circle the room without ever touching the floor. Dennis jumped on the shelves and peed on the wall. I bought pheromone diffusers and different types of litter boxes and even contacted a cat communicator. Dennis peed on the pheromone diffuser and that was the end of that. Over the years, I've had to replace my kitchen counter, my computer monitor, several carpets, and two steel doors that he rusted. He's sixteen now and in the early stages of lymphoma and kidney disease. Despite all the damage he's caused, I'll give him all the love and care he needs for the time he has remaining. Until then, there are strategically placed pee pads taped to the walls in my house.

Joe Miele, TNR project coordinator for Broken Promises SW

~PURR POINTS TO PONDER~

Looking back—with a life that was filled with a revolving door of countless rescue cats and dogs living together under one roof (and rabbits, fish, frogs, and guinea pigs), moving dozens of times, raising children and more, it's a wonder my cats didn't pee on more stuff. I wasn't the knowledgeable cat lady I am today, and I had no idea my cats were probably peeing to tell me I wasn't providing them the best environment to deal with the stresses I was inadvertently forcing them to face every day.

Cats are instinctually territorial—they need to feel in control of their personal space—and I can see now that barking dogs and crying babies probably didn't help the situation. I also didn't create a living space to accommodate their need for high, vertical space.

Back then, I didn't have cat towers or scratching posts, or any cat products designed specifically for them. I don't even remember how many litter boxes I had—perhaps I didn't have enough to suit a multi-cat household. And chances are good that I didn't know enough to carve special playtime out on a regular schedule to bond with my cats. And did I scoop enough? Was it the right litter? I don't remember that either.

Anxiety is one of the main reasons cats inappropriately urinate outside the litter box, so if your cat is doing it, analyze your circumstances. Is it a social issue—is there tension between your cat and a family member or another pet in the household? Or has something changed? Have you moved furniture around, or do you have a new boyfriend or girlfriend? Did you just move, did you have a baby, or did you have company come visit? Or maybe there's a neighborhood cat roaming around outside your dining room window that your cat has caught wind of.

All of these situations can trigger stress in a cat. He might spray near the window to let the interloper cat know your house is his territory. Or he might pee on your personal items to intermingle his own scent with your bed, couch, clothing, etc. Some cats urinate to communicate frustration if something in their world seems amiss—perhaps you're working long hours or traveling too much. Many cats will pee or poop outside the litter box when you're gone, or they may wait until you return to misbehave. It's your cat's way of telling you how unhappy he's been over your absence. Sometimes a cat will urinate in specific places they associate with conflict—a new baby, partner, or housemate might warrant a cat peeing in the baby's crib, the housemate's shoes, or on the side of the bed the partner sleeps.

Many cats also choose a bed to pee on because it helps to alleviate the stress they are feeling. Dogs, children, etc. may bother the cat, and the height of the bed provides more of a visual advantage to see them coming. Most beds have a headboard, removing the worry of being ambushed from behind, so kitty can easily pee on a nice, soft and absorbent surface with minimal worry of danger.

It's important to realize your cat is not being "spiteful" if this happens—much as it's frustrating to you, he's simply trying to comfort himself. If these circumstances don't apply and it isn't stress related, it could be the location of the litter box, the type of litter, or the litter box itself that's causing your cat to stray away from his designated area.

Cats are extremely fastidious by nature, and his litter box needs to be scooped at least once a day (more if you have several cats) and should be given a thorough cleaning on a regular basis. But be mindful of your cat—cleaning with harsh chemicals, such as bleach, can be extremely dangerous to him (if your cats are anything like mine, they are attracted to the smell of bleach, wanting to roll on any surface it's been cleaned with).

When your cat walks on the floor, or scratches in his litter box, the residue from toxic chemicals can get into those sensitive paws of his that he licks every day to keep himself clean. Clean the box with something like a vinegar/baking soda mix and follow up with a **diluted** bleach rinse. Something like a 1:10 ratio of bleach and water is enough to disinfect the box and can deter parasites and diseases transmitted by feces from developing. Slosh the solution around to coat the bottom and sides of the box and rinse thoroughly with water and air dry. Repeat the rinse and air dry process one more time before filling the box with litter. You may want to sprinkle some baking soda on the bottom of the box before you fill it with litter as well.

For spot cleaning and odor neutralizing, keep a spray bottle handy with a baking soda/vinegar solution, but if you don't like the odor of vinegar and would prefer a manufactured pet product, try something such as NOse Offense For PETS. It's a non-toxic, fragrance-free, pet-safe, eco-friendly formula that contains no harmful chemical phthalates (phthalates are found in products made to mask odors with artificial fragrances) which can cause toxic effects related to brain development, immune system functions, birth defects, asthma, cancer, metabolism, and even reproduction.

When deciding what litter is best for your cat, experiment. From fine ground substances to wheat type pellets, there are a variety of litters to choose from. And what about the litter box—is it large and easy enough for your cat to comfortably get in and out of? And those litter boxes with covers—most cats don't like this style, which could be the problem. And where is the litter box located? Does your cat feel safe using it, or is it causing him to be nervous if you have it in a location that makes him feel threatened or is too far away to be convenient to use?

For example, maybe you've constructed a weird getup to keep your dog or toddler away from the litter box and it's upsetting your cat. Try something like the Door Buddy®, an adjustable door strap that mounts to the door and door frame, holding the door open wide enough so cats can easily come and go into the room but narrow enough to keep out dogs and toddlers.

If it's not the litter or litter box, your cat could be crying out for help, and you should take him to your veterinarian to run tests to make sure he doesn't have an underlying problem. Male cats, in particular, are prone to microscopic crystals in their urine, which could plug the urethra, possibly becoming a life-threatening situation.

It's also prudent to stress the importance of spay/neuter. Many cats spray or urinate to mark territory, and this habit can be greatly reduced by having your cat altered. Not only will it help reduce the tendencies, but it's healthier for your cat. Spaying your female prior to her first heat nearly eliminates the risk of mammary cancer, uterine infections, and uterine cancer, and neutering your male before he is six months of age prevents testicular and prostate cancer and greatly reduces his risk for perianal tumors.

Man's Best Friend

It's said that dogs are man's best friend due to the loving and loyal relationships they have with humans. Don't get me wrong—I adore dogs and *do* believe them to be kind and loyal companions. I've had many dogs and hope to have them in my life again one day. But honestly, I feel that terminology could apply to any beloved pet—from rabbits, to ferrets, birds, cats and more—any animal you hold close to your heart is capable of providing you with a loving and devoted relationship.

Me and my best friends!

When it comes to my cats, the depth of their love and devotion toward me often brings me to tears. From their ability to communicate to me when I (or Dan) might be in danger or when

I'm in need of cheering up, or to provide me with support when I'm emotionally vulnerable—everything they do reminds me how blessed I am to have them in my life.

My cats have always been an integral part of my life, but it wasn't until my later years that I began to appreciate and respect them on a different level. It began in 2008 when Zee and Zoey became impending cat parents. I was under the false impression a female cat had to be at least a year old before she could be spayed. Zoey's pregnancy at 10 months proved me wrong. I have since become a huge educator and proponent of spay/neuter, but I also know her pregnancy was a precious gift that changed the direction of not only our relationship, but the direction of my life.

She and I already had a close bond—she was *my* cat—a cat I had wanted for years—one I hand-picked out of a litter to be my forever girl. But when she came to me at 4:30 a.m. on February 12, 2009, yelping with an alarming insistence that I get out of bed, that's when our bond became irrevocable. It was pitch dark at the time—I grabbed my robe and followed her into the living room where she jumped up onto the couch. Sensing she wanted me to be with her, I lay down, and she immediately cradled into my belly, loudly purring while I pet her.

A few moments later, I felt her warm little body contort. She was still purring and since it was still dark, I wasn't quite sure what was going on. A few minutes later, I heard a faint "mew" and realized she had just given birth to a kitten on my lap. She managed to have another kitten on my lap before I could yell to Dan to wake him up to come and help me. She ended up having four kittens total, and I will never forget the experience of sharing that tender, beautiful, and private moment with her. *She came and got me—that was my gift.*

We kept three of the kittens—Mia, Peanut, and Rolz—and the fourth, Zeuss Catt, went to a dear friend, and it was during this timeframe that my life dramatically changed. I was unexpectedly let go from my twenty plus year career in administration and marketing—finding employment in my late forties was nearly impossible, and I was spiraling down a dangerous road of depression and hopelessness. Dan was also laid off at the same time from the same company, and we were precariously close to losing our beautiful home. Through the lessons learned from my cats—primarily the attitude of appreciating the good I did have in my life rather than focusing on what I didn't have—I was able to find the strength and courage to follow a dream of mine—to write a book.

Titled The *Chronicles of Zee & Zoey – A Journey of the Extraordinarily Ordinary*, it's a tribute to Zee and Zoey's love story, as well as a story that explores the human-feline bond, and the bond animals have with one another. Zoey remains the feline love of my life—she can be quite aloof on the surface, but she's also the sweetest, most devoted cat on earth. She adores me and I adore her back. She's also incredibly intelligent as Dan witnessed one afternoon when she came into the dining room, meowing to him that something was seriously wrong. She was visibly agitated, causing Dan to get up. She led him to our guest bathroom, where it turned out a toilet pipe had burst, causing a torrential flood of water on the floor.

When my Jazz was nearing the end of his life, cat-mates Harley and Kizmet rallied around not only me, but him. I was spending the nights with Jazz on the bedroom floor—I'd grab a blanket and lie down next to him. Harley would lay her body into Jazz's, providing him with warmth and companionship, and Kizmet would lay his body into mine, and somehow, together, we all communicated a message of love and compassion.

The last day Jazz was with us was filled with bittersweet poignancy. I woke up and did what I always did—I looked to see if he had made it through another night. On this particular morning, I couldn't find him and my heart filled with agonizing pain. Dan eventually found him under the TV cabinet, his body motionless, and we both held one another and cried. I was overwhelmed with grief, guilt, and profound sadness, lamenting that he died alone and that I wasn't there for him.

Firmly believing cats can communicate and sense emotion, I saw Peanut was getting aggravated while Dan and I were consoling one another. She paced back and forth, between us and Jazz. It became apparent with her persistent body language that she was telling us something about Jazz. And sure enough, she was. Dan bent back down to look under the cabinet and found Jazz was still breathing, albeit ever so slightly.

Dan got a towel and wrapped Jazz in it. He brought him into the guest bedroom where I lay with him for several hours, saying goodbye to my dear friend before we brought him to the vet to ease his journey to the Rainbow Bridge. Until then, at the foot of the bed with me, were Kizmet and Harley. None of us moved a muscle during those final hours, as we paid our respects to him.

It was less than a year later that I unexpectedly lost my precious Harley. I was devastated unlike any other death I've had to experience with a pet. She was with me one minute and literally gone the next. No poignant goodbye, no wrapping our relationship up with a pretty bow of closure. The last spot I ever saw her in my house was my office. When Dan and I came home from the vet, without Harley, Kizmet was in that spot. He stayed there for weeks, on and off, missing his friend. And me, well, Kizmet knew I was missing my friend, too. I tried my best to be upbeat, but the house was cloaked with a veil of sadness that couldn't be disguised.

Out of the blue, one night Kizmet bounded up onto the couch— I was lying on my side with my head on a pillow in a state of emotional duress. He came up to me with complete intention— pressing his nose firmly into mine to tell me he was there for me and that he understood my grief. He then tucked himself into the bend of my belly as closely as he could so I could wrap my arm around him and cradle him. He stayed with me for several minutes, and it was truly a blessed and profound gesture of love and friendship from him.

~MEWS FROM OTHERS~

My tortoiseshell, Sonjay, is nearly ten years old, but she's so tiny she's often mistaken for a kitten. She was also born without a tail, but don't let her small size fool you—she's got a very protective nature, especially with my son, Seren, whom she loves dearly. Like a lot of twelve-year-old's, Seren sleeps with his bedroom door shut. Sonjay will scratch at his door until he lets her in—seemingly to check in on him—because a few minutes later she demands to be let out! She does this several times a night, and Seren always obliges. During the day she'll nap on his bed, no one else's, and if Seren's playing outside, she'll watch him out the window. And if someone dare raise their voice at Seren, Sonjay gets angry! Once my whole family was playing the Wii. Naturally, everyone was being loud and rowdy, including me. Sonjay thought I was yelling at Seren, so she crawled on the couch next to me and "slapped" me on the cheek to stop it!
Lisa Jahn, Abilene, KS

Years ago, I caught my boyfriend cheating and broke up with him. He moved out, leaving me with Figaro and Hobbes—my two lovable cats I rescued from the streets of Briarcliff, Texas. A friend, who will remain nameless, moved in to help me with rent and, shortly thereafter, started dating a girl we didn't know. I went out of town, and when I returned, he recounted a story of what happened one night after he brought his date home: He and his date were parked in the driveway making out. They heard footsteps on the car roof, breaking the mood and getting their attention. Wide-eyed, they watched as Hobbes walked down the middle of the windshield, crouched, and then turned around and stared at them both, growling and hissing, making noises he had never heard come from any animal—and certainly not Hobbes—who continued to audibly berate them. Even though he knew the behavior was out of character for Hobbes, he was afraid to get out of the car, so they remained trapped for nearly a half an hour before Hobbes finally decided to jump off the hood.

The story puzzled me. In all his six years, Hobbes had never scratched, bitten, or threatened anyone. Fast forward two months and the truth came out—the girl turned out to be one of the several girls my ex had brought home when I traveled. Hobbes had an uncanny ability to read the situation; he was protecting me. I called him my "Orangest Angel." He traveled across the country with me twice—thirteen different apartments/houses in the seventeen plus years we shared together. One of his many talents was his ability to duet the song "Brick House." I would sing, "She's a brick..." and Hobbes would sing "...meow," in perfect time, every time (the video is posted on YouTube: "Hobbes sings Brick House"). I still feel the loving presence and protective spirit of my beloved Orangest Angel.

Amy Nelson, songwriter and musician, Folk Uke

I owe my life to Keli—my precious calico cat that lived to the age of twenty. Keli actually saved my life a couple of times. The first time was when I learned I had sleep apnea—a disorder in which you have pauses in breathing that can last from a few seconds to several minutes. Keli normally slept soundly with me but began pouncing on my chest on and off at night, waking me up. It was a mystery until my daughter came to visit and heard me hollering at Keli for waking me up for the umpteenth time. My daughter informed me that just before I hollered, she had heard me snore from the other room—

putting two and two together, I got a CPAP (Continuous Positive Airway Pressure) machine and Keli never woke me up after that. The other time could have ended in tragedy. Keli used her infamous pounce to awaken me, but this time she caused a fuss until she could get me out of bed to follow her into the living room. I didn't know why she was acting so weird, but when I got to the living room, she ran directly to the side of the aquarium where the pump motor was smoking and sparking. Raw wires had crossed each other and the carpet was just starting to burn!

Elizabeth Munroz, chondrosarcoma support group counselor, Watsonville, CA

My huge Maine Coon, Ralphy, shares a morning routine that coincides with mine. I wake up at 5:45 a.m., and he'll be lying on top of my shoes beside the dresser. Once I'm up, I head to the kitchen and typically trip over him on the way because he runs past me like lighting and then slams on his brakes and cuts to the left directly in front of my feet! Once we make it to the kitchen, I fix breakfast for us—I eat mine in the kitchen, and his is served in the laundry room. Somehow he knows exactly when I'm about to finish because he leaves the laundry room and goes to the bathroom where I'm going next. He's always about twenty seconds ahead of me, and after I shower, he shadows me into the bedroom while I dress and so on until I leave.

I began to notice he was no longer shadowing me. Instead of heading to the kitchen with me after waking up, he would be sitting in the guest bedroom window with his head rapidly moving left to right, but when I looked out the window, I didn't see anything unusual. After several more days, I got really curious and investigated. Long story short, directly below the window, were several shrubs—one of them had a bird's nest buried in it, with momma bird sitting in it to watch over her eggs. As she would fly to gather sticks and stuff, Ralphy would eye ball her every move. The birds eventually hatched and moved on. Ralphy and I are now back in perfect sync with our routine, and I never realized how much I appreciated him shadowing me until he wasn't there, which is when it hit me how much deeper our relationship really was.

Scott Johnson, founder and chief executive officer of Wittle LLC, Birmingham, AL

There was a time when I didn't understand the true magic of cats. Until the night, the very late night, when a purring cat wandered into my house as I was moving out and proceeded to sit on my foot. I took him in off the streets, FIV and all, and named him Rosco. Ten years and six rescued cats later, I now take care of one of the most famous and beloved cats in the world—Lil BUB—and I have a fifteen-month-old son named Rosco. My cats have positively impacted my life in every single way—teaching me compassion, empathy, love, and real magic.

Mike Bridavsky, Lil BUB's Dude

In 2004, I was pregnant with my son. My husband, Johnny, and I lived in a town house in Palm Beach Gardens, Florida, and my in-laws and Johnny's sister had come to visit. Johnny worked on race cars in the evening, and sometimes I would go visit him. This particular night, I was feeling extremely pregnant and decided to take a nap (there was a place attached to the workshop). I woke to Johnny saying, "Honey, stay calm." So naturally, I panicked. He went on to tell me his parents had called—Jasper had gotten out and they couldn't find him. Jasper was my beloved cat, and we shared an extraordinarily close relationship. He was an indoor only cat, and our townhouse was located right across a hospital, which put an extremely busy street in front of us. He had gotten out earlier, but no one wanted to alarm me. They had been going all over the neighborhood with bags of food, calling for him. I was understandably upset, and Johnny closed up shop so we could go look for him. On the ride home, all I could do was picture the busy road, the speeding ambulances, and every terrible possible scenario. What if he'd been run over? What if a dog had gotten him? What if someone had found him and decided to keep him? I was a wreck. When we got home, I got out of the car and started to walk around, calling for him. Immediately, he came out from under a car in the parking lot. I think I may have only called out his name once, and there he came—running right up to me, head butts, purrs, and all. Everyone looked at me and shook their heads. They had been looking and calling for hours, and he wouldn't come. But as soon as he heard my voice, out he came, as if to say, "I knew if they told you I was out, you would come home."

Terri Tye, medical billing specialist, Corbin, KY

I'm an actor, writer, and director best known for winning a Golden Globe for the series Wiseguy. My life abruptly changed in 1992 when I was forced to retire due to a severe spinal injury. After I was hurt, everything came to a screeching halt and I went into a deep depression. Were it not for my animals, in particular my cats, I don't know how I would have survived. They gave me a sense of purpose and a reason to get up. I also could relate to them, like Kiddinz—a cat blind in one eye—that my wife, Shane Barbi (of the Barbie Twins—the blockbuster Playboy cover models of the 1990's, turned animal activists) and I rescued after her previous owners discovered she was blind and returned her to the shelter she was adopted from. I appreciated her imperfections and found taking care of her and my animals to be therapeutic, helping me cope with my chronic pain.

Rather than let my pain defeat me, I turned my injury and love of animals into a way to help others—mainly veterans who suffer from Post-Traumatic Stress Disorder (PTSD) by pairing them with service animals. I understood the healing power of cats and dogs and saw it as a great way to save an innocent pet from being destroyed at a kill shelter by training them to be used as service and therapy animals. I especially championed the use of cats, as I felt they were always underappreciated and I knew firsthand just how powerful the warmth of a cat sleeping on my chest and purring was to allowing me to fully relax and sleep. I've avoided publicity over the past few decades, making exceptions only for significant causes I feel passionately about. In 2010, I made headlines for offering my Golden Globe as a reward to help find the killer of a kitten that was found glued to a Minnesota highway and left to die.

Ken Wahl, actor, writer, and director

Shane's twin sister, Sia, also knows the unconditional love of a cat. *My rescue cat, Meanest, was fifteen years old when she died and she spent much of her life wild, not trusting humans, probably because she was badly abused, with a broken back at one point. I had her for eleven years, and she eventually turned into a big love, following me everywhere. Whenever I was sick or sad, she would come and sit on me, purring to comfort me, as if she identified with my pain. Eventually her little broken body gave out, and I had to put her down. I wanted her to be as comfortable as possible and had the vet come to my home so she could be put down in my arms. It tore me up, watching my trusting friend go, and as Meanest left her body, I saw her little grumpy face manifest a slight smile, a beautiful transition—she was no longer in pain. I put my beloved Meanest in her little cat bed and slept next to her that night for closure. I buried her the next day and planted a tree in the forest in memory of her.*

Sia Barbi, former Playboy model, author, and animal activist

For those who rescue a cat from the streets, they know how hard it can be to earn the cat's love, trust, and respect. But when you do, a profound bond is formed that lasts a lifetime. I know that firsthand. One day some kids in my neighborhood told me they saw some kittens in an abandoned house. Immediately concerned, I crawled through a broken window to investigate and wrangled two feral kittens from a pitch-black basement and two more in an upstairs bathroom. I then used a humane trap to catch the Mama Cat. Because I was fostering the kittens for socialization before adopting them out and I already had four cats and two dogs in the house, with a heavy heart, I TNR'd Mama Cat and released her back outside. Over the next few months, this sweet, shy cat frequented my porch for meals and companionship. Eventually I earned her trust, and today, Mama Cat happily lives indoors with her adopted brothers and sisters!

Maggie M. Funkhouser, freelance writer and editor, Ogden, Utah

I noticed that my cat Charlotte was lonely during the day while my husband and I were at work and thought she might like a friend. I went to Craft Cat's website to see what rescue cats they had available, and for a week I scrutinized every cat to find Charlotte the perfect friend. When I finally found a cat I liked, I placed several calls and emails to make sure he was still available until I was able to adopt him. The day I went to pick him up from the shelter, I had every intention of adopting him, but while the volunteer was locating him, a puny fuzzball headed straight for me. He was chatting to me like he had so much to say! I bent down and he crawled right onto my shoulder and kissed my face! Believing full well that sometimes cat choose their people, I told the volunteer to stop looking for the other cat because I was taking this guy home with me. I named him Jasper, and Jasper and Charlotte became instant friends. They are inseparable, and Jasper still kisses my face and tells me about his day! I believe the only reason he was overlooked was because he was meant for me!

Stacey Werner, owner, Felix Katnip Tree Company

My tabby, Nubie, always slept peacefully next to me at night. He didn't walk all over me or meow at 4:00 a.m. like some cats. But one night he changed his routine—I was awakened by him rubbing his furry face all over my cheek and tapping gently on my eyelids. I opened my eyes and said to him, "This better be good. We're not starting breakfast before sunrise." Grateful I was finally awake, he meowed, jumped off the bed, and walked to the bedroom door, continuously looking back to see if I was following him. He walked right past his food bowls in the kitchen and determinedly marched on into the guest bathroom. He then sat down and stared at the toilet. Still groggy, I wasn't certain what was going on, and then it dawned on me what he was trying to tell me—the water was continuously flowing in the toilet! I quickly turned the water off, and we both went back to bed where we both fell promptly asleep.

Beverly J. Harvey, Strasburg, VA

Very often when a person rescues a cat, they say it is the cat who rescued them. This was the case with me and my cat, Bear. Bear was a homeless feral kitten when I came upon him—one of those ferals most people would have considered a nuisance and menace to the community. Had he been captured and brought to a shelter, he most assuredly would have been euthanized. I was undergoing many personal issues—living a life I had nearly given up on—filled with anorexia, self-harm, extreme anxiety, and more. When I started feeding him, he was skin and bones and starving, but he'd ignore the food I gave him for as long as I sat outside with him and pet him. That's all he wanted from me—love. Bear has been with me for years now, and he saved my life. Our relationship has brought me to a new place—I am dedicated to educating people through blogging that every life has value—even one tiny, homeless kitten that most people would have ignored—because I know firsthand the impact a cat can make in a person's life.

Katherine Kern, writer/blogger at *Momma Kat and Her Bear Cat*

~PURR POINTS TO PONDER~

There's no doubt cats can be our best friends and that they provide us with love, companionship, and unwavering loyalty. They have the power to perform miracles with the relationships they share with us, and there are endless, widely publicized stories to prove it. There's Oscar, a ten-plus-year-old tabby who was adopted as a kitten from an animal shelter to be raised as a therapy cat at the Steere House Nursing and Rehabilitation Center in Providence, Rhode Island. Oscar is known by nurses for being notoriously anti-social, yet the miracle moggy has the ability to predict when residents are in their final days, cuddling with them then to provide them with comfort and companionship.

And Iris Grace—a lovely and talented young girl with autism who paints beautiful pictures—has a therapy cat, Thula, an intelligent and gentle Maine Coon who has lowered her daily anxieties and helps to keep her calm. The same is true of Tom, a male tabby adopted from the Animal Care Center of Salem, Virginia as an experiment to see if he could help ease the suffering and stress for patients and their families at the Salem VA Medical Center's Hospice and Palliative Care unit. An end-of-life care facility for military veterans, Tom's presence has been highly successful, allowing the final hours of many veterans easier for families to endure with his calming presence.

Tara the Hero Cat became a national sensation on May 13, 2014, when her human family member and friend, four-year-old Jeremy Triantafilo, was riding his bicycle in his family's driveway when a neighborhood dog came from behind and viciously attacked him on his leg. The dog was violently pulling Jeremy down his driveway when Tara bolted to the rescue, throwing herself at the much larger dog and chasing it away and then returning to Jeremy's side.

And in a story that restores faith in mankind, Dorian Wagner of *Catladybox.com* and the founder of the Cute Transport Network, an all-volunteer organization which ferries abandoned pets by car or plane to adoptive homes, caught wind of a situation local to her. Joan, a woman who suffered from terminal liver disease, had to be rushed to hospice care without being able to make arrangements for her beloved black cat, Isis. Joan continued to pay the rent on her apartment and was desperately contacting animal rescue groups to find Isis a new home. Dorian took heart and launched a social media miracle. Within days, not only did she find a foster home for Isis, but she was also able to reunite Isis with Joan for regular visits. Joan died several months later, but her transformation when Isis would visit was nothing short of a miracle. The story garnered so much attention that Joan was inundated with cards, books, gifts, and more on a daily basis.

There are many, many more heartwarming stories—some make the headlines like those above, but most are humbling stories that never make the news—the everyday stories of the people and the cats who love them—the cats that improve and enrich the quality of their lives. And it's true—studies have proven that our feline friends make us not only happier but healthier. A cat can decrease our depression, stress, and anxiety. They can lower our blood pressure and decrease the risk of heart attack and stroke. But for those of us who have cats, we don't need a study to prove what we already know. Just listening to a cat purr while snuggling on our lap as we pet them is all the proof we need.

Crazy Cat Lady

If by crazy you mean a devoted, passionate, and compassionate person who cares about cats, then yes, I'm crazy. But if you're referring to the negative stereotype that loosely defines a crazy cat lady as a woman, usually middle-aged or older, who lives alone with no husband or boyfriend and fills the empty, lonely void in her life with as many cats as she can, then I'm going to pass on that. Cats (and the women who love them) have enough of an uphill battle without having to deal with fodder that does more harm than good.

And while I'm on the rant, let's put an end to another negative stereotype that does more harm than good—that it's not cool for men to love cats because it's not considered masculine. That's another book in and of itself, but if we ladies can carry the badge of cat devotion, I assure you so can the men. Real men *do* love cats— not only do I have living proof every day with my Dan, but I see it all around me in the cat-loving world I'm a part of.

But back to the topic at hand—what I've done or what I'll do for the feline species ranges from run of the mill to perhaps over the top. There's the basic stuff, such as carrying on a conversation with them. But look, if they meow something to me, it would be rude to ignore them. Mine are an extremely chatty bunch, and communicating with them is a daily part of my life.

And of course if I'm out of town and I call in, I ask to speak to them on the phone—any cat lover would do that. If bystanders happen to be eavesdropping, I'm sure they think I'm talking to a child whom I dearly love and miss, because to me, my cats are my children. And yes, I've also Cat-Skyped. I'm technologically inclined, so why wouldn't I?

When I go to work, more times than not, my pants are covered in cat hair. Some might consider it off-putting, but I consider it me. I've also missed work to take a cat to the vet—whether it's one of my own or one that was part of a rescue effort (because yes, I do travel with a spare cat carrier in my trunk, because yes, I am a stray cat "if you build it they will come" kind of magnet). I've found stray cats in the dark of night, abandoned in a dry-well when I was visiting relatives out of state, at places of work, while on vacation, in my driveway, and more.

I've also been late to work because I can't leave the house until I do a cat head count—sometimes one of them will inexplicably become invisible, and it takes me a while to find him or her. Not to mention, after I lock the door to head out, I'll jiggle the doorknob to make sure it's locked. Then I'll get in my car and get back out to walk back to the door to jiggle the lock again, just to be absolutely certain it's locked.

And I most certainly have taken time off to grieve a cat if they've passed on. I'm nearly inconsolable, and being around people is just too difficult for me. If I know one of my cats is ailing, I will grab a blanket and pillow and sleep on the floor to offer them comfort for however many days, weeks, or months they need me. I've had kittens born on my lap and I've held cats in my arms as they've taken their last breath.

When I go for walks outside, I tuck cat treats inside my bra so if I happen upon a neighborhood cat, I've got something for them. I've also gone to run errands, forgetting I had said cat treats in my bra. I'm also very superstitious when it comes to cats and clothes—if I've had to take a cat to a vet to cross them over the

Rainbow Bridge, I can't wear that outfit again. Part of it seems disrespectful, and part of it's because it's just too painful to relive the memory.

I also no longer get sentimental gifts such as bouquets of flowers. The flowers barely make it into the house before my gang is on them like white on rice, devouring the leaves like hungry little termites. Since some plants can be toxic, if I ever do get flowers, they reside behind closed doors in the guest bedroom where I go and "visit" them on occasion until they gracefully pass away, one delicate petal at a time.

I will always place my cat's needs first—even if I'm desperate to go to the bathroom or heat up my cup of coffee, if I have a cat napping on my lap, I won't disturb them. If I have two, three, or more cats sleeping on me in bed, so be it if my body is contorted to the shape of a pretzel. And if I want a cat, I'll go to any lengths to adopt it. Case in point was the time I coerced my kids into getting me a Ragdoll kitten for Mother's Day.

I turned on the television one day while doing household cleaning—something I typically didn't do. A show flashed on the screen that caught my attention—*Cats 101*—and they were featuring the Ragdoll breed, which, surprisingly, was a breed I had never heard of. I was so smitten that I used the pretext of the upcoming Mother's Day to get a Ragdoll kitten as a gift. The plan worked, resulting in my beautiful, now angel Jazz, but truthfully, I would have found a way to get him regardless of the ruse!

I'm also the one who travels several hours away to attend a pet conference, only to come home with a rescue kitten instead of cat swag. That would be my darling Jazmine—but I dare you to look into her beguiling golden eyes and tell me you wouldn't do the same. And when I travel, I go to extreme lengths to cat-proof the house, such as not only unplugging lamps, but removing the lightbulbs as well so if the lamp accidently got knocked over, no cat would be hurt with broken glass.

My Jazmine. It was love at first sight.

I also no longer decorate my house with the same flair I used to. Fireplace mantels are for my cats to jump up to, not breakable decorations that could potentially be knocked over. That stuff is either packed away or put behind closed, locked doors. My reasoning is simple—it's my cats' home, too, and they need to be happy and comfortable. The physical stuff is only "things," and my cats are far more important to me than an inanimate object.

I've done goofy things with my cats, too—such as playing hide and seek, or "tag, you're it." I love to watch them chase after me and it gives me enormous pleasure to see how much they enjoy the game. I've also done more serious things like turn my whole life upside down by becoming a cat blogger and author. One such incident involved me and a couple other cat cohorts helping to stage a protest when a national hotel chain decided to trap and remove its outdoor cat population that had been peacefully living on the property for years.

In my public persona, I'm known as the "leopard lady" because I'm always decked out in leopard print from head to toe, (and that's just me—you should see the inside of my house!) I'm constantly getting people sending me emails or posting stuff on my Facebook page with leopard print—most of it's stuff to buy, and I try my best not to cave in to temptation, but I'll admit I did succumb to one email—it was for a leopard print hi-rise cat condo, and I bought it minutes after getting the email.

Leopard print for me. High spaces for them. We all win!

My emergence as a writer also resulted in me going on a wild goose chase, trying to get on the *Ellen DeGeneres Show* because I dedicated a chapter to her in my first book, *The Chronicles of Zee & Zoey*, in which I share how her show (and my cats) inspired me to write the book. It never happened, but my devotion to the cause was extraordinary to say the least, with several people jumping on board to help out!

As a child, I always dressed as a cat for Halloween (and as an adult, for that matter), and I proudly wear cat ears to many a public function. As a matter of fact, if I dare show up at a cat-related event not wearing my ears, people yell at me to put them on (I travel with cat ears in my purse, so it's not a big deal).

I also proudly defy anyone who thinks my cats are anything less than precious family members. That includes my allergist, who told me many years ago when I discovered I was allergic to cats, that I should get rid of them. I got rid of the allergist and subsequently learned how to manage my allergies. I also had a kitten once that was born with only one eye. I brought her to the vet—he suggested I put her to sleep. I indignantly left and found a new vet, and she grew into a sweet companion cat that lived with me for over ten years.

I buy my cats Christmas gifts, and as a new tradition, when my family comes to visit for the holidays, rather than watch Christmas movies, we gather in front of my computer and watch a marathon of Simon's Cat videos on YouTube. I also participate in social media birthday parties for other cats, and I know the names of cats but not the humans they live with. When gifts or greeting cards are given to me, 99% of them are cat themed. The majority of books in my office are also cat themed, and a good portion of the decorations in my house center on cats.

On several occasions I've been in the process of writing serious business correspondence, only to realized I've spelled perfect, "purrfect." I've also turned the TV onto *Cute Cats* on Animal Planet many a time so my cats could watch it, and I downloaded a simulated fishing game for them to play on my iPad. I also buy my cats better food than I eat, and I will sit on the floor with them while they are eating to make sure each cat doesn't steal food from the dish of the other cat.

I'm dreadfully homesick for my cats when I travel, and if I'm visiting with someone who doesn't have a cat in the house, I feel out of sorts. I take enormous pleasure Photoshopping stuff onto my cats and turning the picture into assorted memes, cards, and more. And Dan and I no longer celebrate a traditional "green" Christmas—but one that centers on decorating the tree in leopard theme.

I'm eternally bummed I was named Deborah instead of Catherine; whereby I could have had the nickname Cat, and I rejoiced when I found out Monopoly's newest game piece was a cat. I also have super bad eyesight, but when it comes to spotting cats, it's uncanny how quickly I can find one, no matter where I am. Or is it them finding me? In my case, it seems to be the same thing.

When I doodle, it's drawings of cats, and when I need to spell something out for people, if the word has the letter "C" in it, I always say "C" as in cat. The screensaver on my iPhone and computer is of my cats, and most of my passwords are feline related. Choosing which team to root for at a sporting event is determined by whichever team is named after a cat. If there are no cats playing, then there's just no point in watching the game.

One of the greatest moments of my life was being compared to the original cat woman of the original Batman series, Julie Newmar, and even greater, was getting to interview her via email and receiving an autographed book from her. I might not remember when Presidents' Day is, but I do know the day each of my cats was born or when I adopted them. I know events like National Hairball Day, World Cat Domination Day, and Feral Cat Day. As a matter of fact, I even founded a new national day called Rainbow Bridge Remembrance Day that is held on August 28 of every year. I created it in honor of Jazz who passed on that day as special way for pet guardians to honor the memory of cherished pets who have passed on.

Lastly, if you asked me the question "Would you give up your cats for a million dollars?" the answer without the slightest of hesitation would be "no." As a matter of fact, no amount of money would secure a "yes." Cats have always been a significant part of my life, and they always will be. A life without these beautiful creatures would not be a life I would want to live. Through thick and thin, the good and the bad, they've always been my one constant, giving me a reason to get up each and every day. So, crazy cat lady? No, not at all, just a grateful cat lady.

~MEWS FROM OTHERS~

John and Maggie are like the show *Seinfeld* when it comes to their cat, Newt—there's much ado about nothing as evidenced by this text exchange:

> *John: Newt just burped. #nojoke*
> *Maggie: Was it adorable?*
> *John: Yup. #itwasawesome*
> **Maggie Marton, freelance pet writer, Carmel, IN**

I'm the creator of the blog, Three Chatty Cats, *and sometimes my husband, Ross, helps me proofread posts. The only problem—he doesn't "speak cat," so he often has no idea what I'm talking about. It all started with a particular incident in which he completely misinterpreted the term "foster fail." Here's the gist of it: We were walking our dog one evening and were discussing my blog. Ross asked me why cat people talk about their foster fails, almost like they're bragging about them. I said of course they are which Ross didn't understand at all. Sensing his confusion, I asked what he thought they were, and he whispered, "You know...the cat died." I explained to him, "No! A foster fail is when the foster parent ends up keeping the cat because they can't part with it!" Ross responded, "That's a horrible name. You can see why I thought that, right? It's the word fail!" That's when it dawned on me that the less-than-fanatical cat person might need some clarifying, and a list of cat terminology for Ross was created so we could share conversations!*

Rachel Loehner, blogger at *Three Chatty Cats*, Orange County, CA

I'll do anything when it comes to a cat cause. Case in point—I once donned a skintight black cat suit and sang for a music video to raise awareness about stray, feral, and black cats and to overturn misconceptions about cat owners who are women. I'm an attractive woman but not a trained singer by any means. But I'm a good sport—if sexy sells along with bad singing and it can help cats, why not?!

Christine Michaels, award-winning blogger, *Riverfront Cats*, and founder and president of Pawsitively Humane, Inc.

I'm the human to Venus the Two Face Cat—the cat that caused an Internet sensation on social media, known for her distinct facial markings—one half of her face is solid black with a green eye, and the other half has orange tabby stripes and a blue eye. Venus was found as a stray on a dairy farm in North Carolina, and one of my friends posted a picture of her on Facebook. She looked like a mixture of my other two cats—an orange tabby and a black tuxedo—so I fell in love and knew I had to adopt her. Along with Venus, I'm the busy mom of three very active boys, as well as guardian to several other cats and dogs. I have a limited household budget because what people often don't understand is that just because a cat is famous, doesn't mean it equates to monetary wealth.

I had a 1983 CJ7 jeep that I diligently saved for, finally bought, and then a few short months later sold, so I could pay for Venus's emergency surgery and hospitalization when it was discovered she had a urinary blockage, which is rare in female cats. But much as I loved my jeep, I loved Venus more and would have sold a body part to save her if that's what it took.

Christina, guardian to Venus the Two Face Cat

Dancing with the Stars judge, Carrie Ann Inaba, had a cat she adored so much (Shadow) that his death in 2011 inspired her to launch The CAI Animal Project Foundation, an organization dedicated to providing funding to grassroots animal rescue organizations, fostering and adoption of high-risk animals, and spay/neuter services. *One of my favorite rescue stories involves my own beloved Squeaker—a cat I first met as a scared, mangy, and sickly kitten on death row. Squeaker's huge light green eyes, dark tortoiseshell coat, and extra toe that made her walk like a ballerina caused my heart to melt, prompting me to adopt her, only to find out the tragic news; Squeaker only had two weeks to live. Compelled to give her a life full of the love she deserved, I spent every minute with her, even sleeping on the floor with her so she would never have to be alone or afraid in her too-short life. Those two weeks turned into twenty wonderful years and going for me and Squeaker! The doctors couldn't explain what happened, but I knew it was the miraculous healing power of love. She now walks a little slower and she's gone blind, but she's still my love and joy and I'm eternally grateful for every moment I have with her.*

Carrie Ann Inaba, dancer, choreographer, judge on *Dancing with the Stars*, and founder of the CAI Animal Project Foundation

When it comes to people and cats, Amber is as passionate and generous as they come. Not only did she make the decision to donate one of her kidneys to a man she didn't know, but while undergoing a month of recovery after the surgery, she decided to use the time to pick up a couple of foster kittens who needed around the clock bottle-feeding! *I was always an animal lover; however, when I enlisted in the Navy at nineteen, I was without pets for over six years. Once my contract was up, I went to a rescue and adopted a senior cat with serious medical issues. He died a year later of a heart attack, inspiring me to take care of the most vulnerable animals in need, which included taking in "fospice" dogs through the Mr. Mo Project—an upstate New York nonprofit that gets old and sick dogs out of shelters and places them into loving foster homes for their remaining days. I live with my daughter, along with two Mr. Mo fospice dogs—Jill, a former stray with diabetes and vestibular disease, and Saint, who has inoperable cancer. I also have three other rescue pups, a rescue bunny, and two reptiles who were "inherited." My foster kittens—Tillie and Ricki—the first bottle-fed kittens I've ever fostered have since been adopted, and I credit them for helping me heal.*

Amber Noelle Hollier, Kenner, LA

Tigger was abandoned by his owner at twenty years old. His story was posted on Facebook in hopes of finding him a new home, and when my boyfriend, Michael, and I read it, we made the split second decision to adopt him. We were already considering finding a friend for our six-year-old cat, Stuart, and thought, "Why not Tigger?" Tigger was a sight—skinny, full of mats, and drinking up to a gallon of water a day. I took him to Charm City Vet in Baltimore where I work for a full blood panel, with the unfortunate results that he was in kidney failure. Undeterred by the news, Michael and I gave him medication, a prescription diet, a good shave, and lots of TLC. He put on weight and a very handsome ginger cat emerged. A golfball sized tumor was discovered on him, and rather than lament his condition, we created a bucket list of special adventures just for him! His little trips are a blast, and his favorite place is the beach where he can soak up the sun. He has a Facebook page with nearly 20,000 followers, and I share his adventures as well as the joys of adopting a geriatric pet. Stuart was not initially happy with his senior cat-mate but has since warmed up to him, and they've bonded by sharing the many treats, toys, and gifts that have been sent from people around the world for Tigger. I wouldn't trade the experience for anything in the world—Tigger has changed my life, and I joke that he's like a funny, bossy, and endearing young adult trapped in the body of a senior.

Adriene Buisch, former NFL Baltimore Ravens cheerleader, Charm City Veterinary Hospital

I'm so passionate about cats I founded the Peter Zippi Fund for Animals to help homeless animals find homes. Since 1977, the organization has placed over 15,000 animals (95% of them cats), and we even rescued a cat that needed surgery to the tune of $2,000. When complications set in, the fee went to up to an astronomical $8,000 but our team stuck by the little guy, he was saved, and we found him a wonderful forever home!

Dr. Alice Villalobos, DVM, FNAP / *www.pawspice.com*

On those unexpected occasions when a devastating natural disaster occurs, for most of us from afar, all we can do is offer our prayers for recovery. But when I heard about the March 11, 2011, Tohoku earthquake and tsunami in Japan and resulting Fukushima nuclear meltdown, I wanted to immediately leave my comfortable home in Virginia to volunteer with the Japan Cat Network (JCN), an organization devoted to helping save the cats affected by the disasters. My boyfriend and I already had plans to go to Japan—a month prior to the disasters, we had been offered jobs in Japan as Assistant Language Teachers (ALTs)—but it wasn't as simple as packing up and leaving, so all I could do was proceed with quitting my first grade teaching job and get my visa in order. Two weeks later, I was on my way to Japan, and during breaks from my ALT position, I volunteered with JCN, with the five-hour trip (one way) costing $250 in tolls! My volunteer work would vary—from trying to reunite pets with their owners to feedings, cage cleanings, medical care, and more. The biggest challenge I faced was educating people

about the importance of spay/neuter to reduce cat overpopulation. Some of it was cultural—because most of the disaster area was very rural, many people had simply never heard of this as an option. And some people choose not to do it due to the insane costs most vets charged (about 400USD). But thanks to the efforts of my group and other Japanese groups becoming more vocal about the issue since the disaster, it's getting easier.
  Jennifer Koca, animal advocate, Richmond, VA

I'm a proponent of spay/neuter and TNR and my staff and I alter about a hundred cats a week. Many years ago, I went to Louisiana from Texas with a friend, helping in a horse breeding operation. The barn had numerous cats with one semi-feral girl who stole my heart. She was an orange and white beauty, and with bits of BBQ beef and snippets of turkey meat, I courted her affections, slowly building her trust. I noticed she had been injured, probably by an inadvertent kick from a horse, and was having a hard time breathing. I asked permission from the owner of the barn to take her and was given a resounding "no," as she had also caught his eye. Being somewhat wily, I enticed her into the horse trailer we had taken with us and "accidently" confined her in the front of it.

When we got back to Texas, I released her from her confinement and brought her to my new vet clinic. As suspected, her diaphragm had been ruptured, but I didn't have the proper equipment to repair the severe damage. But a colleague of mine did, so with some creative bartering, i.e., five homemade lasagna dinners in lieu of the surgery, the trade was made and she was fixed up. I named her Clinique for the makeup, and after she was fully recovered, I had every intention of taking her back to Louisiana. Until then, she became a greeter at the clinic, welcoming everyone with a purr! When I finally brought her back to her rightful owner, I confessed what I had done and I also told him her care was done at no charge to him. He appreciated that I had stolen the cat to save her and was willing to give her back even though he was obviously taken with her. So she became my cat to love and impressed many people over her fifteen years by just how wonderful a little wild woman could be!

Dr. Cynthia Rigoni, All Cats Veterinary Clinic, Houston, Texas

~PURR POINTS TO PONDER~

There's no doubt people go to extreme lengths for the love of a cat. And why wouldn't they? These beautiful creatures with their all-knowing eyes, jelly bean paw pads, and fluffy bellies have an extraordinary range of personality and abilities. They come in an endless assortment of colors, breeds, sizes, and shapes, seemingly able to convey emotions and feelings. They can be intelligent, angry, jealous, loving, comforting, protectors, predators, aloof, and curious. They have the ability to remember and understand time. They have habits and qualities that exhibit perseverance, fear, anxiety, excitement, affection, frustration, pleasure, contentment, persistence, and petulance. They can be playful, dominant, timid, friendly, scared, bold, subservient, affectionate, aggressive, passive, forgiving, petty, talkative, silent, moody, happy, sad, and so much more. The truth is they're not just "cats," they're flesh and blood, just like we are.

Our cats become an integral part of our lives—sharing the good and bad, the highs and lows, and everything in between, no judgment of the circumstances, remaining loyal and devoted to us. In the simplest sense, they ask for so little but give so much. Food, shelter, fresh water, clean litter, some toys, bedding and veterinary care are some of the staples. But it's our love—the tone of our voice, the touch of our hand, the softness of our lap—those are the things that bring us that uniquely special bond between human and cat.

I remember a time, several years ago, when Jackson Galaxy of Animal Planet's *My Cat From Hell* wasn't the household icon he is today: the guy who fixes cats with severe behavioral problems and a New York Times bestselling author. I had the privilege of interviewing him back then and joked around about the title of his show. I threw the question to him: "The title of your show is *My Cat From Hell*. But what about Heaven? If it exists, what would you like to hear God say when you arrive at the Pearly Gates?" His response, "I really don't need to hear God say anything, but my worst nightmare would be if I got there and there were no cats. I would be lost without them." I couldn't agree more.

Nine Lives

This is where this book is supposed to end. A final chapter, a conclusion—something to tie everything together in a purrfectly pretty bow. But when it comes to cats and their funny or strange behaviors, there is no ending because there will always be cats doing crazy things, and there will always be us humans loving them for it and doing even crazier things as a result of that love.

The real ending is the happy one I wish for all cats, but unfortunately, we're nowhere near fulfilling that dream. As mentioned way back in the introduction of this book, we have an epidemic at hand—upward of 70 million homeless cats are living on the streets and in shelters in the United States alone. It's a combination of feral outdoor cats, abandoned or lost strays, and pet cats that have been relinquished to shelters. A large majority of these cats have not been spayed or neutered, and because cats can reproduce at an alarming rate—an unfixed male/female pair can lead up to 5,000 cats in 7 years—without proper spay/neuter measures, overpopulation will continue.

On the surface, most don't even realize how serious the issue is. We happily live our lives with Fluffy making biscuits on our belly and the Internet is flooded with photos, memes, and videos of cute cats nearly 24/7/365. Lil BUB, Simon's Cat, Nyan Cat, Keyboard Cat, Henri le Chat Noir, Cole and Marmalade, and Grumpy Cat to name just a few are socially savvy cats with millions of collective followers on Twitter, Facebook, YouTube, Instagram, and more. But the popularity is deceiving, and that's what this book is all about.

There's nothing wrong with the social popularity—I love these famous cats myself and many of them promote some great feline causes. But cats are so much more than a funny video or a cute picture and that was my intention with this book—to put everything into perspective, as well as to dispel the myth that cats are too independent and aloof to make good pets, which is one of the reasons they are overlooked for adoption.

Clearly this book, with one anecdote after another, has knocked that myth out of the park. But to truly make a difference, it's not just about sharing our anecdotes. It's about dispelling the dozens of other misinformed myths about cats; it's about educating on the critical need to encourage spay/neuter—not only because it's better for your cat's health and well-being, but because it's the only way to humanely reduce cat overpopulation; and it's about teaching responsibility and learning to "think like a cat" so some of the negative behavioral issues that might land a cat in a shelter can be corrected or avoided altogether.

There are a variety of reasons why someone would dump a cat on the street (which is not only cruel, it's illegal) or bring them to a shelter, but I can assure you the majority of those situations can be managed with some patience and preventative measures. Cat allergies, we have a dog so we can't have a cat, we're moving and can't take our cat, we're going to have a baby and are worried about them getting along, my cat won't stop scratching the couch or peeing outside his litterbox—all are just a few of the excuses/reasons people have for not wanting a cat any longer.

And then there's the other stuff—black cats being overlooked for adoption because even in our modern day society, some people still consider them to bring bad luck. Senior cats are bypassed, often spending the remainder of their life in the confines of a shelter, cats with disabilities or illnesses are overlooked, and then there are the cats brought to shelters that are found to be victims of unspeakable abuses because some people simply don't like cats and want to see them suffer. Since shelters are already overflowing with cats, it could mean a death sentence for these poor cats who are victims of circumstances.

To tackle cat overpopulation, disseminating factual information to the mainstream public on the importance of spay/neuter is step one. Many people don't realize a female kitten can become pregnant as early as four months of age and a male kitten can impregnate a fertile female at the same young age. A "pre-pubertal" spay/neuter with kittens is now recommended—ideally between eight and twelve weeks of age. A nursing mother cat can also become pregnant while lactating, and even if you have an indoor cat and might think spay/neuter is not necessary, it is.

It's healthier for your cat—spaying your female prior to her first heat nearly eliminates the risk of mammary cancer, uterine infections, and uterine cancer, and neutering your male at a young age prevents testicular and prostate cancer and greatly reduces his risk for perianal tumors. And despite best intentions, a cat may accidently get outside and all it takes is one sexual encounter between two ready partners for a pregnancy to occur.

The importance of TNR efforts to control community/outdoor cat populations also needs to be communicated. According to Alley Cat Allies, an organization devoted to managing these cats, only 2% of the outdoor population is sterilized, generally due to lack of funding, community support, or knowledge of the problem. TNR not only reduces outdoor populations, it also deters the nuisance problems associated with them, such as territory marking, fighting, and yowling.

A pet male cat allowed to roam freely outdoors who is not neutered can also be part of the problem. He will do almost anything to find a mate and an unwitting litter of kittens could be the end result if he finds an unspayed female. Accidental litters are often the kittens that end up being brought to an already overcrowded shelter, or worse, dumped on the streets to participate in the endless breeding cycle if they survive. His need to wander might also cause him to run away from home, which could result in an injury to him in traffic or a fatality.

Some of the problem is lack of accurate information. Many cat guardians elect not to have their cat spayed or neutered due to some basic misunderstandings, such as thinking their cat will become overweight after the procedure. While some cats can, with proper exercise, diet, and monitoring of food intake, there is no reason for your cat to gain excess weight. And your cat's personality will not be adversely affected. A male cat will not become "emasculated" if you neuter him—he will be less aggressive and bad spraying habits will be reduced. After a spay, your female cat will be much happier without the undue emotional stress of a heat.

For those who worry they can't afford the procedure, low-fee, or even free clinics offer assistance. Ask your veterinarian or local shelter for options, and the ASPCA has a low-cost spay/neuter provider database available on its website as well.

Some people argue it's not fair to the cat to deprive them of their natural right to reproduce. In light of severe overpopulation and improvement in the overall health of the cat, this should override any need for a cat to procreate for reasons outside responsible breeding.

Lastly is the issue of teaching pet responsibility. I would imagine most people when they adopt a cat do it with the best of intentions. They do the right thing—they go to a shelter and there he is—that sweet face with eyes that melt a heart. They bring him home, imaging a long and happy life, snuggling on the couch together and sharing pieces of their dinner with him. The next thing you know, your cute bundle of fluff has ripped your couch to shreds with his razor sharp claws, used your curtains as a jungle-gym, sprayed the front door with a nasty blast of urine, and treats your boyfriend like he is the most deplorable human being on the face of this earth.

If you don't understand the underlying mechanisms of what makes a cat tick, tensions can mount, the problems can get worse, and out of sheer frustration, your cat is scooped up, stuffed into his carrier and brought to the shelter because you feel it's the kindest thing you can do for him. You wipe back tears but feel hopeful, assuming some other wonderful family will adopt him and he'll have a happily ever after life. It would be wonderful if it were that simple, but the reality is, it's not.

Adopting a pet is supposed to be a lifelong commitment. Your cat is depending on you to take care of him, and if you don't give him the proper tools to be the instinctual creature he was born to be, you're not being fair to him. Or you—by not providing him with what he needs to thrive, you're missing out on what could be an amazing relationship and friendship. That's why before you make any rash decisions to bring him to a shelter; you need to think like a cat. Analyze his behavior. While cats might appear to be complex, they truly are simple. Their actions and behaviors are their way of communicating with you.

And that's my ultimate hope with this book. I want to share it with the world—CATS ARE AMAZING and they make wonderful pets! But to truly thrive, to be happy and healthy creatures, they need the proper environment to be the incredible creature's nature intended them to be.

Epilogue

I was driving home from work. As usual, the rush-hour traffic was bumper-to-bumper, moving at a snail's pace. I'm already exhausted from a long day as it is, so the drive renders me completely drained, annoyed, and thoroughly stressed out by the time I finally pull into the driveway and walk in the front door.

I did what I did hundreds of times before. I tripped over seven hungry cats swarming around my legs, greeting me to hurry up and feed them dinner, as I tried to walk gracefully into my office to drop off my purse before that could happen.

But on this particular day, something was different. I happened to glance over at my computer and I saw something sitting on top of my keyboard. I looked—it was a stuffed plush toy. Only it wasn't just any plush toy—it was one I had made by hand for Zee several years ago using a leopard print fabric in the shape of a heart. Okay. Before I jumped to any conclusions and melted into an emotional puddle of tears, I asked Dan to come to my office to find out if he had put it there.

As you know from reading this book, Zee loves to carry around toys and drop them all over the floor, so maybe Dan had found it and absent-mindedly put it on my keyboard. Nope. Absolutely not. And that's when the floodgates opened. My precious Zee had left me a gift. He associated my computer with me, and the toy was his way of telling me he missed me, probably hoping that by leaving it there, that I would somehow materialize for him.

The symbolism was touching beyond words—a heart just for me—and I was taken aback by the loving gesture, but in many ways I wasn't. I know firsthand how strong the human-feline bond is, but I think in this case, it meant all the more; because it was something I needed without even realizing it. While writing this book was a labor of love and I enjoyed the process, doing it in conjunction with a full-time day job and the routine of everyday life was extremely taxing on me mentally, and I'd been running on fumes trying to meet publishing deadlines.

What an ironic moment—I was writing an informative book about understanding cat behavior, but it was my own cat that was teaching *me*. He was telling me to take a breather, to slow down and to find the time to appreciate what's around me. So that's the real ending of the story, because honestly, when you have the love and wisdom of your cat, what more do you really need?

Resources

While I've shared a wealth of information on cat behavior in this book, it's but a glimpse into the intricate mind of a cat. To learn more, I recommend you check out some of the industry respected books and websites to follow:

~CAT BEHAVIOR AND GENERAL CAT CARE BOOKS~

Cat Scene Investigator: Solve Your Cat's Litter Box Mystery, Dusty Rainbolt, Stupid Gravity Press, 2016

Cats for the GENIUS, Ramona D. Marek, Charity Channel LLC, 2016

Catify to Satisfy: Simple Solutions for Creating a Cat-Friendly Home, Jackson Galaxy and Kate Benjamin, TarcherPerigee, 2015

Catification: Designing a Happy and Stylish Home for Your Cat (and You!), Jackson Galaxy and Kate Benjamin, TarcherPerigee, 2014

Outsmarting Cats – How to Persuade the Felines in Your Life to Do What You Want, Wendy Christensen, Lyons Press, 2004 and 2013

ComPETability: Solving Behavior Problems in Your Multi-Cat Household, Amy Shojai, Cool Gus Publishing, 2012

Your Cat: The Owner's Manual: Hundreds of Secrets, Surprises, and Solutions for Raising a Happy, Healthy Cat, Dr. Marty Becker, Grand Central Life & Style, 2012

The Complete Cat's Meow – Everything You Need to Know About Caring for Your Cat, Darleen Arden, Wily Publishing, 2011

~CAT BEHAVIOR AND HEALTHCARE WEBSITES~

Catalyst Council, http://www.catalystcouncil.org

Cat Behavior Associates, bestselling author and certified cat behavior consultant, Pam Johnson-Bennett, http://www.catbehaviorassociates.com

CatCentric, Tracy Dion, feline care consultant, http://www.catcentric.org

Little Big Cat, holistic veterinarian, Dr. Jean Hofve and cat behaviorist, Jackson Galaxy, http://www.littlebigcat.com

HealthyPet.com - The American Animal Hospital Association's site for pet owners, http://healthypet.com

Healthy Pets with Dr. Karen Becker, http://healthypets.mercola.com

PetMD Cat Care Center, http://www.petmd.com/cat/centers/care

TheCatSite.com, http://www.thecatsite.com

The Conscious Cat, award-winning author and former veterinary hospital manager, Ingrid King, http://consciouscat.net

Veterinary Partner.com, http://www.veterinarypartner.com

~Products for Cats and Cat Lovers~

CatLadyBox https://catladybox.com

CatTipper http://www.cattipper.com/

Hauspanther.com http://www.hauspanther.com

Meow.com http://www.meow.com

Meowbox https://meowbox.com

Meowingtons https://www.meowingtons.com

Old Maid Cat Lady http://www.oldmaidcatlady.com

RCTees (cat themed t-shirts, sweatshirts, and tank tops) https://www.etsy.com/shop/RCTees

Triple T Studios (The Tiniest Tiger Collection) http://triple-t-studios.com

~Low Cost Spay/Neuter Directory~

http://www.aspca.org/pet-care/general-pet-care/low-cost-spayneuter-programs

Acknowledgements

In a book filled a myriad of weird anecdotes, ironically, the most outlandish aspect of it was tackling it in the first place. I'm what's known as a "starving artist," meaning much as I would love to be a bestselling author, I fall into the category that many writers do—I need a regular day job in order to pay the bills. This translated to me writing and formatting the book before and after work hours—i.e., at the crack of dawn, late evening hours, and in-between everything else on the weekends. It was challenging to say the least and I don't recommend the strategy for anyone weak of heart.

That said, it's with mega purrs of appreciation that I thank EVERYONE who was involved in helping this book come to be, because I couldn't have done it alone. I issued an open call on Facebook, my blog, Twitter and more looking for story submissions. I also broached my family and personal friends for submissions as well as complete strangers. I called in favors and I bartered favors back. Talk about corralling cats, I was corralling people!

Then there were the endless follow-up questions and the tracking down of answers. What color is your cat? How did you get him? What's his name? Can you give me more description? Everyone who participated was so generous with me and patient as I tried to paint the best picture I could with each individual story.

And there were many more who submitted stories, but I couldn't feature them because I wasn't able to fit them in the book. It wasn't because I didn't want to, but because I had to limit myself to what I could share, otherwise I would have been writing the next *War and Peace*. But regardless, I thank you all—the outpouring of love, support, and generosity I received was overwhelming. Your stories made me laugh, some made me cry, and many of them, I could easily relate to! But most of all; you allowed a dream of mine to come true. You helped me tell not just my story, but the story of every cat lover who understands the joy of having a cat in their life, crazy habits and all, and want to make the world a better place for them.

I also want to thank Dan as I would not have been able to write this book without his everlasting patience and support. He shares the same love and passion for cats that I do and that love shines through in all the photographs he took that I used in the book.

And thank you to the talented Stephanie Piro for creating the charming illustration for the book cover. I had seen Jazmine making biscuits on the couch one day and knew I wanted that image captured in a whimsical way for the cover. Already a fan of Stephanie's work, I sent her several photos of Jazmine and explained my concept to her. She nailed it on the first try and I love it. She also created the illustration of Jazmine and me for the back cover and no matter how many times I look at it, it gives me reason to smile.

Thank you as well to my editor, Karen Robinson. She helped me with the nitty-gritty details of the book and also provided invaluable insight on what tone and voice the book should take to be most enjoyable to the reader.

Thank you also to all my colleagues and fellow cat lovers who read *Makin' Biscuits* to provide testimonial for the book—I know how busy everyone is and I appreciate you taking the time out of your lives to help out. Having your support means the world to me and I wouldn't be where I am today without you:

Dr. Marty Becker, "America's Veterinarian," contributor to *Good Morning America* and *The Dr. Oz Show*, and three-time bestselling author of 25 pet-related books; Ingrid King, award-winning author and publisher of *The Conscious Cat;* Caren Gittleman, publisher of *Cat Chat with Caren and Cody;* Ramona D. Marek, MS Ed., author, *Cats for the GENIUS;* Debbie Glovatsky, award-winning blogger and photographer, *Glogirly.com;* Amy Shojai, CABC, author of 30 pet care books and a founder of the Cat Writers' Association; Kate Benjamin, founder of *Hauspanther.com* and co-author of *Catification* and *Catify to Satisfy;* Tamar Arslanian, author of *Shop Cats of New York* and publisher of *IHaveCat.com;* Stephanie Piro, nationally syndicated cartoonist and the Saturday Chick of King Features' *Six Chix;* Yvonne DiVita, co-founder of the BlogPaws Pet Community and publisher of *Scratchings and Sniffings;* Christine Michaels, award-winning blogger, *Riverfront Cats,* and founder and president of Pawsitively Humane, Inc.; Dusty Rainbolt, ACCBC, award-winning author of 12 books including *Kittens for Dummies, Cat Wrangling Made Easy* and *Cat Scene Investigator: Solve Your Cat's Litter Box Mystery;* Paris Permenter, author of 33 books on pets and travel and blogger at *CatTipper.com;* and Angie Bailey, author, *Texts from Mittens* and *Whiskerslist: The Kitty Classifieds.*

And a special thank you to Gwen Cooper, New York Times bestselling author of *Homer's Odyssey* for writing the Foreword. I knew from the moment *Makin' Biscuits* started to take shape that her passion for cat welfare epitomized everything the book represented and she would be the ideal person to introduce the story with her trademark wit and style.

Thank you to all the cats in my life as well—both past and present—you all hold a special spot in my heart and have filled my life with unconditional love and companionship. You've given me laughs and smiles, as well as tears and grief when I've had to say goodbye. You are my life and the reason this book even exists.

Lastly, thank you to all of you reading this book. I hope I was able to bring a smile into your day and some knowledge into your life. Cat lovers are a very special group of people and I'm grateful to have been able to share *Makin' Biscuits* with you all.

About

Deborah Barnes resides in South Florida with her fiancé and feline family of seven. She is the author of *Purr Prints of the Heart – A Cat's Tale of Life, Death, and Beyond* and *The Chronicles of Zee & Zoey – A Journey of the Extraordinarily Ordinary*, as well as the award winning cat-related blog, *Zee & Zoey's Cat Chronicles*. She is the Vice President of the Cat Writers' Association and was awarded 2013 "Writer of the Year" by Friskies Purina. She was also honored with the Adopt-a-Shelter Cat Award in 2016 from Adopt-a-Shelter.com for her article "Any Cat Can be a Feral Cat, Even Yours" and is the Secretary of the nonprofit, Pawsitively Humane, Inc. of Miami, Florida. Her freelance work has been featured in *Cat Fancy* magazine, *Kittens 101*, *Catster.com*, *BlogPaws.com*, *TheCatSite.com*, and the *American Association of Human-Animal Bond Veterinarians* newsletter.

Contact Deborah Barnes: info@zzppublishing.com

Book purchasing information: www.makinbiscuitsbook.com

Follow Makin' Biscuits on Facebook: www.facebook.com/makinbiscuitsbook

Follow Makin' Biscuits on Twitter: @Makin_Biscuits

Visit Zee & Zoey's Cat Chronicles: www.zeezoey.com/blog

38074604R00157

Made in the USA
Middletown, DE
13 December 2016